EDINBURGH
EDUCATION AND SOCIETY
SERIES

General Editor: Colin Bell

Computing in Scottish Education

The first decade and beyond

Edited by
Tom Conlon
and
Peter Cope

EDINBURGH UNIVERSITY PRESS

© Edinburgh University Press 1989
22 George Square, Edinburgh

Set in Linotron Palatino and
printed in Great Britain by
Redwood Press Limited
Trowbridge, Wilts

British Library Cataloguing
  in Publication Data
Computing in Scottish education:
  the first decade and beyond.
1. Scotland. Schools, Curriculum
  subjects: Computer systems
I. Conlon, Tom II. Cope, Peter
004'.07'10411

ISBN 0 7486 0150 3 pbk

CONTENTS

NOTES ON CONTRIBUTORS

TOM CONLON is Senior Lecturer in Information Technology at Moray House College, Edinburgh.

PETER COPE is Lecturer in Education at the University of Stirling.

DEREK CURRAN is Acting Assistant Principal Teacher of Computing at Castlebrae High School.

NEIL KENNEDY is Principal Teacher of Computing at Lochgelly High School.

MELODY MCKAY is Lecturer in Computing at Falkirk College of Technology.

BOB MUNRO is Lecturer in the Division of Computing and Business Studies at Jordanhill College of Education, Glasgow.

LAURENCE O'DONNELL is Teacher of Computing at Wester Hailes Education Centre, Edinburgh.

GEORGE PATON is Director of the Scottish Council for Educational Technology.

IAN SINGER is Visiting Specialist in Primary Computing in West Lothian.

BOB SPARKES is Lecturer in Education at the University of Stirling.

RODDY STUART is Adviser in Computing for Glasgow Division of Strathclyde Region.

BILL TAGG is Director of the Advisory Unit for Microtechnology in Education at Hatfield.

PREFACE

The decade of the 1980s was the first in which computing occupied a significant role in Scottish education. It is a very safe bet that it will not be the last.

For those closely involved with educational computing it has been a period of frenetic activity and also of immense change. Perhaps the most dramatic statistic which can be quoted is the quantity of school-based microcomputers, which has grown from almost zero to around 10 000 over the decade. This statistic reflects the seemingly inexorable expansion of the activity of computing in Scottish schools, and we have no doubt that it will be quoted many times in the future.

But, of course, a count of the number of machines provides just one indicator of change. And it is not really very informative: it tells us nothing of the aims and ambitions of educational computing; nothing of the ideologies and policies; nothing of the successes and failures; and nothing of the alternatives for the future. These are things which are surely worth knowing, and they are what this book is about.

NEED FOR DEBATE

The main reason why we felt that a book of this kind would be worthwhile was our perception of the need for debate. The relative dearth of discussion papers, articles, and books in this area suggests that Scottish educational computing has not been particularly good at asking questions about its own directions. Certainly, the contrast between the deluge of technical and scientific literature, on the one hand and the paucity of the educational writing, on the other could hardly be more extreme. Our book is a modest attempt to rectify that imbalance by providing a forum in which some of the most important questions can be addressed.

More specifically, there seemed to us to be at least four reasons why such a book would be useful. First, past experience suggests that frenetic activity by itself is seldom enough to secure the success of a development: if it is not at least occasionally punctuated by interludes of review and reflection, then the expense of energy may be ineffectual, or worse. The turn of the decade seems to provide an ideal juncture for one of these interludes. It is a chance to look back and assess, and also to look forward to the future, it is hoped with wiser eyes. Secondly, the paucity of the educational literature on computing should not be taken as evidence that there are no deeply felt concerns about its progress. On the contrary, we knew from first-hand experience that doubts and anxieties about the direction of many of the Scottish developments were very widespread, even if opportunities for expressing these formally were not. We felt that to give voice to writers from a broad range of perspectives and experiences would be to provide a healthy democratic service. Thirdly, we were aware that no published text existed which could offer insight into the educational computing field to those who are on its fringes or who work in a different, but related, area. We believe that the analyses contained in these pages will be of interest to a potentially wide group of people. Fourthly, we feared that in the whirlwind of change some of the facts might become clouded over or forgotten: this book ensures that the history is documented, however imperfectly, and that many of the facts will be available for inspection by anybody who has the curiosity to look.

COVERAGE OF THE BOOK

Designing a book of this kind is an interesting exercise. We wanted to include coverage of all the main areas and issues of educational computing in Scotland. After much thought, this led us to a tentative set of chapter titles with which we could open the negotiations with potential authors. The contributors whom we approached were selected on the basis of their expertise and experience: we wanted authoritative writers, but it was also important that they should be drawn from a broad cross-section of positions and responsibilities. Contributors understood that they were each writing in an individual capacity, but it was important to the balance of the book that the opinions expressed should cumulatively represent the wide span which we knew to exist in the field as a whole.

In one respect only were we disappointed. Because it has implications for the book's final form, we wish to set on record that invitations to contribute were extended to, and declined by, three people in particular: one is a Scottish Education Department HMI with responsibility for educational computing at national level; and the two others are prominent architects and managers of the current implementations of the secondary school subject of Computing Studies. We were saddened by these refusals: once in ten years does not seem unduly often to contribute to an open expression of views on matters of such great importance. We regret that these omissions make the book less representative than we had wished.

Our editorial hand has been light, although we had many fruitful discussions with contributors, and there was a fair amount of interaction between them. The book is structured as a sequence of chapters which are broadly grouped by area, but they can be read in almost any sequence.

We consider that the book vindicates our thesis that debate is worthwhile and necessary. There is much here that could guide the development of Scottish educational computing beyond the first decade. We hope that others find the book as stimulating to read as we found it to prepare. More ambitiously, we take encouragement from the signs that Scottish society may be embarking upon major structural changes; it seems to us that if the experience of educational computing is any guide, Scottish education has much need of the opportunity to reform. If the book emboldens others to challenge, to develop for themselves a point of view, and to plan for change, then it will have been worthwhile.

TOM CONLON
PETER COPE
April 1989

ACKNOWLEDGEMENTS

Both editors would like to thank the contributors to this volume for their hard work and for their patience with our stumbling editorial efforts. Also, many colleagues and friends have supported the enterprise by undertaking to read portions of the text in draft form. From these efforts we gained much sound advice and numerous helpful comments. Many thanks to all concerned.

We also wish to thank our families, who did not begrudge the many hours which this labour required. Now we can paint that garden gate, fix the shed roof, and try to catch up with the hoovering.

Acknowledgements are due to Alice Brown and John Fairley, in whose book 'The MSC in Scotland' (EUP 1989) some of the material used in our jointly written chapter originally appeared.

More generally, we want to acknowledge those who were the only real heroes in the saga of educational computing in the 1980s: the teachers of Scotland, whose commitment and dedication has been miserably rewarded by government. Their time will come.

1

THE FIRST DECADE REVIEWED

TOM CONLON and PETER COPE

Several factors have been influential in stimulating the development of educational computing in Scotland. One of the most significant was the perception that this was an area which was important politically as well as educationally. Computing and computer technology have become ubiquitous during the past ten years. High technology is now seen as one of the keys to the future economic well-being of the country. The association between computers and employment has been a powerful image which has proved irresistible to politicians. Unfortunately, the exploitation of this image has distorted the way in which computers have been used in education.

In 1981 Kenneth Baker, the then newly appointed Minister for Information Technology, launched the Department of Industry scheme to provide half the cost of a microcomputer for every secondary school. The launch was accompanied by a rhetoric which was unequivocally vocational in nature: 'I want to try to ensure that the kids of today are trained with the skills that gave their fathers and grandfathers jobs' (in Wellington 1988). Both north and south of the border the initiative was widely welcomed. Especially optimistic in Scotland were those teachers (the minority) who were computing enthusiasts and who had long been left waiting for any kind of official support for their efforts. Although some doubts were expressed, these were mainly at the pragmatic level: for example, were the teachers sufficiently prepared, was there enough software to make the hardware usable, and who would pay for repair of the machines when they broke down?

Important though these questions were, they left unchallenged the assumptions which underpinned Baker's initiative. Why was an Industry minister intervening in schools? Since when had it been the role of school education to provide vocational training? Where was the evidence that jobs in the 'sunrise industry' of computing would be the reward for pupils trained in the right skills, even assuming that the schools could offer them? And how could the provision of a single half-price machine make a serious contribution to anything? For the most part these questions were left unasked. Sadly, the shallow response of Scottish education to the 1981 DOI[1] scheme was to foreshadow a decade in which the relationship between education and computing was seldom effectively scrutinised.

That computing has had an injection of resources, and this at a time when public education generally has been starved of them, is not in doubt. Since 1981 the UK government centrally has committed more than £40 million to the school micro and the resources associated with it. This is more than any other item of educational technology in the history of schooling (Wellington 1988). Yet even this sum is dwarfed by the £200 million which has been invested overall in the Manpower Services Commission's Technical and Vocational Education Initiative. The political return for the money spent has been apparent in the numerous Conservative Party political broadcasts which have portrayed a smiling Baker (now elevated to the rank of Minister for Education) surrounded by eager youngsters in a hi-tech classroom. But what is the educational reality behind the media gloss? Have the pupils of the 1980s benefited in any real way from educational computing?

PERSPECTIVES FOR EDUCATIONAL COMPUTING

Hardly anybody denies that computers, and more generally Information Technology, do have a valuable contribution to make to school education. The issues are really those of what the precise goals should be, and of how these can best be achieved. It will be useful here to describe briefly some of the recent thinking.

During the 1980s educationists in many countries have reached a clear consensus on what should be the most important role for IT[2] in schools. This consensus says that the technology ought to be harnessed to support teaching and learning in the existing curriculum. Computers should best be regarded as another type of classroom aid, like the overhead projector or the textbook, but potentially far more powerful. There is much evidence to suggest that learning in almost any subject, and at almost any age and stage, can benefit from software which either teaches the subject directly or which (much more typically) plays a supporting role to the classroom teacher. It is recognised that pupils will certainly acquire IT skills in this way, but these are seen as a by-product rather than the main aim. The success of this 'curriculum computing' approach in practice is known to be critically dependent on the availability of good computing resources and on the teacher preparation which is needed to ensure that the new opportunities are taken up.

The 'curriculum computing' approach definitely regards the study of computing *per se* as a secondary, less important, matter. However, at least three kinds of rationale can be put in favour of computing courses of some kind.

Some education writers, including Caroline Benn (Benn 1987), have presented 'computer literacy' arguments. Typically, these attempt to identify a core of computing knowledge and skills which are claimed to be desirable for all learners: the reasons given are mainly social (that in a 'technological culture' to lack computer understanding is to be isolated) and political (that lack of knowledge is denial of power). The problem for schools is to decide how computer literacy will be achieved. It is important to recognise that computer literacy is presented analogously with basic numeracy and with fundamental skills in reading and writing: it represents a target for all pupils and, hence, demands a response in the core curriculum. But this does not necessarily imply a need for formal computing courses. The knowledge and skill levels suggested by computer literacy arguments are typically low enough that they should easily be overtaken by an effective 'curriculum computing' policy, perhaps together with suitable adaptations within the social science elements of the core curriculum. It can also be argued – somewhat ironically – that if the technology really is as socially all-pervasive as the claims suggest, then (eventually) no special educational provision should be needed, for the children will surely become as casually accustomed to IT as did their parents to telephones and motor cars.

A different kind of rationale for computing courses is one which proposes that Computing Science should become a new subject (perhaps an option, like Russian or Botany) in the secondary school curriculum. It is quite easy to find Computing Scientists who will argue vigorously that their subject has now become a rich and important area of human knowledge. It is much harder to find among them any two who can agree upon precisely what their subject is actually about. What, the perplexed observer of the computing scene may wonder, is there in common between, on the one hand, the blue-suited employees of IBM (whose talk is of executive productivity tools and management information systems), and, on the other, researchers in Artificial Intelligence (who pronounce boldly that for them the goal is 'to build a person, or more humbly, an animal'? [Charniak and McDermott 1985]). But this very diversity can be a source of excitement. Even within the apparently staid world of IBM there is a massively funded research programme in which new discoveries and developments in the uncharted waters of computing are made regularly. The absence of centuries of prior work has the advantage that computing is refreshingly free of the usual rigid taxonomies of topics and domains. Thus, Robin Milner, Professor of Computer Science at the University of Edinburgh has noted that:

> we all find it baffling to try to demarcate between the sciences of Computing, Intelligence and Cognition. Fortunately, there is so much to do that no-one finds any value in boundary disputes!
> [Milner 1986]

If this same spirit of openness and enthusiasm could permeate a school's treatment of Computing Science, then there seems every hope that it could provide an excellent experience for learners. Certainly, there are opportunities as well as difficulties in facing up to a subject in which not only the correct answers but also the correct questions are yet to be determined. Given a willingness to reflect the diversity and to experiment with a variety of syllabus formulations, there seems no reason why computing could not be implemented so as to be consistent with wider educational goals, such as the development of scientific thinking skills, for example. Pupils taking computing as a special interest in this way might, in consequence, become attracted to Further or Higher Education courses in Computing Science.

The crudest rationale for computing courses is the vocationalist one. This regards IT training as the task for schools, and the main problem becomes an accurate identification of what skills the market demands. It follows that teachers should implement courses which offer the precise blend of skills which will match pupils to the jobs available. During the 1980s this rationale has explicitly or implicitly underpinned much of the policy for school computing, and in Scotland, indeed, it has scarcely been challenged. This fact is all the more remarkable since the evidence to justify this position is extremely hard to find.

Of course, there are some strong contradictions within the vocationalist position. First, the new technologies are upheld as the means by which the quality of life should be improved, and the 'leisured society' attained: yet it is implied that this advance depends upon an 'industrialisation' of the school curriculum, with job-oriented skills partially supplanting studies in the cultural and aesthetic areas. Secondly, the citizen who is best equipped for an advanced technological society is widely agreed to be an adaptable, flexible, problem-solver who can rapidly acquire new skills and who will probably hold many different jobs in a working life: yet we are asked to move towards not the broad, liberal, education which seems ideally suited for such a prospect, but rather towards a schooling which looks more like a specialist training. Thirdly, the vocationalists emphasise the rapidity of technological and structural change: yet they claim to be so confident about the precise skill requirements of future employment that educational policy can be safely based on their predictions. The vocational ideology seems to suffer from an extreme case of internal inconsistency.

THE INFLUENCE OF THE SED[3] AND THE SEB[4]

What then have been the objectives of the SED in the educational computing area? From the SED in the 1970s the policy was set out in the 'Bellis Report' of 1972. Bellis, who was headteacher at Daniel Stewart's College (an Edinburgh private sector school), recommended that:

>   work relating to computers should generally be incorporated into the teaching of the various school subjects. Computing Studies

should not be developed as a subject discipline in its own right.
[*Computers and the schools* 1972]

The report proposed that to underpin this 'curriculum computing' approach all pupils should be provided with some computer literacy:

an appreciation of the working and potential of computers as a
necessary basis for future applications in many subjects.

The idea that for some pupils the new area of Computing Science
might have the potential to become a worthwhile subject for study is
dismissed:

they [pupils] could only do this by studying the subject as an
alternative to some other of wider acceptability . . . Computing
becomes meaningful in its application within the area of activity it is
serving.

In some respects the Bellis Report represented an enlightened position.
It contained no hint of vocationalism and its concern was for schools to
respond to computing in such a way as to benefit the all-round education
of the majority of pupils. But the committee's dismissal of the educational potential of Computing Science has a strong flavour of academic
snobbery. And because of the SED's well-known centralist, top-down
style of policy-making, Bellis effectively excluded the subject from all
Scottish schools throughout the 1970s. Evidence of the completeness of
the exclusion is the absence of any mention for computing in the influential 1977 'Munn Report' on the secondary school curriculum (*The Structure of the Curriculum* . . . 1977). In contrast, teachers south of the border
were able to negotiate money for resources and had the freedom to
experiment with a variety of new computing courses.

With little school access to machines, the Bellis 'curricular computing'
strategy had negligible impact. But with the arrival of microcomputers in
the late 1970s prospects looked better. Micros meant that computing
'incorporated into the teaching of the various school subjects' might at
last become a reality. The SED set up the Scottish Microelectronics Development Programme (SMDP) with a four-year remit, costing £1 million,
to develop educational software and to provide support for schools. In
England and Wales there was established the Microelectronics Education Programme with a fairly similar set of objectives.

Very soon there began to emerge disquieting stories about the SED's
management of SMDP. The 'official' line was that all was going well, and
when J. G. Morris, an SED HMCI[6] and the chairman of SMDP's steering
committee, described in 1982 the experience of the first two years of SMDP
in the *European Journal of Education*, he did so in tones of confident
complacency:

Much has been learned in two years about the process of integrating
computers into education. The hardware needs of the main curriculum subjects are clearer and there is enough software to support
training courses. The experience of these two years in Scotland may

the better inform any educational group or system which in 1982 is
at the beginning of micro-integration. [Morris 1982]

But a sharply contrasting picture of the experience came from elsewhere.
In that same year was published an independent evaluation of SMDP by
two researchers from the University of Edinburgh. Their study pointed
to major problems in the centralist, SED-directed control of SMDP, the
work of which was being rated poorly by teachers in comparison to
that of the decentralised MEP[7]. Internal conflicts had led to the resigna-
tion of SMDP's Deputy Director in September 1981 and relationships with
SED had been brought 'near to breaking point' (Odor and Entwistle
1982).

The Edinburgh research report also pointed out that 'curriculum computing' would require far more resources than the SED had been willing
to spend. It identified major problems in the lack of hardware; in the time
required to develop good software; in the requirement for teacher education and preparation; and in the absence of an adequate research and
development programme. The report concluded:

The potential is there – but teachers will need encouragement,
support, and release from class contact to be able fully to grasp the
opportunities offered by the microelectronics revolution.

The implication that heavy and recurrent further expenditure would be
necessary would hardly be welcomed by the SED. Indeed, the researchers themselves describe an interview with the minister at the SED, who at
that time was Alec Fletcher. Fletcher is quoted as saying:

I was delighted . . . that for a relatively small amount of funds we
could get something off the ground, as we did. It is not an expensive
operation in terms of value.

At about that time the SED dramatically changed its line on Computing
Studies. Morris mentions the matter casually in his article:

A joint SCEEB[8]/CCC[9] committee decided in February 1981 that it was
time to offer 'O' Grade computing in Scotland. . . . it has therefore
been agreed by the Secretary of State to run a pilot 'O' grade in 17
schools starting in August 1982 [Morris 1982]

This switch was all the more surprising in view of the fact that plans were
already well under way to withdraw all existing O-Grades in favour of
the new post-Munn Standard Grade curriculum. To introduce an O-
Grade in a new subject at that point meant not just a policy reversal: it
demonstrated an urgency which looked close to panic.

It is often difficult to fathom the SED's motives, but in this case the
explanation has probably at least four parts. First, the 1981 DOI scheme to
provide schools with micros had been launched amid much vocationalist
hype. Without computing courses of some kind in the schools the
propaganda would look ridiculous. Secondly, 'curriculum computing'
was proving to be tricky and expensive: an O-Grade in Computing
may have seemed an opportune means to prevent the machines from

gathering dust and becoming too much of an embarrassment. Thirdly, there was some genuine pressure from teachers for the move, especially from those whose enthusiasm (and possible promotion) had been blocked by the Bellis policy through the 1970s. But the fourth, and most important, factor may have been the MSC[10]. The MSC at that time was at the height of its expansionist phase and was on the verge of extending its educational tentacles outwards from the Further Education colleges and into the schools. The SED will have known that the MSC was about to unleash its TVEI[11] programme: rumours abounded that the SED was making a bid to intercept Scottish TVEI funds *en bloc*. The sudden announcement of the new O-Grade Computing may well have been partly an attempt to give the SED some credibility in its bureaucratic struggle to fend off the MSC.

But the SED was clearly in trouble. The strain of implementing mass-scale Computing Studies courses was likely to damage badly the impact of 'curriculum computing', since these two were in direct competition for scarce skills and resources. Furthermore, after a decade of non-engagement with the subject of computing the prospects for high-quality courses were distinctly poor: teacher training was almost non-existent, for example. Computing Science graduates had been consistently deterred from joining the Scottish teaching profession, not just because of its pay and conditions but also because throughout the Bellis period their subject had gone unrecognised by the SED.

In these circumstances a genuinely sound curriculum development might still have been feasible, but it would have had unattractive implications for the SED. It would necessitate a gradual exploration of the new subject which could slowly accumulate a range of pointers to the most promising interpretations of educational aims, content, teaching and learning styles, and so on. Such a process would be lengthy, and its outcomes (and, hence, its contribution to political propaganda) would be unpredictable. Perhaps worse, a genuine exploration of the subject's potential would probably have required a classroom-led, 'bottom-up', development which would put the teachers in control. Diversity would be inevitable. This would hardly have appealed to the SED with its propensity for leading by the nose.

In this context, the SED's conversion to the need for computing courses which were vocationally oriented can be understood. Such an orientation was not only clearly favoured by ministers, it was also the least demanding in the requirement for trained teachers. A skills-based prescription of approved content, suitably embellished with a rhetoric which was careful to appeal to computer literacy and even Computing Science arguments as well as to the vocational ideology, could be centrally produced quite easily. And to the SED's HMIs, who were themselves overwhelmingly the products of more traditional academic disciplines, 'practical', work-related, courses in computing might be the only kind which could make sense. The old Bellis view that 'Computing becomes meaningful in its application within the area of activity it is serving' still carried a lot of weight, even though the Inspectors would have been indignant had the same comment been made about Mathematics or English, for example. Thus, Morris announced that for the new O-Grade syllabus: 'the emphasis will not be on hardware or logic but on applications' (Morris 1982). By 'applications' the SED meant business and industrial computing skills. It was a decision which maximised the likelihood that the course could be running in a large number of schools within a short period of time. But it also committed computing to the vocational line, and certainly the concept of a creative investigation of a new science was nowhere apparent.

The SED's Standard Grade Computing Studies course which rapidly followed on from the introduction of the O-Grade developed these trends still further. Specified by a working group which substantially comprised individuals who had constructed the O-Grade syllabus, the Standard Grade prescribes a training-style 'case study' approach as the only permissible classroom methodology. Teachers are expected to make their 14–16 year old charges into adept users of business data processing systems, such as those for mail-order, stock control, word processing, and seat-booking. Pupils operate junior versions of these programs (scaled down to fit their BBC micros) and role-play what is portrayed to be the typical work of an IT operative. Certainly, the SED had achieved one thing. Within O-Grade and Standard Grade computing classrooms there was no risk of 'demarcation disputes' between the boundary areas of Milner's 'sciences of Computing, Intelligence and Cognition': none of these things was to be allowed to interfere with learning. Computing was to be interpreted as an arm of commerce, with the 'electronic office' rather than the research lab upheld as the centre of progress. As surely as in the 1970s the subject was decreed not to exist, so in the 1980s its existence, and the dogmatic interpretation of its rationale in commercial applications and vocational opportunities, was decreed also. Sadly, the new position generated scarcely any more debate than did the old.

THE TVEI PROGRAMME AND SCOTVEC[12]

The MSC's announcement in 1982 of the TVEI programme came as a shock to many in education. The goal of the programme was to 'enhance' the curriculum in the area of new technology and to provide pupils with skills which would be directly appropriate to the world of work. This inevitably involved a significant contribution to school computing. All Scottish TVEI projects have featured computing heavily, but the certification has been mainly provided not by the SED's traditional examining arm, the SEB, but by the National Certificate programme of forty-hour modular courses (which had hitherto been associated solely with the post-16 stage) controlled by SCOTVEC. Typically, TVEI pupils have enrolled for one or more SCOTVEC modules, of which the following represent typical titles:

1091: Introduction to Computers
2102: Keyboarding
2129: Introduction to the Information Technology Office
2150: Word Processing
1110: Computer Graphics
4807: Introduction to Computer Aided Draughting

The vocational case for studying such modules as these is highly tenuous. Frequently, claims have been made that their study is 'student-centred' and brings desirable side-effects in terms of the 'personal development' of individuals. But, of course, similar claims about side-effects have been made on behalf of numerous topics and subjects in the past. And it is difficult to avoid the suspicion that the 'student-centred' aspects mean little more than that pupils occupy many hours in sitting at solitary keyboards performing low-level tasks (for which many seem to have an astonishing tolerance). Overwhelmingly these modules present computing at a machine operator's level. It would be the contemporary equivalent of learning how to tend the looms and mind the boilers which were the industrial technology of times past but for the fact – one which could come as a cruel blow to the 60 per cent of TVEI pupils on the SCRE[13] survey who believed that TVEI would help them find a job (*TESS* 1989) – that jobs for 'machine operators' in the IT era simply do not exist.

This is not to deny the possibility that some TVEI computing money may have been usefully spent. A portion of the cash has been allocated to funding 'enhancements' to existing subjects – a strange MSC euphemism for extra cash injections into the budgets of those school subject departments which offered to spend it in a manner compatible with the MSC aims. This opportunity has generated some imaginative proposals from teachers who have found ingenious alignments between their educational goals and the strictives of TVEI. Some welcome resources for 'curriculum computing' have been won from the MSC in this fashion, and it seems unfortunate that the Scottish Local Authorities did not succeed in diverting more of the money in this direction rather than towards the SCOTVEC modules.

Paradoxically, SCOTVEC modules have provided a possible route to an alternative computing curriculum. Although they were originally conceived as being vocational in nature, they have the considerable advantage of offering the opportunity for the bottom-up development of courses. Teachers may submit for approval a module descriptor in any area deemed suitable by SCOTVEC. This is in contrast to the rigid central prescription of SEB courses such as the Standard Grade. A new family of computing modules has been started by a small group of teachers,

computer professionals, and academics (AIMS[16]). The modules are all
related to the area of Artificial Intelligence and are not ostensibly vocational in nature. However, it seems that scotvec's definition of 'vocational' has become quite flexible.

THE NATIONAL PLAN

The dominant themes of the secondary computing curriculum in the
1980s have been concerned with examinable computing and the alternative implementations provided by the SEB and by SCOTVEC. So all-
pervading has this obsession with Computing Studies been that it might
be imagined that it was part of a carefully constructed plan. As early as
1982, proposals for a National Plan for Scottish educational computing
were being circulated to 'interested parties'. The document was the
result of a joint COSLA[14]/SED initiative to try to establish national guidelines for hardware and software in Scottish schools. But the proposals
took a relatively wide view of educational computing, and, of the eight
final recommendations, none was concerned with examinable computing. On 28 October 1982 the *Scotsman* published an article announcing
the proposed standardisation:

> Education authorities and the Scottish Office are drawing up a
> national plan to co-ordinate the introduction and use of computers
> in Scottish schools.

In fact, it took a further three years for the National Plan to make an
appearance, this time under the auspices of SCET.[15] Like its precursor,
the National Plan did not reflect the emphasis on certificate courses
which has been the reality of school computing. Its recommendations
were concerned with standardisation of software and hardware, and
with future equipment and staffing requirements.

Four years later its impact is not apparent. It is not clear whether the
plan has been the instigator of change or merely the predictor. Many of
its recommendations have not been implemented. Possibly a lesson
should be learned from the MSC. The most effective way to ensure that
plans do have a real effect on educational policy is to provide the
resources with which to implement them. Perhaps with this in mind, the
Director of SCET recently claimed that the SED had failed to resource the
National Plan adequately (*TESS* 1989). In any event, the National Plan
missed the opportunity to make any recommendations which would
have challenged the rapidly developing orthodoxy. There was no mention of the need for a variety of approaches to the area; no warning about
the dangers of the premature prescriptions of Computing Studies; and
no real attempt to redress the balance of resources back towards cross-
curricular computing. By ignoring the realities of what was actually
happening, the National Plan paid the price of being perceived by many
as being largely irrelevant.

PRIMARY COMPUTING

Most of the energies of the SED were involved in directing the development of computing in the secondary sector. Primary schools did not attract any serious attention for much of the decade. This meant that the primary sector was at the back of the queue for resources and training. Many primary schools were given inadequate equipment. The teachers were given only the most rudimentary training, often by trainers who themselves were near novices in the area. But, with hindsight, it is possible to view the lack of interference from outside as a considerable advantage.

It is arguable that primary computing has been the success story of Scottish educational computing in the 1980s. The lack of direction was initially frustrating, but it allowed teachers the freedom to experiment with different approaches and varieties of software. There was never any question of the study of computing for its own sake, and the vocational rationale is yet to undermine the primary curriculum. Computers were absorbed into the curriculum and used to support teaching and learning in an integrated fashion. Although there have been difficulties, the success of much of this work puts secondary educational computing to shame.

THE FUTURE

Scrutiny of the development of Scottish educational computing reveals a complicated story of changes of policy. For many of the decisions which have affected the direction of the area, the motivation is both complex and obscure. The SED's treatment of computing has been characterised by its liking for hierarchy, uniformity, and the judgement of a few 'favourite children'. But the SED has also managed to combine these characteristics with a pragmatic willingness to perform an about-turn whenever it seemed in its bureaucratic interests to do so. Thus, the SED committed Scotland to the Bellis 'curriculum computing' policy at a time when it was barely meaningful, and then deflected resources away from it when the arrival of microcomputers made its success seem a possibility. The SED excluded the subject of computing from Scottish schools, due largely to an academic disdain in the 1970s; then in the early 1980s it introduced vocationally inspired computing courses wildly and almost overnight, using prescriptive syllabus formulations which effectively excluded liberal and academic interpretations of what the subject might be. Perhaps what is most surprising is that the SED has managed to do these things in the almost complete absence of scrutiny, and still less criticism, from anyone inside or outside Scottish education.

In a decade in which educational computing has developed from almost nothing to become a significant part of the school curriculum, one might have expected the area to have stimulated lively debate amongst policy-makers and practitioners. The lack of evidence of any

such discussion is only one of the symptoms of the malaise which has
gripped the area from the moment of its birth. Educational computing
will come of age only when it ceases to be considered undesirable to
make searching evaluations of its progress. The authors who have contributed to this volume have made a start to that process. It remains to be
seen whether their efforts will have any lasting effect: at least they will
have tried.

NOTES

1. Department of Industry.
2. Information Technology.
3. Scottish Education Department.
4. Scottish Examination Board.
5. Scottish Microelectronics Development Programme.
6. Her Majesty's Chief Inspector.
7. Microelectronics Education Programme.
8. Scottish Certificate of Education Board, now the Scottish Examination Board.
9. Consultative Committee on the Curriculum, now the Scottish
   Council on the Curriculum.
10. Manpower Services Commission.
11. Technical and Vocational Educational Initiative.
12. Scottish Vocational Education Council.
13. Scottish Council for Educational Research.
14. Convention of Scottish Local Authorities.
15. Scottish Council for Educational Technology.
16. Artificial Intelligence Modules for Schools.

REFERENCES

Benn, C. (1987). *Technology, Education and Training*, SEEDS, Brighton
    Technology Conference.
Charniak, E. and McDermott, D (1985). *Introduction to Artificial
    Intelligence*, Wokingham; Addison-Wesley.
Computers and the Schools ('Bellis Report') (1972). Curriculum Paper
    11, HMSO.
Milner, R. (1986). *Is Computing an Experimental Science?*, LFCS Report
    Series, Department of Computer Science, University of
    Edinburgh.
Morris, J. G. (1982). 'The use of the new information technologies in
    Scottish education', *European Journal of Education*, 17(4), 369–82.
Odor, P. and Entwhistle, N. (1982). *The Introduction of Microelectron-
    ics into Scottish Education*, Edinburgh: Scottish Academic Press.
*The Proof of the Pudding: A Study of the Views of Pupils in Lothian Pilot
    TVEI Schools* (1988). SCRE.
*The Structure of the Curriculum in the Third and Fourth Years of the
    Scottish Secondary School* ('Munn Report'), (1977). HMSO.
TESS, 6 January 1989, p.1.
Wellington, J. (1988). *Appendix to Policies and Trends in IT and Education*,
    ESRC Occasional Paper ITE/28e/88, University of Lancaster.

2

A MINIATURE LEADERSHIP CLASS

PETER COPE

INTRODUCTION

The title of this chapter is derived from Walter Humes's analysis of the way in which Scottish education is controlled (Humes 1986). Humes contended that educational policy was determined by a 'leadership class', whose members are drawn from the ranks of SED[1] civil servants, HMIS[2], Directors of Education and their staffs, and others, including carefully selected teachers. Members of the class are characterised by their positions on various national bodies such as, for example, the CCC[3] and the SEB.[4] This relatively small group of what Humes describes as 'mutually admiring' people are able to steer the development of Scottish education by their control of the different elements of the Scottish educational system. Apparently independent bodies are controlled indirectly by the patronage of individuals who are likely to conform to the values of the leadership. Policy decisions are concerned with the accumulation of, and the preservation of, power rather than with the quality of the educational experience of pupils. Informal contact between members of the leadership class is an important vehicle for the formation of policy. Rationalisation of educational organisations, a frequent feature of the current quest for economic efficiency, is used as a method of drawing the strings of control to the centre and further extending the power of the leadership class. Humes's conclusion was that the image which is projected, an image of consultation and democratic decision-making, is in stark contrast to the reality of the tight self-serving control over Scottish education exercised by this group.

Humes's 'leadership class' thesis has not passed without criticism. Raab (1987) has taken issue with the methodology of the analysis, particularly with the absence of interview material from leadership class members. McPherson and Raab (1988) present an analysis of the government of Scottish education based just on such material. Since the interviews were with retired members of the Scottish educational establishment, the result is partially historical. Indeed, the application of such techniques to educational computing would involve a wait of some twenty years before the policies of the 1980s could be examined.

If we accept Humes's thesis as to the existence and purposes of a leadership class, then we might predict that there exists a set of 'miniature leadership classes' whose function is to implement the policies of the 'global' leadership class in each area of the curriculum. This chapter will explore the contention that Humes's 'global' analysis of the Scottish educational system can be applied 'locally' to a particular section of the curriculum. Educational computing provides a useful opportunity for such an analysis because of its recent arrival on the scene. The origins of a miniature leadership class in educational computing should be relatively accessible to examination.

Members of the global leadership class occupy prominent positions in the national bodies of Scottish education. Miniature leadership class members should, therefore, be found to occupy similarly prominent positions in the committees charged with overseeing the development of particular curricular domains. Control of the development of educational computing has been in the hands of a number of committees set up by the CCC and the SEB. Membership of the miniature leadership class, however, would be indicated by invitations to join more than one of these committees. In a sense, the first appointment to a committee is a test to see whether the individual is 'sound'. Those who pass the test can look forward to more patronage in the form of further such appointments. The reward for successful conformity to the values of the system is sometimes measured in terms of elevation to a higher position in the system. But it also includes the power to control the area. Paradoxically, this control cannot generally be used in any original innovative way. Innovations other than those sponsored by the leadership would be construed as 'rocking the boat'. Thus, power is often used to restrict the activities of others working in the field rather than to exert a creative influence.

This interpretation of the role of those prominently involved in the development of educational computing might be considered to be cynical. There is an alternative explanation for the way in which such committees are appointed and for the ubiquity of certain individuals. The official view concerning SEB and CCC committees is that they are devices by which power is devolved throughout the system in order to achieve consensus. Hence, each such committee has at least one teacher on it; there will usually be an adviser, a university representative, someone from the colleges, miscellaneous 'consultants' – and there will always be a member of the Inspectorate. Policy-making is, therefore, shared by representatives from a wide spectrum of Scottish education, and the invitation to participate in the process is the mark of the expert. Humes (1986) describes this conventional view as the 'received wisdom', and it is in terms of the received wisdom that members of the miniature leadership class describe their own role.

There are, however, several reasons for questioning the received wisdom, particularly in the area of educational computing. It is demonstrable that members of the various committees involved in its development were not expert. This does not necessarily reflect on their ability; it simply describes the state of knowledge in educational computing at that time. It seems unlikely, therefore, that an invitation to join the formative committees was an indication of expertise. More probably, such invitations were a sign of approval by the SED. Thus, a system of patronage allows the appearance of wide-ranging consultation without any danger of the inconveniences of its reality. Although it remains important to pay lip-service to the received wisdom concerning consultation and debate, in practice, such debate would be restricted to avoid conflict with those more knowledgeable and less conformist. Finally, membership of the miniature leadership class involves absorbing the bureaucratic conventions rather than demonstrating any deep understanding of the domain. So, we would expect its members to identify strongly with official policy.

Thus, the miniature leadership class thesis generates hypotheses concerning the expertise of its members, the reality of their consultation with outsiders, their patronage by the SED, and their assimilation of the values of the global leadership class.

BACKGROUND TO SCOTTISH EDUCATIONAL COMPUTING

The major groups from which the membership of the miniature leadership class may be drawn consist of the Advisorate, the Colleges of Education, and the Inspectorate. The origin of the appointment of many members of these groups goes back to the early 1980s and before. Most teachers, advisers, and members of the Inspectorate knew little or nothing about computing at that time. An apparent answer to the requirement for knowledgeable people appeared in the shape of a few individuals who seemed to be comfortable with the new technology. Their expertise was very limited, but 'in the country of the blind, the one-eyed man is king'.

This 'one-eyed man' effect has had a considerable influence on the key appointments in the area of educational computing. In the late 1970s and early 1980s the possession of skills which we now know to be easily attainable by primary school children was regarded with awe by the uninitiated. This marked the start of a significant trend: the confusion between superficial and profound computing knowledge which has become the hallmark of Scottish educational computing. It takes no more than a few days to learn how to use a range of applications packages, yet these skills were taken to imply a level of knowledge far above their true significance. In one region, for example, the Adviser in computing was appointed by the simple expedient of changing the remit of the existing adviser in environmental education. The criterion upon which the decision to make this change was based appeared to be that the individual concerned occasionally used a BBC microcomputer.

However, one of the characteristics of computing is that qualifications are even less reliable as a guide to competence than they are in other areas. The domain is developing so rapidly that qualified people can quickly become out of touch, especially if they are no longer intellectually engaged with the subject. Conversely, people who start with 'very limited' qualifications can develop a high degree of competence – 'one-eyed' individuals can develop binocular vision. But while the former process is all too easy, acquiring competence which transcends everyday software familiarity is not. Busy people tend to be more willing to learn how to use new software packages than to take on more demanding goals associated with new areas of Computing Science or Artificial Intelligence. But computing is a much wider and richer area than can be encompassed by a focus on bread-and-butter 'utility' software.

THE ADVISORATE

The formal qualifications of the current computing Advisorate in the domain of educational computing vary considerably. Some have none at all; others have the 'crash' SATQ[5] which was provided by Jordanhill College of Education in early 1984. This course covered a period of six months and involved attendance at the college for one day per week during this time. To put the course into context: consider the acceptability of taking a teacher of, say, French and sending him on what amounts to a thirty- to forty-day course in order to prepare him to be an Adviser in maths. This order of retraining seems cursory. Current Diploma courses for retraining in educational computing require attendance for one day per week over a period of two years, or one year of full-time study, and even this is regarded as barely sufficient to cover the basics of the subject. The SED's view of SATQ courses in computing was given by an HMI at a meeting convened at New St Andrew's House on 14 November 1988 to persuade university Computing Science departments to become involved with INSET[6] for teachers of Computing Studies. She described such courses as 'very, very limited indeed'.

The other normal requirement for membership of the Advisorate is a substantial background in teaching the relevant subject area. But the appointment of most of the current members of the group from the classroom in the early part of the 1980s effectively removed them from any meaningful experiences of teaching current courses in Computing Studies, or from participation in the use of computers in other subject areas. There are now many members of the computing teaching force, therefore, whose qualifications and experience far outweigh those of the people charged with advising them. However, computing Advisers have the means to wield considerable power over teachers in their area. Many teachers have seen computing as a way of gaining promotion in an otherwise logjammed system. Furthermore, computing teachers are dependent on their Advisers for the equipment which is essential to their teaching. Such pressures do not encourage outspokenness among the teaching force.

COLLEGES OF EDUCATION

Colleges of Education in Scotland have had Departments of Computing since the early 1970s, notwithstanding the lack of any significant school computing until the advent of the microcomputer. Up to that time their duties could not be described as arduous. They maintained mainframe computers with which they provided a service to the few schools which required the compilation of batch processed programs or the running of administrative software. Their hitherto gentle existence was rudely interrupted by the IT revolution, which required them to undertake the training of teachers, a task which was routine to their colleagues in other departments but for which they were not well prepared. Computing staff found themselves in the position of having to create and teach courses for the first time. How well they responded to the demands for the training of new teachers in computing is examined in another chapter of this book. Here, we are concerned with their other new role – that of 'expert' consultants to the process of curriculum development. It is this role which rendered suitably conformist members of this group eligible to be recruited into the ranks of the miniature leadership class.

The first problem was that college Departments of Computing did not have sufficient personnel to carry out the new tasks which confronted them. Colleges of Education usually recruit their staff from experienced teachers and, as we have seen, there was a dearth of these in the computing field. The curricula vitae of College of Education staff are published in submissions of course descriptions to validating bodies such as the CNAA,[7] and, for colleges which have been active enough to submit such courses in computing, it is possible to examine the background and development of the staff. Typically, these may be divided into the 'old guard', who were recruited in the 1970s; and the newcomers, who were a result of the expansion of the early 1980s. Many of the latter were Assistant Principal Teachers of Mathematics and, typically, they have five to ten years of teaching experience. Many of the former held no promoted teaching post and their teaching experience is limited to two or three years.

Whatever the background of College of Education personnel, it is reasonable to expect their contributions to the subject area to be significant. An area such as educational computing should have provided many opportunities for research, software, and textbooks. The paucity of evidence for any of these (with a few notable exceptions) is a striking

feature of the curricula vitae of these individuals. One head of department, for example, entered his college in 1971 after only two years
of Mathematics teaching. His listed interests include 'methods of
teaching programming' and 'assessable computing at school level' – the
latter presumably referring to his position as principal examiner
for O-Grade Computing Studies. Yet, apparently, these have not stimulated him to a single publication in eighteen years. One is moved to
question the management strategies of departments where there seems
to be so little published output when so much innovative work
is so obviously required, and is, indeed, being carried out elsewhere.
More serious, however, is the contribution to the control of the development of computing that is made by people whose horizons appear
to be so limited.

HER MAJESTY'S INSPECTORATE

The Inspectorate are charged with the inspection of education and with
steering its development. It is an important component of the received
wisdom that they are experts in their particular field of education. As
such, they appear on all committees of the SEB and CCC. Another function
is to provide advice and feedback to their political masters in the Scottish
Office. That there is an inherent conflict in this dual role is not readily
acknowledged. What happens if the political wing of the executive
chooses to ignore the proffered advice and dictate policies which conflict
with the 'expertise' of his Advisers is a question never directly addressed. When asked recently to elaborate on this theme, Donald Mack,
HMDSCI,[8] replied somewhat tersely: 'The constitutional position is well
understood; officials offer advice and ministers take the decisions'
(*TESS*, 3 February 1989, p. 6). Members of the Inspectorate are not
allowed to articulate publicly any areas of disagreement which occur
between them and the Minister responsible for Education, nor are they
permitted to demonstrate any dissension from SED policy generally.
Thus, the crucial skill necessary for survival and advancement in the
Inspectorate is to be able to interpret and conform to policy. But that
policy is then presented to teachers as if it emanated from an impartial
expertise akin to that of consultants in non-political areas such as
medicine.

  The psychology of the Inspectorate is illuminated in another quote
from the above article in which Donald Mack speaks of the need to take
the wider view rather than see things 'through your own distorting
prisms'. These statements from a senior member of the Inspectorate
comply perfectly with Humes's descriptions of the mechanisms used by
members of the leadership class to rationalise such conflicts:

> The suppression of personal doubt can be looked upon as a kind of
> self-denial undertaken for the greater good of the organisation.
> Thus it is the person who silences his or her personal reservations

about approved policies, not the one who insists on speaking out, who becomes the paradigm of the good administrator. [Humes 1986 p. 204]

Humes concludes that although the Inspectorate has been successful in projecting itself as a body possessed of considerable educational expertise, this reputation is not fully justified (Humes 1986 p. 79). An examination of their role in computing tends to lend support to Humes's analysis. The collective experience of the Inspectorate in educational computing is not significant. No HMI has a Computing Studies teaching qualification, and none of them has ever personally used computers in support of other areas of the school curriculum.

How do HMIS in computing gain the 'expertise' to inspect teachers who are often better qualified and have more experience? The Inspectorate couch their descriptions of educational computing in terms of 'good practice'. Humes suggests that the criteria used to identify good practice are vague and ill defined, and that it is often a synonym for what happens to be fashionable at the time. But another interpretation of 'good practice' is that it represents knowledge accumulated by what is essentially a plagiarism of teachers' expertise during the inspection process. HMIS do not often acknowledge the source of their information. The recent HMI report on microcomputers in education (SED 1987) contains not one single reference or acknowledgement, although it abounds with eulogies about good practice. The reason for this apparent insularity is not clear. However, it has been suggested (Kent 1988) that HMIS withhold sources of information because of a desire, conscious or subconscious, to control that information in a manner which protects their image of superiority. Thus, the Inspectorate is seen as the source of the knowledge rather than as merely the messenger.

Another important area of activity for the Inspectorate is in curriculum development. HMIS have appeared on every significant committee concerned with the development of educational computing. Humes (1986) suggests that HMIS are able to exert considerably more informal power on the educational system than that which stems from their formal position (Humes 1986 p. 8). The 'Rendle Report' suggested that there is some concern that HMIS are inclined to dominate educational committees of which they are members. It refers to their 'disturbingly powerful influence' and to the deference which such committees automatically accord to members of the Inspectorate and their opinions (Rendle 1981). Members of educational computing committees are especially vulnerable to such pressure due to the dearth of experienced and qualified personnel, which has been discussed earlier. It is difficult to imagine many of them having sufficient confidence to oppose any position or policy being forcefully presented by an HMI. Thus, HMIS can be seen as representatives of the global leadership class, whose task is to control the miniature leadership classes to which they are assigned.

THE COMMITTMENT TO OPEN DEBATE

An important part of the received wisdom is that the process of curriculum development is one which is open to debate and discussion among all concerned professionals. Indeed, the impression is given that such debate is welcomed by members of committees involved in planning for the future of Scottish education. Thus, much is made of the distribution of Joint Working Party reports for comment before the final arrangements documents are published. The H-Grade JWP in Computing Studies even went so far as to distribute a draft interim report document in 1986 so that comments could be considered before the official report was written.

A typical example of the received wisdom on consultation is contained in a letter, dated 25 November 1986, from HMI Dr George Gray to the Borders Secondary Schools Computer Group (BSSCG). In it, Dr Gray refers to the 'open and very publicly oriented approach' of the Higher Grade JWP, and of his aim to 'promote open and free debate on all aspects of computing'. However, the letter was a response to a specific and detailed complaint from the BSSCG concerning a conference on the Higher Grade proposals. This conference, which was held at Moray House College in September 1986, was unusual in that it was open to all. Individual teachers, who are normally left out of such discussion, were able to put their views on the draft syllabus. Attendance was undoubtedly boosted by the circulation of a rumour that the SED had attempted to prevent it from taking place. The BSSCG's letter addressed itself quite specifically to this issue as the following extract shows:

> At the recent Higher Grade Computing meeting, one of us ... expressed our collective concern to you about approaches which were made by the inspectorate to Moray House College with regard to the Higher Grade conference which was held there on 29th September ... The interpretation being placed on the above approach is, rightly or wrongly, that it was an attempt to restrict a legitimate discussion of the Higher proposals

Curiously, Dr Gray, while reaffirming the received wisdom in general terms, made no mention of the substance of the letter at all.

The reality of the consultative processes listed by Dr Gray as evidence for the open nature of the system is less effective than it sounds. In fact, responses to SEB JWP reports are considered only if they come from 'interested parties', and the SEB decides who is classified as 'interested'. Individual teachers are not so classified. Any comments from teachers on an SEB Report must be directed through their union or professional organisation. This system is ostensibly designed to protect the SEB from the risk of being overwhelmed with individual opinions. However, it provides an effective filtering process which allows for the dilution of criticism during the collation process. It also allows the SEB to disregard criticism on the grounds that it does not come from a 'proper' quarter.

The inescapable conclusion seems to be that it is unlikely that effective criticisms of the current educational computing ideology can emerge from the protective layers of bureaucracy. Only the chosen can have any influence, and only the conformists are chosen. In early 1987, an article in *TESS* suggested that there was cause for concern in the way that educational computing was being developed (Conlon and Cope 1987). This article prompted a series of contributions from interested and concerned professionals (Paton 1987; Sparkes 1987; Hill 1987; and Sorensen 1987). The level of interest and the obvious anxieties of the contributors prompted an editorial article in *TESS* which called for a reassessment of educational computing policy:

> At the very least the keenness of teachers to express their worries raises questions which should not be brushed off because HMIs and local authority advisers tell good news stories. Such is the investment in educational computing and so important is it for Scotland to make the right decisions for the classrooms that a dispassionate assessment of the state of the art ought to be set in train. [*TESS*, 17 April 1987, p. 2]

No dispassionate assessment has since taken place. In fact, the response of the miniature leadership class to all this was a deafening silence. Such lack of participation does not reinforce their continuing contention that they are eager to discuss issues openly.

THE SEAL OF APPROVAL

The committees which have shaped the development of educational computing have been staffed largely by members of the groups described in the preceding sections. It is an interesting exercise to follow the adoption or rejection of a particular individual by tracing his or her path through the committee chain. A name which appears only once is usually a sign that the favours of patronage were withdrawn, presumably for some transgression. A number of names appear again and again, suggesting that the individual concerned has been approved as a sound and reliable recruit to the miniature leadership class.

For example, the software consultant for S-Grade Computing Studies went on to become principal examiner for the same course. The FDO[9] for S-Grade Computing Studies became full-time consultant to the H-Grade Computing Studies JWP and is now an HMI. An Adviser in computing was a member of the S-Grade JWP for Computing Studies, chairman of the H-Grade JWP for Computing Studies, and is now principal examiner for the latter course. A senior Adviser was on the Joint Committee (1979–81), was the convenor of the Joint Steering Committee (1981–4), and was the Chairman of the S-Grade JWP. A College of Education Lecturer was a member of the S-Grade JWP for Computing Studies, was scds Curriculum Officer to the H-Grade jwp for Computing Studies, and was on the Computing Studies Examination Panel from 1985 to 1986. The list goes on.

Now it is possible to argue that these multiple roles are a result of the demonstrable shortage of suitably qualified and experienced people in the area. But the knowledge and experience of those involved does not seem to be significantly greater than that possessed by many others working in the area at the same time. It is possible to claim that sticking to a small select group provides continuity, and that this is a desirable and deliberate policy. But the repeated occurrence of the same names is also consistent with the thesis of the miniature leadership class. The confidence of the SED, which is conveyed by a second appointment of some nature, is not gained by drawing attention to the flaws in the consensus position. Humes points out the consequences of non-conformist behaviour on such committees: 'The culprit would soon merit the description "forthright", which in Scottish education is a widely recognised codeword for "troublemaker"' (Humes 1986 p. 98). We may deduce, therefore, that the foremost qualities of these miniature leadership class members are more to do with their reliability and 'soundness' than with their capacity to shape the development of educational computing in any innovative fashion. Reliability may be assessed by the HMIS who oversee all SEB/CCC committees and whose excessive influence has already been discussed. One particular inspector (now an HMCI[10]) was present on every major educational computing committee convened between 1979 and 1985. It may be assumed that his was the hand which steered educational computing through its early development.

THE SED AND DISSENT

If individuals do not prove to be susceptible to the allures of the patronage system, the SED has other methods of ensuring the boat is not rocked. Tom Conlon has consistently argued against an attempt to lay down a prescriptive framework for teacher education in educational computing. According to the plan, all courses will comply with arrangements decided upon by a committee of college representatives plus the ubiquitous HMI. Already the SED controls the submission of Diploma courses to the CNAA for validation. There seems to be no reason for this except a desire to vet and control the contents of such courses. The Moray House College DPSE[11] in Computing was duly sent to the SED for their approval. There was some disagreement about the course contents. In a letter to the Assistant Principal of Moray House College, Hugh Perfect, dated 21 April 1988, HMI Gillian Campbell sought to clarify the areas of dispute. The tone of the letter is openly authoritarian. For example: 'The College might wish, in its own interests, to remove the reference to lack of debate contained in paragraph (c) page 31, since this comment was factually incorrect.' The offending paragraph is one which suggests that surprisingly little debate had been generated by publication of the SECT National Plan and the 1987 HMI Report on microcomputers in the secondary school. However, there is, according to HMI Gillian Campbell, to be no debate about the lack of debate! More sinister is the insistence that SED approval for the DPSE would be given only 'subject to confirmation of your undertaking that there would be no further obstruction to the development of the consortium course on the part of the Moray House representative in the field group'.

Persistent refusal to conform is met with the threat of a totally arbitrary sanction. This sort of crude pressure appears to be unusual, presumably because of the general reliability of the more subtle method of patronage. However, it does illustrate the importance which the SED attaches to the suppression of dissent, should patronage fail.

IDENTIFICATION WITH THE VALUES OF THE SYSTEM

The 'miniature leadership class' thesis leads to another prediction about the behaviour of its members. We would expect enthusiastic development of themes perceived to be those endorsed by the prevailing educational ideology even if the results of such development were not greeted with approbation by the teachers who are eventually saddled with the task of implementation.

The S-Grade JWP for Computing Studies produced a syllabus of staggering tedium, which is criticised elsewhere in this book. It is the amount of energy which went into the design of the assessment procedures which tends to confirm the uncritical assimilation of leadership values. The use of GRCs[12] was precisely the sort of development which was being pushed from above, and represented an important element of the value system of the global leadership class. GRCs appeared to provide the benefits of criterion-referenced assessment with the discriminative power of norm-referenced assessment.

Although objections to the practicalities and principles involved in their use have been made (Drever 1988, see also *TESS*, 17 February 1984, p. 2), members of the miniature leadership class would be expected to implement GRCs unquestioningly. Thus, criticism of GRCs would be ignored and suppressed even in the face of overwhelming evidence of their impracticality. The history of S-Grade assessment is well known. The original specifications were so out of touch with reality that they had to be revised by SGROAG[13] and the subject-specific SLWGs.[14] It is possible to argue that the general failure to communicate the problems associated with S-Grade assessment back to the higher echelons of the SED was the result of their unquestioning adoption by a buffer layer of miniature leadership classes.

As far as Computing Studies is concerned, an examination of the original S-Grade assessment procedures confirms that the JWP did, indeed, produce a system which was excessive even by the standards of the time. There were four assessable elements which the JWP claimed to have 'identified' by some unexplained process. In the first draft of the JWP Report, each of these was broken down into a further three or four sub-elements. In total, there were fifteen sub-elements, each with its associated GRCs designed to discriminate six different grades (SEB 1984). Everyday assessment by teachers, therefore, was to involve consulting a table containing ninety cells. The contents of each cell consisted of arcane 'content-free' criteria which the teacher was supposed to use to discriminate between grades. The following examples (accurately transcribed) show the original GRCs used to discriminate Grades 2 and 3 in sub-element 1 of knowledge and understanding:

> Grade 3: demonstrate knowledge of simple and some complex computing facts and concepts
> Grade 2: demonstrate knowledge of simple and complex computing facts and concepts

By the time the 'Arrangements' document was published (SEB 1986), the number of sub-elements had been reduced from fifteen to eleven. The GRCs had metamorphosed into another bizarre form which required the teacher to discriminate between such activities as classifying, categorising, comparing, and contrasting. The assessment of a single sub-element of knowledge and understanding required interpretation of a table containing fourteen entries.

Two interesting conclusions may be drawn from these examples. First, the miniature leadership class adopted GRCs with an enthusiasm which suggests that they had genuinely assimilated the values of their superiors. Secondly, the suspension of normal critical faculties implies powerful psychological pressures to conform – or a total absence of knowledge and expertise.

THE CONTROL OF KNOWLEDGE

If much of this chapter has seemed concerned with Computing Studies rather than with computing across the curriculum, it is a reflection of the major focus of the miniature leadership class. In Computing Studies, an important function of the power of the miniature leadership class has been to delineate and contain the extent of the legitimate knowledge base. Computing encompasses a wide and rapidly growing body of knowledge. By careful selection of those parts which are considered suitable for education, the miniature leadership class is able to prevent any challenge from those who have knowledge outside the tightly prescribed domain. This 'defining out' of challenging new areas of computing has been a constant feature of the development of examinable computing.

The early years of educational computing were pregnant with an excitement which is unusual in the relatively staid circumstances of education. Scotland had the potential to develop an original and dy-

namic approach to the area. The University of Edinburgh is an international centre of excellence in Artificial Intelligence, and much of the
experimentation in educational computing in the 1970s was stimulated
and, indeed, carried out by members of the Artificial Intelligence Department of the University of Edinburgh. Apparently, capitalising on this
initial effort was not considered by the leaders of educational computing
in the 1980s. It is now an expected feature of British innovation that any
early advantage is squandered. Educational computing has proved to be
no exception. The kindest thing that can be said about the miniature
leadership class is that they have snatched 'compulsory mediocrity' from
the jaws of originality.

THE SUFFOCATION OF DIVERSITY

The preparation of this chapter has been an illuminating, if somewhat
depressing, process. Many individuals have expressed grave and deeply
felt misgivings about the current state of Scottish educational computing
and the manner in which it is developing. Very few are willing to be
quoted. Potential non-conformists are afraid to criticise the system
openly. The overall impression is of a repressive, inflexible, system
which is conducive to conformity but totally intolerant of novelty, imagination, and creativity. Some of those involved closely with the development process justify their own role by claiming that they are
working quietly to change things from within. Others have stated that
their job is to motivate teachers and that this is incompatible with taking
an overtly critical stance of the establishment.

The rapid development of computing led to opportunities which
many seized enthusiastically. It is a measure of the poor management of
the system in which they work that their initial enthusiasm has been so
badly misdirected. Instead of evidence of diversity and experiment, we
have witnessed centralised prescription. The agenda has been rigidly set
before the new area has had a chance to find its feet. There has been no
shortage of volunteers to assist in ensuring that we all have to wear the
same blinkers. These dispensers of wisdom see nothing wrong with
confining discussion to within their own ranks, confident that in such
close company, their limited knowledge will not be challenged. Some
can now measure considerable personal success: elevation from the
'local' miniature leadership class to the 'global' leadership class itself.

CONCLUSION

Scrutiny of the actions of those involved in the control of educational
computing provides powerful indications of the existence of a miniature
leadership class. There has been evidence of lack of expertise, of patronage, of suppression of legitimate debate, and of the uncritical production
of schemes which were unrealistic but consistent with wider leadership
thinking. Influence has been used to constrain the area rather than to
promote its diversity.

Humes concedes that the picture of the leadership class which emerges from his analysis is not marked by 'unbridled adulation'. It will be apparent that similar reservations concerning computing's miniature leadership class have been expressed in this chapter. It is not the uncertainty and the lack of knowledge which prevailed in the early stages of development which is open to criticism. These are inevitable consequences of attempts to assimilate a new technology, with all of its educational potential, into the curriculum. Rather, it is the absence of insight and the intolerance of alternative views and philosophies which have caused the greatest offence to those who have also been involved in the development of educational computing.

A tribute to those who have retained their sanity and a sense of real educational priorities is an appropriate way to end. It is taken from the analysis which has provided the basis for this chapter and describes an altogether more wholesome definition of success:

> What is truly remarkable – and this is where credit for real achievement is due – is that many classroom teachers . . . continue to work with enthusiasm and dedication. It is perhaps some small consolation to them that intelligence employed with integrity carries a measure of intrinsic worth, even if, in terms of extrinsic reward, the mixture may be regarded by their superiors as a tiresome liability. [Humes 1986 p. 203]

NOTES

1. Scottish Education Department.
2. Her Majesty's Inspector.
3. Consultative Committee on the Curriculum.
4. Scottish Examination Board.
5. Supplementary Additional Teaching Qualification.
6. In-Service Training.
7. Council for the National Accreditation of Awards.
8. Her Majesty's Deputy Senior Chief Inspector.
9. Field Development Officer.
10. Her Majesty's Chief Inspector.
11. Diploma of Professional Studies in Education.
12. Grade Related Criterion.
13. Standard Grade Review of Assessment Group.
14. Short Life Working Groups.

REFERENCES

Conlon, T. and Cope, P. (1987). 'Why the micros fantasy is heading for a crash', *TESS*, 27 February, p. 4.
Drever, E. (1988). 'Criterion Referencing and Grade Related Criteria: The Experience of Standard Grade', in S. Brown (ed.) *Assessment:*

A Changing Practice, pp. 90–103, Edinburgh: Scottish Academic Press.

Hill, R. (1987). 'Yesterday's syllabus', *TESS*, 3 April, p. 4.

Humes, W. M. (1986). *The Leadership Class in Scottish Education*, Edinburgh: John Donald.

Kent, D. (1988). *A Study of the Dissemination of Educational Research Findings and Innovation in Scotland*, University of Stirling.

McPherson, A. and Raab, C. D. (1988). *Governing Education*, Edinburgh: Edinburgh University Press.

Paton, G. (1987). Letter to *TESS*, 13 March.

Raab, C. D. (1987). 'The "Leadership Class" Dismissed: Humes' Critique of Scottish Education', in D. McCrone (ed.) *The Scottish Government Yearbook 1987*, Unit for the Study of Government in Scotland, Edinburgh.

Rendle, P. (1981). *Scrutiny of HM Inspectors of Schools*, Scottish Office.

SEB (1984). *S-Grade JWP in Computing Studies Report: Experimental Course Guidelines* (First Draft).

    (1986). *S-Grade Arrangements in Computing Studies*.

SED (1987). *Learning and Teaching in Scottish Secondary Schools: The Use of Microcomputers*, HMSO.

Sorensen, I. (1987). 'Ask the parents', *TESS*, 17 April.

Sparkes, R. A. (1987). 'Let it crash', *TESS*, 27 March, p. 4.

3

THE NATIONAL PLAN AND ITS IMPLICATIONS

GEORGE PATON

BACKGROUND

The bookshelves of educationists throughout Scotland may well be strewn with national plans, but the title as such rarely appears on front covers. Her Majesty's Inspectorate (HMI) have regularly offered opinions on the state of education, or some aspect or some stage of it, which, because of their origins have assumed national importance. As often as not, the writers have then been indefatigable in pursuing any recommendations made in their document, and in persuading others to see them as national preoccupations and take them as seriously as possible. While the results have not always been profound they have, to be fair, very often been for the good.

Most other contributors to national debate have been careful to avoid any overtones of prescription or authoritative guidance. There is something in the Scottish psyche which does not react well to the term 'National Plan' for anything. 'National Plans' imply centralism; the Scottish system is legally and structurally at the decentralised end of any spectrum. Regional Authorities have legal responsibility for everything in school education in their areas. National bodies abound, but act separately, and to that extent are weakened in their impact. They all seek to collaborate, however, and usually mean it. The Scottish Consultative Council for the Curriculum (SCCC), Scottish Examination Board (SEB), Scottish Council for Educational Technology (SCET), Scottish Council for Research in Education (SCRE), Scottish Community Education Council (SCEC), and Scottish Vocational Education Council (SCOTVEC) are all separate bodies or private companies with their own specialisms, but are trying to operate in a collaborative network all the same. The function of size means that Scotland has a recurring belief or dream that 'a country like us ought to be able to get things to work'. The truth is that, historically, to outsiders, south of the Tweed and elsewhere, we have usually appeared to have our house more in order than most. Only rarely have Scots themselves ever taken that view. A paternalistic Scottish Education

Department (SED) characteristically tries to work in partnership with all the various nodes in the network, occasionally cracks the whip, and always retains ultimate fiscal powers. The resulting balance of forces is both the strength and the weakness of our system, but it is a very potent strength indeed when all the various forces support any move for change. When time is also taken to win hearts and minds in Colleges of Education, teacher organisations, and staff in schools, the system works at its best.

Reversion to centralism comes periodically, and especially at times of massive technological innovation. Scotland was no different from most countries, developed or developing, in the strong central drive and central control or management exercised over the introduction of new information technologies (IT) into the school system. The establishment of the Scottish Microelectronics Development Programme (SMDP) and the Microelectronics Educational Development Centre (MEDC) in 1980 were twin evidences of that drive in Scotland after a decade of experimentation; and the later initiatives from outside education by the Department of Trade and Industry (DTI) underlined the massive importance of the whole issue in industrial and economic terms. The need to combat what was perceived as drift towards fragmentation by Local Authorities in terms of purchasing policies led, in the autumn of 1982, to the issue of a joint letter by the SED and the Convention of Scottish Local Authorities (COSLA) urging the idea of a National Plan, and suggesting a structure of working groups under various bodies to lay some of the groundwork for this. The SMDP, the Colleges of Education, and the Scottish Schools Science Equipment Research Centre (SSSERC) were asked to play initiatory roles. By the nature of Scotland no National Plan can ever be imposed; it can only be accepted. From the nature of its origins this idea for a National Plan had every prospect of success. A powerful national group called the Microelectronics in Education Committee (MEC) was established in SCET late in 1983, comprising all the relevant interests, with the SMDP as its executive arm. It inherited the thinking begun in the Working Groups and completed its own document within eighteen months. It was, therefore, quite a remarkable illustration of national will at work, and it was accepted in principle by both COSLA and the SED, and very quickly indeed. In November 1986, just fifteen months after restricted publication, a follow-up meeting in SCET attended by senior representatives of all the regions demonstrated that all regions were taking the National Plan seriously into account. Some had adopted its words as part of their policy statements. And over the country as a whole, local government was playing its full committed role under the plan, with varying levels of achievement to that point. Central government inputs were already problematic, and have continued to be so. A Revised Strategy was issued for consultation in the summer of

1987, and it is clear at the time of writing (January 1989) that further possibly radical reappraisal is required.

WHAT WAS THE NATIONAL PLAN ABOUT?

The National Plan was firmly rooted in the general curriculum. That was its strength. It was not about massive injection of capital in order to create a platform for a specialist optional subject (Computer Studies) for a minority of pupils, although this topic was not forgotten. In essence, it was about computer-assisted learning across the curriculum, something which affected all learners at all stages, albeit in different ways. It took note of underlying drives in the curriculum arguably over the last forty years but articulated explicitly in and since the great reforming documents of the 1960s both in primary and secondary schools. These may be summarised as drives to encourage or promote independent learning, through a learner-centred, individualised, differentiated curriculum appropriate to the needs of the learners themselves, and seeking to make as effective as possible the shared political aspirations towards equality of opportunity, regardless of geographical or social context. All of these high causes were already being pursued in one way or another. The National Plan clearly perceived in microcomputers in the classrooms, and in the increasing capacities of these, a tool of great flexibility and power which would help teachers to achieve better what they already wanted to do – and by a methodology which involved learners in living the independent roles described, either individually or in collaborative activity. To underplay such aspirations is to devalue education itself.

In summary, the MEC believed that most educationists would wish to encourage, among other attitudes, capacities, and skills:

the growth of problem-solving capacities in the learners;
the capacity for increasing independence in the learning process;
the capacity to make choices and be faced immediately with the need to cope with the consequences of these, which derive from problem-solving and independence in learning;
the capacity to go beyond problem-solving to problem-modelling by hypothesising about changes in key aspects of the problem;
and also to develop:
the capacity of the system to individualise learning provision in appropriate ways, so far as is practical;
the capacity to provide rapid diagnostic feedback on performance which would direct the pupil to appropriate remedial materials;
the capacity to facilitate school-based assessment through producing tailor-made tests through effective item bank selection systems;
the capacity to store, access, and retrieve large amounts of learning material easily, and inexpensively, in order to achieve this individualisation or meet the needs of small groups;

the capacity to simulate fairly simply or create models of external real-life situations not easily brought into schools;

the capacity to do all this in a lively interesting way felt by the learners to be of relevance both inside and outside the school. [see 'National Plan' pp. 12–13]

Within this context, the elements of the National Plan took shape. It was seen as a strategy into which Local Authorities would move in their own way, within their own resource plans, building on the precise situations in their own areas over a period of some ten to twelve years, and seeking to establish by this means a flexible but secure basis for coping with further change, whether educational, technological, social, political, or economic. Inevitably there were elements of forecasting, of prophecy even, about likely technical/technological developments. And inevitably there were varying degrees of accuracy in these. For example, the National Plan advocated levels and types of hardware provision both in primary and secondary schools from actual case studies and models in existence. Technological change has confirmed some of these judgements and undermined others. Changes of policy with regard to the educational market by major multinational manufacturers, followed by varied responses by educational administrators, have been even more potent factors in the changing kaleidoscope since 1985.

Hardware and operating systems

The MEC believed that, following massive and very varied investment in the preceding years, from 1981 anyway the bulk of purchasing in Scottish schools had narrowed in focus, and by 1984 almost all the machines being purchased by authorities were either BBC or Spectrum. Factors leading to this '*de facto* standardisation' included the effect of government (DTI) schemes, the emergence of commercial software in sufficient quantity for these machines plus RML, and the software contribution of the SMDP, which, by following the narrowing trend in purchase of machine systems, helped in turn to confirm that trend. None of these developments had come from any national policy. There was some belief that either BBC or Spectrum would become the national 'standard'. Earlier front runners like Apple and Commodore were less in evidence. While the MEC saw advantages in diversity, notably the freedom from dependence on one manufacturer, it saw more strength in a degree of standardisation with a view to reducing unit purchasing costs, simplifying servicing and maintenance systems, and creating a basis for easier software development. Above all it argued that the transition to the next generations of equipment, the sophisticated 16- and 32-bit systems then emerging, would be facilitated by the establishment of a more common base.

The MEC argued, therefore, for a degree of national standardisation in computer systems which would result in software compatibility between the different systems being used; compatible communication links to peripherals and to other systems; the development at national level of software application packages; sufficient flexibility to allow for experimentation; and independence from a single manufacturer. And it saw the need to develop definitions of hardware functions and a software environment within a common national operating system so that all software producers could be readily assured that their programs could run. After some doubt it identified the UNIX systems as the potential front-runners for education, and recommended exploratory and evaluatory studies. This was in spite of the need in systems running under UNIX for much larger amounts of memory than were currently available to school systems; but was in the confident hope that not only would the cost of memory fall quickly but that also 'within five years a single UNIX work station operating as a stand-alone device or as part of a network might cost roughly the same as the current price of the work-station being used in schools'. We are still, in 1989, at least five years away from that point. In the transitional phase then forecast, the National Plan identified those machines common in Scottish schools for which it would be reasonable to keep producing software through a national programme like that of the SMDP (namely BBC, Spectrum, RML, and Apple) and urged that no new machines be added to the list unless they were capable of being developed for stand-alone or networked use under the common national operating system, and unless they had adequate graphics capabilities.

Software development

The National Plan put forward unequivocally a national system of software development funded on an agreed basis by central government and Local Authorities, not at the expense of commercial input, but to underpin such input by materials produced out of a national consensus on where education was going and on what were the priority areas in the curriculum. It envisaged a central software development unit comprising programming staff and some educational interface officers, working with teams of teachers who would work out the specifications for an agreed succession of programs. A two-year production cycle was designed, involving especially the then Consultative Committee on the Curriculum (CCC) and also Local Authorities, who would help to define priority areas and identify appropriate teaching staff. In addition, a network of Regional Development Units (RDUs) was to be established, according to the needs of the relevant Regional Authority, probably by extending existing Resource Centres, and fulfilling a range of specified functions, including software production if the region wished. Such regional software from the RDUs could either enrich the priority areas by adding to central unit national production or extend them by choosing other curriculum areas of more immediate interest to that Authority, perhaps in advance of national priority. By these means a two-stream corpus of material or library of programs would emerge, although materials from RDUs might need some 'polishing' and/or 'versioning' (in the absence of a national common operating system) before entering the national library.

Suggestions were made about the type of staffing required in these RDUS, the nature of the training support which could be given to programmers in them from the central unit, and the range of services they might provide to teachers in their area. In terms of unit size, it was believed that each RDU should serve an area containing approximately 180 primary schools, twenty-five secondary schools and twenty special schools, each equipped to a recommended level of hardware provision. It was further suggested that College Development Units (CDUs) be developed out of existing provision in Colleges of Education, albeit with fewer functions than the RDUS.

National information services

It was envisaged that the whole national system so far would be underpinned by a national information network involving the central unit, RDUS, national advisory bodies, Colleges of Education, commercial publishers, regional directorate and advisory staff, teachers in schools, and curricular working parties.

Other areas of the system

The National Plan focused on general provision in mainstream primary and secondary schools. It had little to say about special education, and advocated a consolidating process in view of the national funding already channelled into the area of Special Educational Needs. Full recognition of the importance of this area was given. It had even less to say about Further Education, in view of the fact that the MEC had already intended to publish a separate National Plan in this area, issued in July 1986 under the title *Microelectronics and Information Technology in Further Education – A Plan for Scotland*.

There was much more to say about training, especially of teachers, but also of technicians in schools. Targets were identified, and types of approach to staff development clearly set out, in close co-operation with the Colleges of Education and the MEDC, who would play the leading national roles in this, in association with the Local Authorities.

Reference was also made to the implications of all these ideas for accommodation, especially at the early stages of building planning and design.

Research and development structures

It was clearly argued that a central unit, now defined as SCET into which SMDP had been integrated, should take over the Research and

Development (R&D) programme of the Research and Intelligence Unit of
the SED in the broad field of microelectronics. Thus a balanced programme could be maintained of research projects mainly external to the
SCET, using expertise wherever it might exist, in universities and colleges, and also in Local Authorities, which the SED could not fund. Great
weight was placed on 'action research' defined as being of immediate
relevance and use in schools; and very close links were forged with the
CCC, whose proposals for projects were given high priority. The MEC
established an Innovation Research and Development Committee (IRD)
to design and monitor this programme on a national basis, with some
programmer support and a small budget. Partly because of this and
partly because many of the proposals emanating from the CCC were
more for software development rather than innovation and research, the
MEC later established a Software Development Committee to siphon off
proposals of this kind and forge links with the emerging RDUS. Over the
years since 1985, the IRD has obtained additional funding from other
sources in order to extend its work, notably in the field of Special
Education on a large collaborative project with spin-off advantages for
the National Plan. In addition to this external project programme, the
IRD has monitored the 'internal' programme within the SCET to carry out
some of the exploratory R&D work associated with the National Plan
itself, UNIX-related work leading towards the common operating
system.

WHAT HAS HAPPENED SINCE 1985?

It has already been suggested that those elements in the National Plan
involving direct action by Local Authorities have taken purposeful steps
forward. RDUS have emerged, albeit patchily and usually without a
software production capacity. Computing Advisers have been appointed in most regions, who liaise well with SCET while retaining their
total independence of action within regional policies. Even during the
dark times of the teachers' action, work on micros continued in schools,
at least a trickle under the ice; and now there is a welcome resurgence of
professional teacher interest which must receive support from staff
development programmes.

The Colleges of Education have been in convulsion for long periods,
but a new system of teacher education has now almost emerged which
should give the strong support envisaged from that quarter. CDUS have
not emerged as such, but some of the best and most widely used micro
materials in Scottish schools have come from the in-service staff in
Jordanhill, the computer-assisted topics materials (CATO) strongly supported by SED, SCET, and Strathclyde Regional Council. The Moray
House work in interactive video (the IVIS materials) has also opened up
new avenues for teachers. There is no doubt about the colleges' capacity
to contribute and their willingness to do so.

The CCC has itself gone through a period of trauma only now being resolved in its new form as the Scottish Consultative Council for the Curriculum (SCCC). As a result the envisaged two-year rolling plan for software development has not received the kind of support expected from the SCCC itself. Other agencies, especially Local Authority staff and subject Working Groups, have also submitted suggestions around which the SDC has constructed development programmes. The original intention of producing fifty smallish subject-specific programs per year has been replaced by a target of about twenty major packages with a wider variety of support materials, of the more sophisticated 'open-ended' type. Support for this trend through the Joint Working Groups has been a valuable contribution to staff development nationally. With the SCCC itself moving away from a subject-orientated basis for its committee structures, this process will undoubtedly be strengthened in the future.

The R&D 'external' programme has supported smallish pieces of work all over the country and the MEC/IRD has established a niche for itself, particularly valuable in that the SED imposed on itself a moratorium for work in micros while HM Inspectorate were carrying out work for their official Task, the results of which were published in October 1987 in *Learning and Teaching in Scottish Secondary Schools: The Use of Microcomputers*. The SED will now fund directly certain follow-up work to the Report, of an R&D nature, but in close consultation with the MEC.

Moves towards a national information system have been patchily successful. The SCET produces a variety of publications including SCET *News Education* and *Micros in Scottish Education* (MISE), but these do not have sufficient guarantee of reaching targets to be sure of making an impact. The same might be said of most publications. The most promising vehicle for information may be the UK viewdata system of the National Education Resources and Information Service (NERIS) of which the 'Scottish end' operates through SCET. Certainly, the welcome DTI initiative to supply modems for all schools, in 1986, gave the opportunity for easy on-line access to such databases. Scottish-based NERIS staff have worked hard to extend the awareness of its usefulness as well as its availability.

The main difficulties have stemmed from the fact that, in spite of the best efforts of the SED, the promised additional funding from central government has not been forthcoming to enable the planned evaluatory and exploratory development work on the development of a common operating system to take place. Some small funding has been possible. SCET has also diverted some of its income generated from other sources to aid the work, which is given very high priority by both Department and Council. The pace of the work has been slower in consequence, and has run the danger of becoming *ad hoc*.

A Revised Strategy in the summer of 1987 advocated collaboration between SCET and bodies during similar work in other countries in order to cut costs and save time. The Province of Ontario in Canada, roughly comparable with the Scottish situation and closely aligned in philosophy, was doing valuable work in defining functions for a national machine and was about to enter work on a common software environment. Mutual advantage led to an agreement to collaborate, confirmed at Provincial Government level, but the results are not yet striking. More realistic was the close relationship with the new Microelectronics Educational Support Unit (MESU) in England, which boded well for the articulation of a National Plan at UK level. Such work was 'frozen' by the sudden decision to merge MESU into the CET in 1988 to form the new National Council for Educational Technology (NCET), and may yet bear fruit. Collaboration with the Inner London Educational Computing Centre (ILECC) has produced promising work on graphics within a broader software operating environment.

Now, at the time of writing, significant technological development has produced a far more compelling set of reasons for rethinking these parts of the National Plan. After years of indifference, IBM has decided to enter the educational micro market. IBM and IBM clones running on MSDOS have swept the European market. The UK would have had to take that seriously into account, even if Acorn and the BBC family had not been in difficulty. Amstrad, an IBM-clone, bids fair to take the Business Studies market in Scotland: cheap and efficient, it runs the generic software, broadsheets, etc. which the school departments want. We may be seeing in this only one striking illustration of a move in schools towards the subject-specific provision of machines in some areas of the curriculum. Apple has decided to compete strongly again in the British market, and in the Apple Mac has excellent graphics capability, the basis of good, efficient and cheap desktop publishing capacities in schools generally. Some Regional Authorities appear to be concentrating their BBCs into primary schools and creating a new, varied, secondary provision, using BBC Masters, or Archimedes, or Nimbus, or Apple, supported by Amstrad. Extension of networking facilities makes its own impact on choices. The situation has become much more fluid than it was in 1985. UNIX may yet emerge as the common operating system and events are moving towards that end in industrial terms. Bodies like SCET or NCET will not really have the resources to promote such work on their own, and it is arguable that education should simply await the outcomes in five years or so. Perhaps, in the meantime, the effort should go more strongly into smaller scale activities simply to extend portability of programs through the development of a more flexible software operating environment.

At an even more radical level, it could be argued that, in national terms, the need is more for staff development and increasing teachers' confidence in using the materials already available to them. Such an argument would also have to accept the need for some innovative software development, but emphasis might pass, to some extent, away from a massive national software development capacity and towards training materials for self-help, or supported self-help at school level. Whatever the outcome, it is now clear that SCET will have to fund all of the central government elements from its own SED grant, which has hitherto supported a broader range of activities across the field of educational technology. Its programmes in open learning or flexible learning systems and in production of media other than micros will have to be slanted to support these National Plan elements in the new form of the strategy now taking shape. A meeting of all interested parties is to be called by the MEC in May 1989 to seek consensus on the shape of the new strategy and agree on the basis of funding it.

4
A VIEW FROM THE SOUTH
BILL TAGG

What a daunting prospect. How can anyone from England understand Scottish education well enough to be able to comment. I suppose I was approached because I have been watching computer education develop in Scotland for over twenty years, I have many friends in Scotland – professional and personal – and I have been an examiner for two courses for teachers, off and on, for about ten years. Despite my 'qualifications', I still do not understand how you come to your philosophical priorities and I certainly do not understand your politics. (I do not understand my own either for that matter.)

THE CONTEXT

Before we start looking at computer education in detail, perhaps it would be a good idea to compare England and Scotland more generally:

Population – England and Wales has about ten times the population of Scotland.

Geography – England and Wales is warmish and mainly densely populated, while Scotland is decidedly cold and sparsely populated outside the Glasgow to Edinburgh belt.

Politics – England and Wales is mainly Conservative, while Scotland, despite what many would have you believe, is mainly Labour.

Education – England and Wales has always had a devolved education system (but not for much longer) while Scotland's has been centralised. If you go a little further north, to Iceland for instance, you will find a country which to us southerners appears even more extreme, more Scottish than the Scots. There, they do not even pretend to speak English. Their population is even more minute (a mere one-third of a million), hardly anyone lives outside Reykjavik, it is even colder, and their education system is centralised to the extent that even text books are prescribed.

COMPUTER EDUCATION – ORIGINS

In the early 1960s, computer education (we could not have used capital letters at this stage), started apparently simultaneously south of the border in Twywn, Hatfield, Romford, and Dover. In each case, the initiative was local and school-based, usually it was the work of one or two people, and it had nothing to do with systems. Colleges of education were not involved. Indeed, it was many years before computer education was to be found routinely as part of initial teacher training.

In Scotland, only marginally later than the English *ad hoc* approach, the Scots came out with the 'Bellis Report', five Colleges of Education were equipped with batch-processing ICL computers, and punching cards became a national pastime. (South of the border we were more used to paper tape.)

So it was that using computers in schools became respectable in Scotland as early as 1972, but in England, nobody took us seriously (although we were still doing it), until James Callaghan watched the television programme *Now the Chips are Down* just before his government fell in 1979.

GOVERNMENT INITIATIVES

It is always understood that the government's Microelectronics Education Programme (MEP) and the Scottish alternative, the Scottish Microelectronics Development Programme (SMDP), had their origins in this 'road of Damascus' conversion of our erstwhile Prime Minister, but whether that is true or not, Scotland used their pot of government silver in a very different way from us. Again, you went for a centralised approach whilst we set up fourteen regions.

With hindsight, it is clear that neither the MEP or the SMDP were a success. Their failure was more to do with government perceptions than that of those charged with carrying out the programmes. The total sum of money was small (£22m in England and £5m in Scotland) but more important was the fact that it was never perceived as a totally inadequate budget. Thus, instead of trying to make limited and achievable objectives, both programmes attempted the impossible and failed.

The MEP worked with the model shown in Figure 1. The curriculum was split into four 'domains' called Computer Based Learning, Communications and Information Systems, the Computer (which really meant Computer Studies), and Electronics and Control. Regions were resourced to provide in-service training in these areas and appointed regional co-ordinators who related to national co-ordinators in the same domains. Curriculum development, including software production, was organised both nationally and locally.

The MEP failed for a number of reasons. First, LEAs were virtually ignored, yet it was these organisations which were left to pick up the pieces at the end. The MEP was described by the Government to be 'pump priming', but there was no encouragement to keep the few pumps going at the end of the programme. Indeed, where there were successes, DES seemed to go to some effort to remove the water which had primed the pumps.

In the wake of the MEP, there have been several factors which have meant that the anger felt by many at the end of the MEP has been kept hot. The general programmes of high funding for in-service training have enabled time to be found for more teachers to come to terms with technology and the regular windfalls from the DTI, which have usually cost as much to administer as they have provided, have allowed computer education to continue with a high profile.

In England, the Microelectronics Education Support Unit (MESU) was set up when the MEP came to an end. (Later, the MESU merged with the Council for Educational Technology to form the NCET.) At last, then, we had been provided with a permanent structure, and one which talks directly to LEAs. Now, however, the difficulty lies with the LEAs themselves. Until recently, all matters relating to computer education were routed through the computer education adviser or someone else who served in a similar role. This no longer works because there are too many interests in the typical LEA for all of the communications with the NCET to go through one person. The NCET has recognised this and has made sure that it directs its attention to LEAs more generally. This has accelerated the fragmentation of LEA policies, so that it becomes increasingly difficult to maintain a coherent LEA policy over hardware and software,

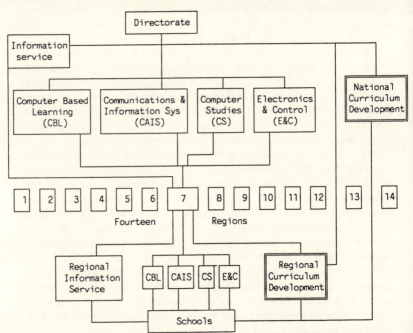

for instance. With the emergence of the Education Reform Act and local management of schools, this fragmentation was inevitable and it remains to be seen whether those who, until recently, have been responsible for *all* aspects of computer education, can adapt to provide *support* for those who want to take the initiative themselves.

In Scotland, the result is likely to be the same although the route there is interestingly different. From the outset, the SMDP has never been highly regarded in Scotland. Few seem to feel that they have seen much benefit from an organisation which seemed to start with so much money. Teachers have felt that 'SMDP does not know what real teaching is about' and that it has squandered its money producing materials which no one wants instead of providing support for real teachers in real classrooms.

In neither country has anyone counted any of the cost of providing every teacher with the resources – hardware and software, technical and pedagogic know-how – required for computers to be used routinely rather than on an experimental basis.

COMPUTER STUDIES OR INFORMATION TECHNOLOGY?

In the early days, nearly all computing in schools was concerned with *studying* the technology rather than *using* it. This was not surprising because at that time it was not much use anyway so you had to be a particularly dedicated subject teacher before you took it seriously in terms of what it could deliver. By 1968, we had the Certificate of Secondary Education (CSE) to supplement o levels, and a whole set of new examination boards to administer them. The CSE was easier than o-level, contained assessable course work for the first time, and schools were encouraged to present their own syllabuses for the boards to agree and moderate. This provided an opportunity for the development of locally moderated examinations in what became known as Computer Studies. Typically, groups of schools which were enjoying (suffering?) the same computing resources were producing idiosyncratic syllabuses and asking the examination boards to approve and moderate them.

Numbers grew rapidly and, as they did, standards declined. Soon, it was not just the dedicated few who were involved, and since there was pressure to 'keep up with the Jones's', teachers found themselves teaching a subject for which they had had no professional training and with little or no access to computers. Indeed, at this time, the shortage of computing resources was so great that anything marginally better than the norm was regarded as satisfactory. Some schools managed with a service whereby children wrote their programs on coding sheets which were sent off to a local firm. Here they were punched and run on a grace-and-favour basis and the results – usually a list of error messages – returned some three weeks later. Imperial College offered a postal service in FORTRAN which meant that *any* school could take part if they wanted to.

At that time, I was teaching in Hatfield, and because I had been doing it longer than most and because I had enjoyed 'ridiculously expensive on-line facilities' to a mainframe, I was asked to advise on what level of on-line access we should plan for schools in the future. I felt vary daring when I said that I thought that one day, a school might be able to make sensible use of an on-line terminal for as much as fifteen hours per week!

Computer Studies was more than just programming. It had to be, because the computing facilities were so poor; so, additionally, there were sections on hardware and on applications. It was all very unsatis-factory because the hardware developed so rapidly that we could not keep up with it and found ourselves teaching about obsolete technology. (I would not be surprised to learn that there is still some school where ferrite core memory is being explained to children – as a contemporary technique not a historical phenomenon.) The applications side was not much better because at that time almost all applications were commercial and their contexts were totally outside the children's experience. It should be noted that the commercial orientation of Computer Studies was seldom motivated by a desire to make the subject vocational; it was just that there was nothing else to do.

In short, Computer Studies, despite its rapid growth in the 1970s is now regarded with suspicion, and in England we tend not to use the term. Instead we sing the praises of 'Information Technology' but it does not make a good deal of difference because we probably mean the same. For some, however, the name is important, and Information Technology (IT), they say, concentrates on applications not the technology. Further-more, it is now possible to concentrate on applications which are much more within children's experiences as the breadth of possible appli-cations is now so wide. We are pretty confused, however, for while IT has achieved respectability, it has not received recognition, and no syllabuses with that title seem destined to stay the course. 'Computer Studies', on the other hand, although it has gone to the trouble to bring itself up to date, has recognition but no respect.

I do not know whether you are having the same futile arguments north of the border, but certainly IT is more highly regarded in Scotland. In England (and probably Wales, too) more than half the computer edu-cation advisers would probably like to see Computer Studies disappear completely. Of the remainder, most would give it lower priority than a broader approach to computing. The picture is the same when you talk to teachers. Even when the computer has not successfully spread across the curriculum, most schools would agree that a broad approach to computing was what they were looking for. If there are arguments, they are about how this Utopia might be achieved.

When I talk to teachers or teacher educators in Scotland, I do not get the same message. There seem to be structural difficulties which I do not understand, but apart from these, computing across the curriculum does not have the same high profile.

COMPUTER AIDED LEARNING OR COMPUTERS ACROSS THE CURRICULUM?

Again, it has been much easier to change names than priorities, but the change in name is coupled with a gradual move away from topic-specific to generic software. You are more likely these days than would have been the case, say five years ago, to see a history teacher using a database package rather than a specially written program about the Second World War.

There are several reasons for teachers moving in this direction. First, it is now more fashionable to use a database. Secondly, many teachers feel that open-ended software encourages open-ended learning. (It is not true, it is just that teachers who believe in open-ended learning choose open-ended software.) Finally, if you use general purpose software, you will need less in total to support your whole curriculum. This means lower costs, less software to look after, and less to come to terms with.

Additionally, such software is commercially more viable because it has a bigger potential market and it commands a higher price. Often, the generic software used in schools – particularly secondary schools – has been produced for the commercial market and has perhaps been adapted for school use.

Perhaps it is the entrepreneurial spirit of the SMDP which has been more able to keep the spirit of CAL alive in Scotland, or perhaps it is just that this aspect of computer education appears less important to you than Computer Studies. Whatever the reason, where the computer is used outside the Computer Studies room, it is more likely to be called CAL north of Hadrian's Wall.

SOFTWARE TRENDS

Often, in England, but less frequently in Scotland, the list of software which an ambitious secondary school might feel the need for might look something like this:

a word processor and possibly a desktop publishing package
a database package
a spreadsheet
a communications package capable of dealing with PRESTEL, electronic mail, and a local viewdata database
Logo (with an emphasis on problem-solving rather than programming) and an opportunity to undertake some Control Technology
a graphics package
software to enable children and teachers to build models.

(This particular list was adapted from an internal document produced by a school in Hertfordshire.)

Much is available from the suppliers of commercial software (and is expensive) but a large proportion is still produced specifically for education. At the Advisory Unit in Hatfield, we sell a good deal of our own software to Scotland and hope very much that you will continue to buy it from us. Writing software for education is a thankless task, as the SMDP has discovered, so the bigger the market that we can aim at, the better.

Recently we have been writing mouse-driven software (every computer, in my opinion, should have rodent capability) to run under 'MS Windows'. This environment provides portability across a range of machines. More importantly, it provides a consistent, user-friendly, and powerful interface so that users (teachers and children) can concentrate on the topic being supported rather than on the technology. You can expect more and more of our software to be written this way in the future.

THE INFLUENCE OF IT ON THE CURRICULUM

There is yet another aspect of computer education which we should talk about (and I am not sure where Scotland stands on this one). This is best illustrated through one small aspect of the English curriculum. (I mean English as opposed to Maths, not English as opposed to Scottish) but it pervades all aspects of the curriculum.

In the past, English teachers have rightly made a clear distinction between oral English and written English. They describe different skills and see different opportunities in the communications game with children being encouraged to use the right kind of language for the occasion. Children are even encouraged to write down examples of the spoken word using speech marks. Now, however, in the world of business and more generally we are developing new methods of communication which are establishing new styles of the English language. Viewdata and electronic mail are good examples, and some teachers of English are taking the opportunity to broaden the curriculum to take account of these advances and are making sure that children are able to use forms of English which are appropriate to the new media.

This is just one of the grey areas of computer education where we have difficulty in categorising curricular activities. Is it Computer Studies or is it English? I think that we spend more time worrying about these distinctions than you do.

ADVANTAGES OF A DEVOLVED EDUCATION SYSTEM

In the debate about the emerging National Curriculum, there has been little opposition to its concept, most have been content to criticise the detail. The arguments in favour have been obvious and frequently stated: an entitlement for all children; maintenance of standards; fewer problems when children move from school to school, etc.

The arguments against are less obvious so it might be as well to state them here in a bit more detail:

(1) *Entitlement*. Children are certainly entitled to *good* education, but to say that they are entitled to a *particular* education leaves much unsaid. Who knows best what that education should be – government? the parent? the teacher? Certainly, there can be no single answer, it all depends on the child. Clearly, if this is the case, it is more likely that the teacher would know rather more about what suits little Alice than Kenneth Baker.

Telling Alice's teacher what Alice should be learning at this time does not legislate for better teaching. Teaching is a human activity and if you are going to do a good job, you have to believe in what you are doing. Thus, the old method of curriculum definition by consensus is more likely to achieve results.

In the end, however, whatever government, schools, parents, or teachers may say, it is Alice herself who will make the real decisions. Perhaps we ought to start talking about what she is entitled *not* to learn about.

(2) *Maintenance of Standards* There are only two ways of attempting to maintain standards. Either you use police tactics, which are very expensive if they are to be effective, or you attempt to persuade, in which case you have to face the fact that you may not succeed. Either way, simple regular testing will achieve negative rather than positive results. Testing only finds out *what* children are learning, but a more important question is *how* they are learning.

There is plenty of evidence from other countries, that regular testing actually interferes with the *how*. It is not surprising that this should be so. Good teaching and learning styles are associated with taking risks and putting children in the driving seat. For the teacher, such learning activities can be a nail-biting experience. Many teachers lack the courage to take those kind of risks as it is (although the rewards can be very great), but if you have a system which is perpetually looking for short-term results, the longer term benefits of more open-ended learning are put on one side.

(3) *Children moving schools*. This can be the only really valid reason for a National Curriculum. Again, however, it is overstated. It implies a linear approach to learning so that you can pluck Alice out of one school and slot her in at the right place in the new school.

Moving schools can cause problems (and many opportunities too), but these are more likely to be associated with social factors – like being removed from her friends – than with a disruption in the curriculum at a syllabus level. There may be problems about differences in attitude on the part of teachers towards the curriculum and levels of expectation, but it is only the syllabus content which will be considered when all the talk has quietened down.

There are much more compelling reasons for *not* having a National

Curriculum (although these apply more to England and Wales than they do to Scotland).

I can perhaps be excused for considering computer education for a moment rather than education more generally. (The same arguments apply to the more general situation, but the focus may not be quite so sharp.)

Travelling abroad, and seeing many other countries introducing computer education, one cannot fail to be amazed that anything can be made to work at all. If a country has done nothing until now – the position for many countries until recently – it must, simultaneously, produce teacher expertise, hardware, software, space on the timetable, and an appropriate curriculum. Clearly, it will need to make careful plans and will need to be thorough because the problems are great, so it will take several years. A country will have to evaluate the hardware and software to see what they are capable of delivering. Then it will have to see how that matches its hoped for curriculum. Mismatches will result in commissioning new software and it will not be able to embark on its teacher training programme until that is complete. In any case, it will first need to 'train the trainers'. The training process will take quite some time because although children easily come to terms with computers, this is not the case with their teachers.

If a country has enough resources (which is unlikely) it may reach its launch in about four years. By then, of course, the goal post will have moved. Technology has moved on and now has much more to offer: that affects the new curriculum, the software needed, the training . . .

If the country you are talking about is Russia, then you clearly have a bigger problem to contend with than if it is Iceland. In Iceland you really do need to prescribe text books because your population is so small that leaving that kind of decision to the publishers and market forces would mean no text books at all! However, we are not talking about prescribed textbooks here and there is no *need* for Scotland or England to go for centralised decision-making and every reason for not doing so. Standards we must have, but not uniformity.

However, Scotland is smaller and it ought to be easier for those making the decision to get near to real classrooms so that the decisions have some practical as well as theoretical relevance. The Scottish reader must judge for himself/herself whether or not the decision-makers have succeeded. For me, I simply note that a National Curriculum (of sorts) is nothing new for you, but it is my biggest regret for Scotland that you have been this way for so long.

IMMEDIATE FUTURE

There is no getting away from it, in England at least, the effect of the National Curriculum and the rest of the Education Reform Bill will be very significant for us as far as innovation in computer education is concerned. Always, in education, we have to talk about *opportunities* not *problems*, but perhaps on this occasion, the opportunities are harder to find. When teachers feel threatened or under extreme pressure, they react by sticking to the safe (and well-tried) option, so if they are not using computers already, they will be reluctant to try. Even if they are *made* to use them, little will be gained, because as we have already discussed, they will not take risks, so the applications are likely to be unexciting.

On the other hand, teachers are more likely to be receptive when they are looking for new solutions to new problems. They will certainly have plenty of new problems.

What we have to do, therefore, is to be extraordinarily supportive. We must make sure that schools are encouraged to have high standards but are not undermined. We must remember, too, that it is the Alices of this world who are the real innovators. They are the real agents of change.

THE LONGER TERM FUTURE

Whatever the outcome in the short term, the effect of the continuing enhancement of the technology and its continuing price reduction mean that the dust has not yet settled on computer education.

There are many new aspects of the technology – CDROM, expert systems, photographic quality graphics. Windows environments are now making all this much more accessible to the user, and once the temporary world shortage of memory is overcome, the opportunities of systems with very large amounts of memory are legion.

At the cheap end, we already have every eleven-year-old in one class in Stevenage with a personal lapheld computer (even if it is only a Z88). By the turn of the century, not only will this be routine (with much better hardware), but the school network will be robust enough to give genuine access to all who want it.

We shall not be dependent on teacher courage by then. The children will have voted with their feet. As more and more learn the real advantages of word-processing, the sale of the number of ball point pens must fall. If the only piece of software to survive was the word-processor, it would all have been worth while.

5

EDUCATIONAL COMPUTING IN GLASGOW SCHOOLS

RODDY STUART

BACKGROUND

In June 1979 the first microcomputer was placed in a Glasgow secondary school. It came as part of a national project – 'Education for the Industrial Society' – although the specific educational objectives of placing a micro-computer in six secondary schools around Scotland were far from clear.

Within ten years the number of microcomputers in Glasgow schools has increased by over 2 000. It is tempting to see this as a success in itself. But schools are about learning and not about stock-taking; and it is necessary to consider the processes which have stimulated this pro-digious growth in numbers.

By any historical standards, the development of educational comput-ing in the 1980s, especially since 1983, has been a major phenomenon in Scottish education. This has happened during a period when difficulties stood in the way of any educational innovation. Among other inhibiting factors schools in Glasgow have experienced the following.

There has been a severe downward spiral in pupil numbers, made worse in the city than the trend elsewhere because of considerable net emigration. For example, most of the 30 300 fall in the population of Strathclyde as a whole between 1976 and 1984 is accounted for by the 27 000 fall in the population of the city of Glasgow over the same period. This has created problems for teacher morale, funding, and organis-ational flexibility. At another level it has led to a growing disproportion of available funds being allocated to the maintenance of a surplus of buildings, at the expense of cash for more directly curricular priorities.

The abolition of traditional forms of disciplinary control of recalcitrant pupils, at a time when the employment market for young people was conspiring to remove the incentive attraction of secondary schools for a large proportion of the young customers, has added to the burden which teachers have experienced, and has, therefore, made no easier the likeli-hood of taking new aims or new methods on board.

There have been the traumas of the lengthy period of organised collective disruption of the processes of curriculum development by teachers in pursuit of the restoration of pay levels in the mid-1980s.

Also, there have been considerable changes in the curriculum and·in the means of its delivery. This has been most clear in secondary schools, with the uneven development of the Standard Grade programme and the introduction of Action Plan, in 1984. Development in primary schools may have been less spectacular, but no-one who maintains regular contact with primary schools could deny that the changes which were articulated by the Primary Memorandum of 1965 were having their effect on the primary schools of the 1980s.

The stability in curriculum planning which may provide the background for innovation has been made more difficult by the various legislative changes and other central government policies which have affected all schools: including the right of parents to place their children in virtually any school; moves towards a National Curriculum; the introduction of TVEI and other centrally funded curriculum projects; and punitive central government control over local financing of the education service.

In the face of this litany of excuses, it really must be accepted as proof of some success that all those involved – pupils, professionals, managers, and parents – have felt that educational computing is worth the effort to overcome these real and daunting problems. Why has this been so? A report approved by Strathclyde Regional Council in December 1988 outlined a curricular philosophy, based on observation of the best practice in schools in Glasgow and elsewhere in Strathclyde, and not on a theory of learning, which saw the following substantial benefits from the appropriate use of computer and related technologies in the learning process:

> The motivational power of the computer with pupils of all ages and all levels of ability is unequalled. To many disadvantaged and alienated young people with limited literary skills it offers for the first time a serious educational medium not wholly dependent upon the written and printed word. It is already clear that the new technique of interactive video has even greater capacity to capture the imagination and attention.
>
> Computing stimulates creativity. It may free the imagination by overcoming shortcomings in technique (e.g. through word processing, computer graphics, statistical experimentation).
>
> Computers encourage independent learning. At the simplest level they can be used for 'drill and practice'; in a more sophisticated way, to develop problem-solving abilities using elaborate simulations.
>
> Instant feedback to the learner and the teacher makes computer assisted learning a useful tool for formative assessment and diagnosis of difficulties.
>
> The computer encourages logical analysis of complex tasks both by

the teacher and the learner. In this way it both tends to enhance teaching technique and to allow for easier identification of necessary skills.

Computer assisted learning stimulates collaborative as well as individual work. It provides a highly suitable context for pupil/pupil as well as pupil/teacher discussion.

Pupils can be offered a wide range of genuine investigative experiences within the bounds of the classroom. The computer is readily adapted to a problem-solving approach to learning. [*Educational Computing in Schools* 1988]

The report went on to indicate that education computing has a role in three major aspects of planning the curriculum:

the development of appropriate life skills – these are as much in the affective domain, coping with the new and the changing, as in the cognitive domain, where the development of certain information seeking and handling skills are seen as essential for life chances.

the development of work skills for the high technology industries and services which every pundit predicts will be essential for economic survival in a hard world.

the development of learning skills from the earliest stages of education.

'Learning is, for the most part, an intrinsically individual activity. Yet, for financial and logistical reasons, schools have always been obliged to deal with pupils in groups. New technology offers for the first time a serious prospect of resolving one of the fundamental dilemmas of universal education [*Educational Computing in Schools* 1988]

It will be obvious to anyone who maintains contact with schools that everyday practice in each and every one of the 440 schools in Glasgow does not provide irrefutable proof of the revolutionary nature of computers and related technologies in schools. What, then, have been the clear and outstanding successes, and where have failures been evident?

PRIMARY SCHOOLS

Without question the most significant development in the use of computers has been the use of word processing. This has enabled pupils, working alone or in groups, to develop practical language skills by drafting and redrafting, which the older technology of pencil and jotter made unattractive. It has allowed experimentation with language – in a variety of forms, both prosaic and poetic – which lies at the heart of any good learning. It is not only written work which has shown benefits in many classrooms from this approach; because of the work being done in groups, oral language skills have been developed. This has helped to reinforce practical co-operation by groups of youngsters. Many teachers have indicated, sometimes against their initial expectations, that the use of word processing has enhanced pupils abilities with the older technologies of writing. It is almost never the case that pupils study word processing *per se*; neither does the study of the computer as a whole feature in many classrooms. A wide range of programs now exists which supplements word processing for aspects of language development: simple (and not so simple) desktop publishing packages (e.g. 'Fleet Street Editor' from Mirrorsoft); software for the development of word banks (e.g. 'Easy Type' from Sherston Software); software related to specific commercial reading schemes (e.g. 'Reading 360' from Ginn); software for a range of word attack skills (prominently the use of 'cloze procedure' techniques and the use of context clues to rebuild passages which have been seen briefly); spell-checking software for the reinforcement of standard spelling (e.g. 'Edspell' from LTS); software to stimulate creative writing (e.g. 'Podd' from ASK/ESM or adventure programs); and software to produce distinctive displays on paper (e.g. 'Folio' from Tedimen Software).

The use of word processing has permitted teachers to help pupils to concentrate on one particular skill at a time: perhaps the first draft will concentrate on narrative structure; a second draft will place emphasis on correct spelling; punctuation may be the focus of the third draft; and narrative colour may be the aim of a fourth draft.

In Glasgow, where the BBC Micro in all its variants has reigned supreme in primary schools, the most common word processing packages have been 'Wordwise Plus' from Computer Concepts, 'Writer' from MEP, 'Folio' from Tedimen Software, and 'PenDown' from Logotron.

The use of adventure programs has been closely related to the development of language, although such programs have also been used for number work. The range of adventures – including 'Granny's Garden', 'Flowers of Crystal', and 'Dragon World' (all from 4Mation); 'Dread Dragon Droom' from RESOURCE; and 'Yellow Brick Road' from Northern Micromedia – has been wide, and teachers have reported levels of excitement and preparedness to write which have been unusual. Children have sometimes gone on to write their own adventures with some of the adventure generators which exist (e.g. 'The Last Adventure' from LTS).

The series of topic studies which have come from Jordanhill College – 'Desperate Journey', 'Fantasy Islands', 'The Travelling Shop', and 'Whale' – have offered ample opportunity to integrate word processing into a range of work, some directly involving the computer while other aspects are stimulated by it but take place away from the computer (e.g. the design of tartan in 'Desperate Journey'). These computer-assisted topic studies from Tricia Watterson's team will surely occupy a significant place in the history of educational development in the last fifteen years of this century.

There has been a debate as to whether word processing is an addition to the curriculum or an enhanced means of its delivery. Concepts which have been accepted as the business of schools since the 1496 Act put upon parish heritors the obligation to build and maintain schools can be enhanced by the use of the computer. It is clear that less long-established skills are being learnt by the use of the computer: practical skills in the manipulation of the QWERTY keyboard and in storage media; organisational and social skills in working for a purpose with other people; conceptual skills about the nature of information and its perception by others. Some would claim that these skills are wholly additional to skills which can be tackled by other means; others concede that the computer is one valid means of developing these skills; still others would claim that the computer is a richer means of accomplishing these aims. While resolution of this debate would occupy those who worry about the angelic crowd capacity of the head of a pin, such considerations will be of little interest to pupils, parents, or their teachers. All seem to concede a worthwhile place for the computer in the learning processes.

Another area in which, some argue, the use of computers has added to the curriculum in primary schools is that of information handling. This can be used in a number of subjects and at a number of stages. The evolution of coherent programmes of environmental studies and the development of information handling using a computer have sometimes gone together. Teachers have reported that the use of the computer can focus the children's information-searching efforts to produce good quality information, thus helping to practise that most elusive of skills: the derivation of evidence. At its best, the child who would have copied a whole entry from an encyclopaedia for inclusion in a jotter has to face a sterner discipline to fit the information found in the encyclopaedia entry within the headings or fields of a (simple) information-handling program such as 'FactFile', 'Quest', or 'Find'.

The information which can be handled can be varied. The handling of factual information, usually verbal, has been established for a relatively long time; one of the applications of the first computers installed in Glasgow primary schools in November 1983 was for information handling. The use of spreadsheet programs is beginning to be explored. Graphical information can be manipulated both to develop drawing and painting skills and to produce decent output for those who seem to display little talent for this. Recent developments in the use of computers for monitoring and controlling the environment have begun to excite a number of teachers and their pupils; the use of a suitable interface unit – the Cambridge Microtech 'In Control' unit is spreading in Glasgow – with suitable construction kits (e.g. 'Lego') offers one basis for the introduction of technology in a practical and stimulating way.

While it is impossible to state that any application is universally successful (although word processing comes close) it is never easy to dismiss an application as wholly a failure. Among those notions which have been tried and which appear not to have taken root are the following.

The use of full implementations of 'Logo' has singularly failed to develop – problems with the reliability of floor turtles have not helped in this. Teachers have made use of turtlegraphics programs, but few of them seem to have been motivated to progress to other applications of the 'Logo' environment.

Another project which received some support but which seems to have flopped is the use of authoring packages. Simple tutorial routines, permitting the teacher to customise material to suit the particular reading scheme or topic, do not (yet) seem to have become common. An experiment with the use of 'Microtext' did not succeed.

One curricular area where developments have been limited to date includes most aspects of the expressive arts. While there has been a modest interest in the use of videotex emulation for language work, the demand for software for artwork and for music has been limited. Simulations of aspects of topics which are covered in schools' environmental studies programmes have met with partial and patchy success.

The main problems which would be identified in a randomly assembled gathering of primary school teachers would almost certainly be the lack of equipment and their own lack of understanding. While the first can be solved by the availability of more cash, the resolution of the second problem is less susceptible of simple solutions. After five years of experience of the use of computers in primary schools, the strategy in Glasgow is now to introduce teachers to computer applications – word processing and topic studies featuring prominently – rather than to run courses about computers themselves. The response of a significant number of teachers – and not just those with the longest service – is that the teacher needs to be thoroughly familiar with the technology and the software before they will risk exposure in the classroom with pupils. Others have found that it is not essential to take this preliminary step. This is part of a larger issue of staff development (in all sectors): how to help teachers to take a more enterprising and less authoritative view of the function of the teacher in the classroom.

SECONDARY SCHOOLS

While few would doubt that the sensible integration of computers has made a contribution in a very large majority of primary schools, the position in secondary schools is far less clear.

One unconditional failure was the initial use of computers in secondary schools. The author remembers spending several months on the development of an introductory course on BASIC for the Cromemco computers which were installed in six Glasgow secondary schools in 1980. The lack of software was almost total; it was felt that teachers would develop the ability to write their own. This wrong idea was shared

by a lot of teachers – there really was a lot of demand for the author's
introductory course, although I have never yet met anyone who shows
any signs of benefiting from it.

The problems in secondary schools which have impeded progress in
relation to the exciting developments in primary schools include the
following:

the competition for resources (hardware, software money, staff) between the use of computers as educational tools (as in primary
schools) and their use in courses where they are an object of study

the timetable constraints in secondary schools, reduced by the adoption of the twenty-five or twenty-seven/twenty-eight-period week.

the demands of detailed externally determined syllabuses, which
most teachers feel are already full and which offer little freedom for
experiment in either content or method

inexperience in the use of single computer systems linked to individual learning schemes, group methods, or a workstations approach

a lack of software which reflects peculiarly Scottish concerns (e.g.
using the terminology accepted by the Scottish Examination Board
[SEB] in O-Grade Physics, or for peculiarly Scottish subjects such as
Modern Studies).

In spite of these inhibiting factors, some successes are in evidence. As
in primary schools, the use of word processing in a range of contexts is
striking. A significant proportion of teachers now uses the computer as a
personal productivity tool, with word processing being the dominant
application – this is used to provide greater flexibility in the production of
learning materials. The use of desktop publishing packages is enhancing
this established use.

Other applications which have made an impact, albeit unevenly,
include the following:

Information handling: much good work has been done in history
classrooms throughout the city to sift and sort through real historical
data (such as Poor Law applications in Govan or the census in areas of
the Gorbals in 1851 and 1881) to permit pupils to experiment and to
speculate.

Interfacing for monitoring and control is growing in science teaching,
and, in a more limited way, in technical education, to permit students to
measure and to control common and not so common phenomena. This
varies from the measurement of acceleration or heat gain to an ambitious
project in biotechnology in a secondary school not used to the attention
of the educational press.

The development of skills in the use of colour, texture, and shape in art
and design helps to overcome imperfections of technique and allows
concentration on perspectives and understanding.

Computer-aided design (CAD), linked to computer-assisted manufacture using lathes, in craft and design permits pupils to accomplish

more polished results than pencil and ruler often give, and to link design to execution.

The use of on-line (and stored examples of) videotex services is giving language practice in French.

Linking the use of computers with electronic keyboards is gradually opening up new opportunities for experimentation in learning for both specialist and non-specialist students of music.

The simulation of dynamic phenomena or difficult experiments, such as weather patterns or volcanic activity in geography, molecular change in science, work in genetics, or the working of markets in economics, permits difficult concepts to be tackled in a more interactive way than can easily be done with video or other teaching media.

The use of adventure programs – perhaps linked to a book – for stimulating creative language in English has achieved some of the same success as in primary schools.

The use of computers is enriching the methodologies which are available to teachers of established subjects and, in the ways outlined above, it is extending the realistic curriculum in many of these subjects.

The computer has also added to the range of subjects. Office and Information Studies is not just a new name for Secretarial Studies; even in its early stages, there is evidence that a large number of boys will be attracted to this traditionally female subject. Technological Studies is an amalgam of significant technologies, many of which (computing, pneumatics, electronics) were not seen in secondary schools at the beginning of the 1980s.

Computing Studies has had a considerable impact in the second half of the 1980s. Many teachers were sceptical of the specialist courses in computing, and there was much debate as to the value of the courses being formulated for O-Grade Computing, Standard Grade Computing Studies, and National Certificate Computing Modules. Many of the teachers who were reluctant to support specialist computing courses have changed their minds. The uptake of computing and word processing modules, not least among the several thousand adults who have been attracted into Glasgow secondary schools in recent years, has been striking. The demand from pupils and parents for the qualifications deriving from Standard Grade Computing Studies and Higher Grade Computing Studies has been forceful. Several Glasgow schools have demand for places in Standard Grade Computing Studies from over 50 per cent of the S2 cohort. Many teachers give heartening reports of achievement and hard work encouraged by the practical nature of the course; this is highly significant in an area where a very large proportion of pupils is conditioned to expect little success from its efforts at school work.

The overriding failure has been the inability to convert the particular successes into a general trend. Few subjects have, as yet, a coherent plan to exploit those areas in which the computer can offer the maximum benefit. Indecisiveness in staff development is both a result of lack of clarity as to curricular priorities and a factor reinforcing continued lack of subject policy for information technology. Perhaps the challenge for non-specialist applications of the computer in secondary schools is this: how can teachers working away quietly pass on their best practice to others?

SPECIAL SCHOOLS

Many of the benefits and problems outlined above for primary schools and secondary schools apply to special schools, too. There has been a big increase in the use of microelectronics devices – e.g. pressure pads and other switches, special keyboards, braille printers – to meet the challenge of a wide range of physical, learning, and emotional needs. Success has been uneven here, as elsewhere. Special needs are often individual and solutions must be customised accordingly. There are perhaps fewer patterns in special needs than in any other sector. The record of achievement is piecemeal; perhaps it will always be so, but we can hope that the progress will be more comprehensive and offer solutions to a wider range of special needs.

POLICY FOR THE FUTURE

Developments to date have been characterised by a pattern whereby 'better' learning has provided the spur, and extraordinary effort on the part of professionals (and their young charges) has provided the means. Better learning is one of those concepts which is easier to recognise than to define, but it certainly includes extension of concentration span, deeper conceptual understanding, the ability to correlate elements of conceptual understanding, the reinforcement of a realistic and positive self-image, and improved communication.

Much of the effort which professionals and students alike have given freely to develop the uses of educational computing has been because of the flexibility, even excitement, which computer-based learning brings to the business of learning. The challenge of the future will be to extend the sense of adventure which the pioneers experienced, not least in making do with inadequate resources of hardware and software, to a wider range of professionals in such a way that diversity and experimentation is not trained away and submerged in standard provision.

NOTE

This chapter expresses the personal views of the author.

REFERENCE

Educational Computing in Schools: The Report of a Working Party (1988). Strathclyde Regional Council.

6

BEYOND THE TROJAN HORSE: EDUCATIONAL COMPUTING AFTER TVEI

DEREK CURRAN

THE NATURE OF THE BEAST

With Mrs Thatcher well into her stride in her third term of office, the culmination of changes in education look likely to produce the sort of major transformations which we have already seen taking place in the nationalised industries and in the social services. Such changes are likely to have a massively enhanced role for the private and semi-private sectors. If these plans are carried through, it may well be that the face of education in the early 1990s will be unrecognisable compared with that displayed at the beginning of Thatcher's first term of office. This is, therefore, perhaps an important juncture at which to reflect upon those changes which have so far been thrust upon us.

The breathtaking pace of these changes, many of which have been extremely radical in nature, are typical of the style of the present government. None so far, however, has had the sort of transformatory potential as that initiated through the Manpower Services Commission's (MSC, now renamed the Training Commission) Technical and Vocational Educational Initiative (TVEI). Announced by the government in November 1982, this was presented as a major innovation which would explore and test ways of managing the provision of technical and vocational education. As one of its main selling points, the government put forward the idea that through it 'youngsters should receive an education which will enable them to adapt to the changing occupational environments'.[1]

At first sight, this is a very laudable aim. But how was this 'adaptable' and 'flexible' young worker to be created? In the first place, the scheme was to direct its attention towards the links between education, training, and industry; and computing and information technology was to be a central component. The idea was that TVEI was to be a major element in the government's strategy for dealing with the problems of sustained increases in unemployment, particularly youth unemployment, which had been a major political problem in its first two terms of office. As David (now Lord) Young suggested that: 'By the time they leave, our youngsters will be highly employable'[2] as a result of the scheme. If nothing else, the scheme recognised that there was an urgent need to revamp and modernise the provision of industrial training. Whether or not, however, schools should in fact be producing practical skills for particular ends as Young implies, we need to question. In particular we might refer to Bailey (1984), who, in defence of a liberal philosophy of education, has argued that such a philosophy is one which directs us towards involving pupils in knowledge and understanding which is fundamental, and hence towards providing them with that knowledge which has most utility value throughout their lives. The adoption of such ideas would preclude any narrow vocationalism on the grounds that it constrains an individual's horizons.

The concept of a liberal education has fuelled much of the debate surrounding TVEI. Concern over its theoretical basis and the practical nature of much of the TVEI curriculum has produced a great deal of opposition to, and unease with, the scheme. The thesis put forward by the MSC as its rationale for the scheme was that the technological illiteracy of the workforce was a major factor in the problems facing British industry, and that this stemmed in large part from the education they were receiving. Whilst there is little evidence to support this point of view (see, for example, Senker 1986; Stonier 1983), it commands support across the political spectrum. The pervasive nature of this notion has even led the HMI to state:

> It has in recent years become a truth 'universally acknowledged' that education should be more closely linked with the world of work and with the country's economic performance; and there has been increasing pressure on schools to assess the relevance of their curriculum to their pupils' future working lives. [DES 1982]

From a more radical perspective, Benson and Lansley (1987), for instance, have argued that average and below-average students compare badly in terms of performance with our industrial competitors both in terms of the qualifications they achieve, and in terms of the training they subsequently receive. However, as Senker (1986) has shown in comparisons drawn from the role of vocational education in West Germany and Japan, this has much more to do with post-school vocational training and education. In West Germany there exists an extensive system of intermediate qualifications of a vocational nature (such as City and Guilds) which is employer-led in terms of its control and administration. In Japan, on the other hand, substantial vocational training takes place on the job within individual companies. This has the advantage of quickly meeting the rapidly changing needs of new technology, particularly where this necessitates the retraining of staff. What is significant about both these systems is the flexibility inherent within them. If the problems of British industry are related to the relative inflexibility of Britain's industrial training, then it would seem unlikely that a greater degree of industrially and commercially relevant curricula in schools, as per TVEI, would improve matters.

Amongst educationists, debate on whether vocationalism in education is desirable has continued unabated, contrary to the line expressed by the HMI (see above). And, whilst many of the wilder fears concerning the scheme – such as the fear that it might bring about the reconstruction of a two-tier education system (see Simon 1985) – have failed to materialise, there remains a concern amongst more radical educationists as to the overall impact of the scheme. These reflect a suspicion that the scheme has had more to do with social control – with inculcating attitudes in students (punctiliousness, obedience, co-operation, for example) which would turn them into more efficient and reliable workers – than with overcoming the widely held perception of a dearth of skilled and technologically literate workers. The replacement of the MSC with the Training Commission, a body with a far narrower remit and without many of the MSC's educational concerns, indicates perhaps the government's attitude to this question, and at the same time reaffirms its faith in vocational answers to the perceived problems of the economy.

TVEI AND COMPUTING

But what has the implementation of TVEI meant for educational computing? Ever since the introduction of the O-Grade and Standard Grade, there has been a strong vocational element in the subject. The MSC placed emphasis upon computing and information technology in the scheme, and, as a result, one would expect to have seen an impact on the place held by educational computing within the school curriculum. In the teaching of the subject, its heavy vocational content is one area likely to have been affected, with consolidation of those more strictly vocational elements of the present syllabus.

In terms of curricula, from the beginning the MSC has remained firmly, though flexibly, in control of the TVEI curriculum. The scheme's criteria represented a very radical departure from what had been the norm until that time. No longer would schools or the LEA's have overall control over the curricula in their areas: curricula now had to be planned in a way which made great reference to a loosely defined 'technology' within the school and to the world of work outside it.

One result of TVEI has been that within educational computing we have seen a mushrooming in schools of Scottish Vocational Educational Council (SCOTVEC) modular courses, and alongside those a growth in Scottish Examination Board (SEB) certificated short courses, lasting in the region of forty hours. For the most part, those courses offered to S3/S4 students in computing have been information technology related – mainly 'Introduction to Computing,' 'Information Studies', and the set of 'Introduction to Applications'. More recent courses have included

'Graphics Processing' and the plans for a short course in 'Desktop
Publishing'. What all of these courses have in common is a hefty vo-
cational/applications bias – most of the applications packages in use in
Computer Studies attempt to simulate data-processing tasks which take
place at a very low level in the world of information technology, and
students often do little more than simulate the jobs of such data-processing operatives. The implementation of such courses could hardly be
likely to do anything other than reinforce the vocational view held of
Computer Studies – a view which owes much to the 'computer literacy'
model discussed elsewhere in this volume by Melody McKay. This
model emphasises the study of computer use and pays little attention to
the science of computing.

On the other hand, however, it may be that the development of these
courses might subsequently allow an optional educational computing to
concentrate to a greater extent on the non-vocational, more scientific
side. Whilst this has so far not happened, a Computer Studies devoted
more to a scientific understanding of technology, its possible uses, and
its development could emerge in the long term if short courses were to
continue beyond the TVEI period. There have been rumblings in some
quarters of education for such an interpretation of the subject to be
implemented in the short courses on offer in schools – for instance in
interfacing, and in expert systems. But, given the nature of short courses
with limited time on the timetable and generally completely mixed
ability classes, it is difficult to see how such courses could be introduced
in S3/S4.

If we return to the rationale behind such short courses, we must ask
some questions concerning what TVEI hopes to achieve from them. From
the scheme's aims and participatory criteria, the government's central
concerns would appear to have been with equipping young people with
skills and qualifications increasingly related to the world of work and to
the sorts of job opportunities which are likely to be open to them. In a
world of rapid technological change, it is assumed that the skills most
likely to be in demand are those associated with the new technologies
and especially with information processing. But can we seriously
assume that the courses we provide in school are the means through
which students acquire new skills and qualifications which would facilitate job transfer as the government implies? To go further, can we accept
the general claim made by the MSC that the elements of the curriculum in
question are easily identifiable and transmissible? Given the less than
predictable nature of the future facing us, especially when we consider
the pace of technological development, the answer to that question
should hardly be in doubt.

Quite how schools were to prepare curricula which included elements
broadly related to potential job opportunities, in a world of rapid technological change with the likelihood of frequent, often unrelated, job

changes, remains a mystery. In the world of educational computing, the reliance, even in the late 1980s, upon 8-bit technology and simulation software bears little relationship to the world of work. What 'skills' could be taught within this field which would enable young people to 'adapt to the changing occupational environments' (Young 1983)? Can the use of obsolete technology be used to enhance the individual's ability to acquire new skills and qualifications which would in themselves facilitate job transfer?

It needs to be said that only a small number of students are likely to require a great deal of specialist training in a particular vocation; the vast majority, particularly in the service sector, is unlikely to require any more than that which can be provided by a few weeks on the job. In information technology, the much more powerful computers used in the workplace, and the improved human – computer interfaces they tend to confer, are liable to render redundant any 'skills' in these areas conferred within schools. The most important attributes required of such workers are adaptability in changing from one job to another, and flexibility within a job. This is confirmed in recent studies (see, for example, Wellington 1987) which suggest that the qualities required by employers of young people have less to do with qualifications or school success than with personal skills and qualities.

Placed in such a light, the thesis that there is a direct link, capable of manipulation, between what happens in our schools and the problems facing the economy *vis-à-vis* high unemployment and the lack of a technically qualified workforce becomes absurd. That there are strong and complex links is not in doubt, and what TVEI does raise is the question of what the proper nature of that relationship ought to be. For educational computing this raises the question much more sharply of what sort of content the subject should contain – the creation of morally autonomous individuals, long the central idea of the liberal philosophy which has dominated educational theory, if not always its practice, in this country, can hardly be enhanced by the Standard Grade reliance on a 'case-study' approach which seeks to simulate the functions of computer applications in the workplace. It is this reliance which in my view has narrowed the scope for development within school computing for so long. In the eyes of guidance staff, pupils, and parents there is an almost banal faith in the utility value of computing as a qualification for the world of work. Indeed, there would appear to be a belief that there exists a direct link between educational computing and the activities of the workplace. It is this factor which I would argue has ensured that educational computing has not been viewed in particularly high academic regard, with the consequence that the majority of pupils entered for S-Grade examinations have been at the lower end of the ability scale. This status problem obviously has serious implications for the develop-

ment of the Higher Grade in computing and in the creation of truly
mixed ability groups within the subject.

RESOURCING THE FUTURE

Without a doubt, the overriding success of TVEI from the teachers' point
of view has been in terms of resourcing. The scheme has provided
impressive resources to a school system so often starved of any large-
scale injection of funds. The provision of large injections of cash has not
been wholly successful, however. The divisive nature of the way funds
have been allocated, mainly to subjects which have claimed a technological (whatever that means) basis, has left a residue of resentment amongst
teachers whose subjects have not been so impressively resourced. Furthermore, such funding has produced a clientele in the areas which
benefit from the scheme who are less than critical of its wider implications. As Harland (1987) has speculated, to some extent one of the
factors which may play a role in this respect is the relatively privileged
position which some staff have achieved as a result of their involvement
in the scheme and the enhanced status which TVEI has given them. She
suggests that such teachers are more likely to lend support to the utilitarian policies of the government in this sphere, because of the detri-
mental effect upon their professional identity of doing otherwise. Within
educational computing the lack of any real debate upon what TVEI might
have meant for the subject would seem to give some support to this point
of view. This does not bode well for those who see a need for a far more
widespread and better informed debate on the future of educational
computing as a subject in the school curriculum.

On the positive side, the funding received by educational computing
through TVEI has enabled many computing departments to upgrade the
technology in use in schools. Computing received, on average, 25–33 per
cent of a school's TVEI funding. This has enabled upgrading to take place
at a rate much faster than would have been possible solely on the basis of
Local Authority funding. The benefits of such funding have been immediate: the old 8-bit technology of the BBC, running simulation software, is being replaced by 16- and 32-bit machines which have enabled
the use of much more powerful application packages and opened up
horizons in educational computing which we can only now begin to
introduce to schools.

An important area of consideration is obviously what happens to
school computing when the finance provided by TVEI goes. The nature
of the schemes developed in schools – mainly reinforcing a vocational
trend – will be relevant here, but I would argue that this is of secondary
importance. Of more importance are the changes which have taken place
at the more subtle level of the terrain upon which educational discourse
takes place. Whilst it is apparent now that TVEI has not succeeded in
having any obviously indoctrinatory or directive role, it has succeeded in

altering the terrain and that is now pregnant with implications for the future.

SCIENCE OR STUDIES – IDEOLOGICAL IMPLICATIONS

One of the problems of most approaches to teachers and their relationships with vocational training is the lack of an ideological element in the analysis. This is true even of many critical approaches to TVEI. What is at stake in current attempts to redirect Scottish (and for that matter English and Welsh) education is an attempt by the government to reconstruct an educational reality more in line with a radical Conservative philosophy: to reconstruct the whole relationship between the education system and the world of work. The discourse of TVEI has been concerned with the attempt to redefine and rearticulate the desired relationship between education and work. The notions of 'relevant skills', 'learning experiences', and 'product' have been instrumental in shifting the way we think in schools about the relationship between education and industry. Unless we intervene in the construction of such notions, we risk allowing the present dominance of utilitarian ideas and meanings to become further entrenched.

This suggests that there is a clear need to elaborate more succinctly on the nature of the relationship between the economy and educational institutions, as well as the proper function of education in a technologically advanced society. The current direction being followed, with its new and rapidly expanding vocabulary, risks becoming a new educational dogma. By incorporating the concepts of TVEI uncritically into our educational discourse, we allow some spurious and ill-founded assumptions to become 'fact': that a liberal schooling is deficient and of questionable relevance to low achievers; that education is responsible for society's perceived lack of the 'suitably skilled people' required by the economy; and that a vocationally orientated education is likely to redress this position, and slot people into the occupations required by society. The fact that there are elements of truth in such statements, even though they are a gross distortion of the education/industry relationship, confers a spurious legitimacy upon them. There can be little doubt that the links between education and training require reconstruction. But if we recognise this, we cannot simply defend traditional education against vocational incursion without also articulating what should be the nature of the links between them. Failure to do so would be to allow a skills-based, utilitarian, culture to become pervasive. One which, dangerously, derives much of its utility value from its ability to socialise the young into acceptance of the values required for the workplace. If computing is to take its place as a subject of academic stature, as it currently lays claim to, there is a need to develop much more thoroughly a thought-out picture of exactly what sort of links the subject should have with the world of work.

The current success of the TVEI scheme lies, as we have said, mainly in the extent to which the language of its discourse has managed to permeate staffroom discussion on vocational education. Discussion is now couched in terms of what degree of vocationalism is desirable rather than whether or not vocationalism *per se* is desirable. The novelty of TVEI consists of the fact that, in its implementation, much of the debate has focused not around the philosophical issues raised regarding the content and aims of education, but around the more practical questions of the manner in which the scheme could achieve its aims. This is the most significant measure of the scheme's impact: its ability to transform the terrain upon which debate takes place.

It is this more insidious aspect to TVEI, particularly since in most of the schemes underway it has moved a long way from its short term aims of simply increasing the vocational element of schooling, that it has fulfilled the Trojan Horse analogy. It has raised fairly fundamental questions regarding the nature of the relationship between education and the world of work: questions concerning the proper role of education in a technologically developed society; of the interconnections which exist between the education system and the workplace; and of how change is affected in the economy. Yet the initiative fails to address any of these questions whatsoever, and in subjects such as Computing Studies its effect has been to mask them, thus inhibiting the development of serious debate on the content of courses. The very limited debate which has taken place has involved few teachers – the majority having been more concerned with the extraction of maximum benefits from TVEI than with the niceties of a debate on the practical and philosophical questions facing the subject, thus further entrenching a Computer Studies approach. Those who promote the scheme make no attempt to question the basic assumptions underlying it. Even the most cursory of economic analysis is likely to show that the reasons for the UK's poor comparative economic performance are complex, and have at their base the failure of British industry to invest to the same extent as our competitors and a disregard for training which matches that failure. From comparisons with our competitors, it would appear that where we differ radically is not so much in the area of compulsory education and in the attention paid to vocationalism there, but in the area of post-school vocational training (see Wellington 1987; Senker 1986). And it is in precisely those areas that the impact of the scheme has been the least. If, therefore, the prime purpose of TVEI is to bring about improvements in our relative economic competitiveness, the superficial and wrongheaded nature of its analysis render it unlikely to bring about any major improvement.

A TECHNOLOGICALLY LITERATE WORKFORCE

In its own introductory material, the MSC made much play of the problem of technological illiteracy, and we must ask to what extent TVEI has resolved this problem. A great deal of money has been used to introduce and expand the technological facilities available in schools – and educational computing has benefited more than most – and these facilities have, without doubt, been put to good use. Yet, and this is of importance when we consider the prevalence of vocational elements in computing, it is difficult to imagine how the use of such equipment *in itself* is likely to affect technological literacy except in the most cursory way. Technological literacy has more to do with the study and science of technological advance than with the application of new technology. For most users of technology in an industrial or office environment, as we have already noted, the necessary 'skills' for a job are most likely to be acquired in a few weeks at work. As Wellington (1987) has noted, the language of skills which accompany publications on vocational education are frequently biased towards behaviourist, psychomotor conceptions of skill: those at rudimentary levels such as 'answer a telephone' or 'use a keyboard', or 'use delete key in a wordprocessor'. In abstracting these skills from a context or knowledge base, they become totally meaningless.

If the scheme is not likely to have achieved any real improvement in levels of technological literacy, we must ask exactly what has been achieved. As we have noted, a range of benefits has accrued, most notably the provision of resources but also in the collaboration which has taken place between institutions. At the same time, whilst we have not seen the emergence of a dominant vocational education, we have seen a significant shift in the educational world's perception of vocational education. This has important consequences for education, in general, and, in particular, for any initiatives in educational computing. Future developments in computing are not likely to be well served by the sort of ill-defined and superficial commitment to the elements of vocationalism already established in schools and which TVEI has served only to strengthen. Already, at a common sense level, we find an acceptance amongst teachers of the need for increased vocationalism in schools, with few questions asked as to its nature or content. This does not auger well for the future of a liberal education. Furthermore, concern with the issues raised by TVEI distracts our attention from attacking the very real problems faced by the education system as society moves rapidly towards a future in which work is likely to play a far less central role in people's lives than it has in the past.

As we consider the future for educational computing, we would do well to note the comments of Gramsci (1971), who, commenting on the growth of specialised vocational schools, wrote:

> the last phase of the common school must be conceived of as the decisive phase, whose aim is to create the fundamental values of 'humanism', the intellectual self-discipline and the moral independence which are necessary for subsequent specialisation – whether

it be of a scientific character (university studies) or an an immediately practical–productive character (industry, civil service, organisation of commerce, etc.). The study and learning of creative methods of science and in life must begin in this last phase of the school, and no longer be a monopoly of the university or be left to chance in practical life.

We can achieve this within educational computing only by combating the current pervasive nature of vocationalism within our subject.

NOTES

1. Quoted in 'The TVEI programme: past, present and future', *Education Digest*, 168 (12), 19 January 1986, p. i.
2. Quoted in 'Mailed fist and velvet glove from Mr David Young', *Education*, 19 November 1982.

REFERENCES

Bailey, C. (1984). *Beyond the Present and Particular*, London: Routledge & Kegan Paul, p. 167.

Benson, G. and Lansley, S. (1987). 'Failing the masses, passing the buck', *New Statesman*, 114 (2496), 11 September.

DES (1982). *Teacher Training and Preparation for Working Life*, HMSO, p. 1.

Gramsci, A. (1971). *Selections from Prison Notebooks*, edited and translated by Q. Hoare and G. N. Smith, London: Lawrence & Wishart, p. 32.

Harland, J. (1987). 'The TVEI Experience', in D. Gleeson (ed.) *TVEI and Secondary Education: A Critical Appraisal*, Milton Keynes: Open University Press, p. 41.

Senker, P. (1986). 'The Technical and Vocational Education Initiative and economic performance in the United Kingdom: an initial assessment', *Journal of Educational Policy*, 1(4), 293–303.

Stonier, T. (1983). *The Wealth of Information*, London: Methuen.

Simon, B. (1985). *Does Education Matter*, London: Lawrence & Wishart, p. 170.

Wellington, J. (1987). 'Skills for the Future', in M. Holt (ed.) *Skills and Vocationalism*, Milton Keynes: Open University Press, p. 32.

Young, D. (1983). *Circular to Directors of Education on TVEI*, Sheffield: MSC, p. 2.

7

EDUCATING EDUCATORS: THE COMPUTING EXPERIENCE

TOM CONLON

TRAINED FOR LIFE?

One of the ironies of Scottish education is that its practitioners cannot, generally, afford to devote much time towards their *own* education. Teachers are kept so busy teaching that opportunities for learning – other than 'experiential', on-the-job learning, which is important but limited – are few. It is as though there were some secret rule saying: 'learning is for *other* people; teachers are professionals who are trained for life'.

Of course, this is absurd. On paper, at least, the 'trained for life' assumption has long been rejected by the managers of education, and the professional rhetoric, if not the practice, of teaching is replete with emphatic endorsements of the necessity of continual 'staff development'. But if there is agreement on the importance of staff development, its nature and content are highly controversial. Who should take responsibility for it and what form should it take? Should it be compulsory or voluntary? Should it be controlled by the government or by the teaching profession? Should it be academic or pedagogical in orientation? Should it pursue the needs of the individual or the needs of the system? And in either case, who should determined what these 'needs' actually are?

At the start of the 1980s it was clear to everyone in educational computing that the 'trained for life' assumption was untenable. The almost overnight arrival of microcomputers caught the entire profession unprepared, and provoked an instant crisis of staff development. This chapter analyses Scottish education's response to that crisis, concentrating mainly on formal course provision (the accepted acronym for which is INSET[1]). Chronologically, it ranges from the early courses associated with the DTI[2] 'Micros in Schools' scheme through to recent developments associated with the centralisation of the award-bearing INSET curriculum which is now being vigorously pursued by the SED.[3]

The analysis which is offered will suggest that three recurring weaknesses have badly damaged the information technology (IT) staff development effort. The first has been a basic lack of suitable resources. Secondly, IT INSET[4] has been characterised by a frequent failure to debate and analyse needs, and to evaluate experiences in an open and honest fashion. Thirdly (and perhaps this is the issue which has been least publicised) has been the damage done by the pursuit of an increasingly centralist and bureaucratic model of INSET. The trend has been particularly evident in the area of IT award-bearing courses, central control of which has now reached the unprecedented and extraordinary level of course prescription at national level. This chapter traces that process in some detail and it concludes that radical changes will be necessary if IT INSET is to play its full part in developing Scottish education.

THE SCALE OF THE PROBLEM

From the outset it was clear that the staff development implications of the new technology were immense. Computers without teachers who know how and when to use them are just useless boxes, and the history of educational technology is littered with stories of 'innovations' which have become dusty cupboard-fillers for want of the relevant teacher expertise. Many of these stories relate to quite mundane technologies, such as overhead projectors and video recorders, for which the skill requirements are rather modest compared with that which is typically associated with microcomputers.

A combination of other factors made the task especially daunting. First, the challenge which came from IT represented only one of many to which Scottish teachers were expected to respond in the 1980s. In the secondary sector, for example, demands for attention included those arising from the Standard Grade programme, the Action Plan, and TVEI;[5] pressures arose, too, from such changes as those associated with multiculturalism and special needs. Second, falling pupil rolls had been used by government as the justification for a near-freeze on recruitment into the profession. Without 'new blood', the teaching force was ageing fast; and although home computers were to become rapidly entrenched as part of youth culture, the bastion of the staffroom would be more difficult to penetrate. Third, educational computing in Scotland scarcely existed in the pre-micro era and there was no significant pool of experience on which an INSET team could be based. Although computing staff did exist in the Colleges of Education (traditionally the major INSET provider), most had a background in commercial data processing rather than in schools.

Exhortations that the staff development problem would need to be solved are to be found in most of the official IT-related documents of the 1980s. Notable among these is the Scottish Council for Educational Technology (SCET) 'National Plan' (*Microcomputer in Scottish Schools ...* 1985), which interpreted the needs of four different groups of teachers on a spectrum from 'all teachers' to 'spearhead teachers'. For the former group was recommended the provision of a range of skills, including 'basic technical competence' and 'ability to evaluate software packages'; whilst the latter group was to become competent in the ability to design and produce software ('the programs to be written by programmers') and to 'promote innovation'. The National Plan envisaged an extensive range of courses and distinguished ten different varieties of these, recognising in a commendably forthright manner that

> the needs are immense ... the future resource implications are considerable to mount the comprehensive programme of inservice-training required and maintain an ongoing programme of refresher/updating courses. Staffing levels will have to be sufficient to allow release to teachers to attend the courses. Money will also be required to maintain and replace hardware as necessary and to acquire and develop relevant software

But by that time the first major INSET exercises had already been completed. Perhaps it is significant that the National Plan makes little mention of them, for these courses (funded by the DTI) had been far from successful.

THE DTI 'MICROS IN SCHOOLS' COURSES

When Kenneth Baker's DTI announced in 1981 the half-price micros scheme for secondary schools, one condition was attached to the offer. Perhaps in anticipation of criticisms that the scheme was an obvious political 'stunt', a training element was included: it was made a requirement that schools accepting the subsidy should nominate two teachers for participation on a short (three-day) introductory course. Subsequently, the scheme was extended to primary schools, and from 1981 to 1984 thousands of teachers attended DTI courses. For the majority this experience represented their first-ever contact with micros.

In Scotland the DTI handed the administration of the scheme over to the SMDP (notwithstanding that body's lack of an official remit for INSET). However, the courses were delivered mainly by College of Education staff. Mostly the content focused on 'familiarisation' with the hardware components (typically a BBC model 'B' machine with a domestic cassette-tape recorder to serve as a storage device). There was also an introduction to such software as could be mustered – often this meant the 'Welcome' tape provided by Acorn, although later courses featured the Microelectronics Education Programme's (MEP) 'Microprimer' package – and perhaps a little BASIC programming. According to the 'cascade' model of INSET, on which the courses were supposedly based, teachers attending these courses were expected to pass on their new-found skills to their colleagues on return to school.

No formal Scottish evaluation of the courses was undertaken. However, the University of East Anglia has evaluated the scheme within the

UK as a whole. Its report (*Evaluation of the DTI Micros in Schools Schemes . . . 1988*), based on forty-four questionnaire responses from teachers, course providers, and LEA Advisers in areas including Scotland, tells a depressing story. A summary of the main points is as follows:

(1) Not a single respondent felt either that the courses had been adequate or that the 'cascade' theory had worked. Coverage of the bare technical necessities was not enough without consideration for the educational uses, and the software used was roundly condemned (with only 15 per cent regarding the Microprimer material as worthwhile).

(2) Overwhelmingly, it was felt not to have been useful to introduce schools to microcomputers without disk drives. The disk drives available at the time were expensive, but, in the words of one respondent, 'the cost of the frustration/in-service training/turn-off/replacement has been hugely greater'.

(3) Serious doubts were expressed about the real aims of the scheme. The commitment of the DTI to genuine educational objectives was questioned, and political and commercial motives were ascribed instead.

LEARNING THE LESSONS?

Of course, it would be unreasonable in appraising the DTI-led INSET to ignore the difficult context in which the courses arose. It could be fairly pointed out that educationists did not ask for the DTI scheme: they had little or no say in its design. The government carrot of half-price micros caused a stampede which caught the inexperienced INSET providers unprepared. It was hardly the fault of the colleges that the software was not available and neither could they be blamed for the inadequate hardware: they did their best with the resources which were available at the time.

It is more difficult to justify the absence of any retrospective analysis. There was potentially a great deal to be learnt from the DTI courses; they represented the first substantial IT-related INSET initiative after all. Unfortunately, the Scottish courses appear not to have been monitored or evaluated in any way and, for whatever reason, they generated negligible discussion. One of the very few published references to them comes in a report by the HMI (*Learning and Teaching in Scottish Secondary Schools . . . 1987*). This report (which has 'evaluation' as one of its principal objectives) contains the single sentence: 'Attendance at courses related to the provision of DTI-funded hardware provided an introduction to microcomputers for many teachers.' Sadly, this bland level of comment reflects fairly typically the failure of those involved with 1980s INSET to evaluate experiences in a forthright fashion.

The INSET providers (if not HMI) had one possible excuse for the failure to reflect on what had happened: lack of time. For, before the DTI scheme had finished, they were already reeling under the demands which had come from a different source: Computing Studies had arrived.

COMPUTING STUDIES DEEPENS THE INSET CRISIS

When, in 1982, the SED suddenly reversed its policy of ten years' standing by announcing support for examinable Computing Studies courses, first at O-Grade[7] and (later) at Standard Grade and then Higher Grade, the INSET problem grew to crisis proportions. Other contributors to this book have discussed the development of Computing Studies, which teachers often saw as the only route by which they could secure recognition, time, and resources for their efforts. But the number of teachers genuinely well prepared to teach computing as a subject was negligible. It is certain that no teachers were 'qualified' in the formal sense, for the Teaching Qualification (TQ) in Computing did not exist until the SED added it to its Memorandum (approved list) in the year of the O-Grade announcement. On the forecast that the new subject would require two teachers in every secondary school, it could be estimated that 900 teachers of computing would be needed (*In-Service Report . . .* 1987). Furthermore, by the nature of computing, it seemed unlikely that the problem could be solved on the basis of a single diet of INSET. The requirement for updating would be continuous.

For the Colleges of Education, the establishment of Computing Studies caused immense strain. College computing staff were fully stretched, and not merely with DTI courses. They were also providing teaching and support to students and staff within their own institutions. Two colleges – Moray House and Jordanhill – had launched ambitious two-year CNAA[8] validated Diploma programmes in Educational Computing, and, after the languid years of the 1970s, the struggle to establish the reputation and quality of these Diplomas was proving extremely difficult. The situation was particularly hard for the minority of lecturers who had attempted (sometimes in the face of opposition) to undertake research and development work. Furthermore, the college computing departments were still carrying the baggage of mainframe management chores which had been their bread and butter in the previous decade.

Partly in recognition of the scale of the problems, the SED introduced in 1984 a 'New Blood' scheme, whereby Colleges of Education were able to recruit additional computing staff. But these new posts were very few: Moray House gained one, for example, but, taking resignations into account, this brought its Computing Department's lecturing strength up to only six – the same level that had existed in the pre-micro era of the late 1970s. The new computing staff, who were invariably recruited from the schools, had great difficulty in establishing their credibility. Nor were they much helped by the 1970s vintage staff, few of whom had made any significant contribution to the field.

From another and perhaps more cynical perspective, however, things may not have seemed all that bad. First, there is no requirement in Scotland that a teacher should be qualified in a particular subject. Much of the computing teaching would certainly be done (and this could be presented as a 'temporary' measure) by those whose qualifications were in other areas. Secondly, the vocational interpretation of the new subject to which the SED had become committed greatly softened the perception of the INSET crisis. The approach taken by Standard Grade Computing Studies, which was variously represented as 'practical', 'skills-based', or 'applications-oriented', minimised the scientific and theoretical content of computing. By using its influence over the SEB, the SED could effectively 'seal' the subject's school definition within a highly prescriptive syllabus. IT INSET might then be narrowed to a specific training in the approved syllabus content. Thirdly, the SED effectively controlled also the definition of 'qualification' and this made possible a simple bureaucratic means whereby the numbers of teachers holding the Computing TQ could be inflated at minimal cost.

THE RUBBERSTAMP TQ

The last factor was particularly significant. For almost all teaching subjects, the usual entry requirement into a College of Education secondary TQ course was the equivalent of a degree containing at least two graduating passes in the subject concerned. The SED decided that for the TQ in Computing, just one Computing pass would be sufficient. It was assumed that this was an emergency measure, but in fact 'normal' requirements were not instated until 1988. In the case of entrants to PGCE[9] Computing courses the 'emergency' entry level could effectively operate until 1991.

Thus, many teachers discovered that the TQ could be gained with ease. If they could show that their degrees had included a solitary pass in computing, then a two-week course in a College of Education was all that was required. It was not necessary to claim that the pass was recent, and, indeed, the holders were frequently astonished that what they had considered to be a relic of ancient history now assumed such significance in the eyes of authority. These In-Service Teaching Qualification (ISTQ) courses were inevitably seen as rubber-stamping affairs. Among the College of Education tutors they left a nasty feeling of being used; unfortunately, the private unease was never translated into anything more public. The teachers were glad of the 'free gift' of a TQ, but most were realistic enough to recognise that a prize so easily won cannot be worth much. Nobody could mistake the rubber-stamp for a real preparation for the challenge of teaching computing. Perhaps only the SED gained, for the ISTQ route rapidly generated an impressive quota of 'qualified' teachers and for 1984–5, for example, they were able to point to 150 teachers who were undertaking the TQ (quoted in *Learning and Teaching in Scottish Secondary Schools* . . . 1987).

COMPUTING IN THE PGCE

The experience of the pre-service Computing TQ has been better. Since 1982 the Colleges have offered Computing among the other subjects available to students entering the one-year full-time PGCE, a course which recruits mainly from newly qualified graduates. Most colleges by now had coherent and fairly well thought-out PGCE programmes for these students, combining subject with professional studies and with substantial components of placement in schools, and these courses provided a strong supportive framework within which Computing could be integrated. Computing tutors worked hard with their more experienced College colleagues and with teachers and LEA Advisers to make these courses successful.

Unfortunately, the PGCE courses have failed badly in the competition with industry and commerce to attract the best-qualified IT graduates. Relatively few of the PGCE Computing applicants have held qualifications which exceed the minimum requirement of the one pass – a pass which is typically already three years old by the time that students reach College of Education. It has been a frequent complaint that there is little opportunity, either during or after the PGCE year, for students to develop their knowledge of the subject. A key assumption on which the PGCE course is built is that academic 'content' provision is unnecessary, since the course entry requirements ensure that the knowledge base is already in place: in the case of Computing that assumption has clearly not been justified. This would not have been so important had provision existed (as it generally does in industry and commerce) for ongoing IT staff development, but predictably the SED's willingness to allow for exceptional entry requirements has not been matched by a keenness to offer a correspondingly exceptional degree of post-qualifiying INSET opportunity.

In fact, the newly qualified young IT teachers have been perhaps the worst off in terms of staff development provision. Traditionally, head-teachers expect their newest young staff to be academically the most fresh and up to date. Frequently, but unreasonably in comparison with the situation with established subjects, they have expected the IT recruits to become involved immediately in extensive curriculum development work in their first posts. It is a challenge to which the young teachers have generally responded amazingly well. But headteachers should be made aware that Computing is not like the Latin or Geometry of old; nobody in IT can remain credible who must rely upon on an increasingly obsolete knowledge base.

LEA AND MSC FUNDED INSET

By the mid-1980s virtually all Scottish LEAs had recruited staff to support their own educational computing developments. Many had appointed Advisers with specific remits for IT and some, such as Lothian and

Tayside, had extensive resources at their disposal, including INSET support facilities. But the turn to Computing Studies was a source of immense strain here also. LEA Computing Advisers, like College tutors and indeed schools, were expected to support both the new school subject and the wider curriculum applications of IT. The tension between the two responsibilities was apparent everywhere and, since the Advisers were usually highly influential in a region's IT-related staffing and equipment deployment policies, much depended on that individual's perception of priorities. But, whatever their views, it was inevitably the case that a vast amount of resources was occupied in attempts to make a success of Standard Grade Computing Studies.

There appears to have been no systematic monitoring or evaluation of LEA INSET provision. Some efforts, such as the early attempts to make teachers into BASIC programmers, were clearly misplaced, but others (notably the work with primary schools) seem to have been very worth while. The LEAS appear to be well suited to supporting the less-formal type of school-based INSET, particularly pedagogically-oriented INSET conducted by a seconded teacher who is able to spread enthusiasm and knowledge without arousing anxiety or resentment.

In the mid-1980s a second source of IT-related regional INSET emerged. To support its rapidly unfolding TVEI programme, the MSC launched the TRIST[10] initiative, in 1985. Although directed by the MSC (with SED collaboration), TRIST was managed at local level by the LEAS. Like TVEI – with which its connection in Scotland was actually very slight – TRIST was relatively luxuriously financed: within a two-year period (1985–7) it injected £2.5 million into the INSET budget. On TRIST, the previously mentioned HMI report offers only another bland comment: 'This initiative offered many teachers the opportunity to learn new skills and teaching strategies, including those associated with new technology' (*Learning and Teaching in Scottish Secondary Schools . . .* 1987, p. 12).

Fortunately, TRIST has been more helpfully documented elsewhere. An evaluation of it has been provided for the MSC by the SCRE[11] (Butts and Turner 1988). The SCRE researchers point out that throughout the period of TRIST, Scottish in-service work was 'severely inhibited' by teachers' industrial action. Those involved with TRIST overwhelmingly welcomed the initiative, but the explanation was an echo of the response to TVEI itself: 'The best thing about TRIST, for many of those involved, was the money'. (Part I, p. 50).

Measured as a short-term 'skills-based' project which pursued specific needs, TRIST was a success. But the success may be short-lived, for although an intensive injection of resources over a short period of time may produce impressive results: 'Once the external stimulus is withdrawn, the effects tend to die away and the system reverts to the *status quo ante*' (Part I, p. 49). Furthermore, the evaluators (quoting a study by Cumming *et al.* 1985) point out that the TRIST approach to INSET is based largely on skill-specific training: as a model of professional development this can be criticised as far too narrow. In an unusually forthright passage, the researchers spell out the dangers:

> Given the SED's insistence that national and regional priorities must take precedence over individual interests it may be that 'identifying needs' at the institutional level will increasingly become a matter of discerning the competencies that teachers must acquire to enable them to implement centrally ordered imperatives. [Part I, p. 54)

In the context of INSET for Computing Studies, there was evidence that this was happening already. Developments in nationally organised INSET particularly confirmed the trend.

NATIONALLY ORGANISED INSET

Throughout the 1980s a small amount of IT-related INSET has been nationally organised. In the first few years, annual conferences were provided by the Scottish Computer Education Group (SCEG): these tended to be somewhat chaotic events, but they were open to all teachers, they were cross-curricular, and they spanned the primary–secondary divide. The SCEG conferences were imbued with the optimism (and perhaps naïvety) of their time.

By the middle of the decade the SCEG's funding had been withdrawn by SED, and a very different pattern of nationally organised computing INSET emerged. Although there were still conferences, these were mainly tightly controlled by the SED (often operating through a College of Education), and they were usually geared to a very specific purpose, such as the implementation of local training programmes for Standard Grade Computing Studies. 'Training' was by now the key word. Attendance was confined to a strictly limited group, typically comprising college lecturers, Advisers, and a few selected teachers. For these events the agenda was invariably predetermined in such a way that serious debate on major policy questions was effectively precluded. It would have been almost impossible to raise the key questions, such as (say) whether the proper balance of resources had been struck between Computing Studies versus cross-curriculum computing; or whether the effort being asked could possibly be justified by the questionable educational worth of the prescribed syllabus; or whether there might be better ways to tackle the IT INSET crisis.

On at least one occasion the presentation of *fait accompli* was sufficiently crude to provoke the sending of a protest from three participants to the joint colleges' highest management body, the Committee of Principals. At the National Conference on Higher Grade Computing Studies in November 1986, the three protested that the published purpose of the conference, which had been to seek 'consultation' on the state of the Higher Grade proposals, had been undermined. Papers detailing extensive and complex changes to the draft Higher Grade syllabus had been issued on the spot instead of in advance of the day, and the conference chairman (a College Head of Department) had opened the event by saying that the status of the meeting was merely to 'provide information'. An angry scene arose when the chairman disallowed an amendment to the conference programme to be proposed from the floor of the hall.

But this occasion was untypical. More generally those participating in the nationally organised INSET events were compliant: some presumably because they agreed with this approach to doing things; others perhaps because they preferred not to expend energy in resisting what seemed to be inevitable. Sadly, the result was that what might have been crucial opportunities for appraising developments and evaluating policy alternatives seldom rose above the level of the stage-managed set piece attended by the loyal, the meek, and the dutiful.

THE COLLEGE DIPLOMA PROGRAMMES

Probably the most significant INSET achievements of the Colleges of Education were the Diploma courses. As mentioned earlier, Jordanhill (jointly with Paisley College of Technology) and Moray House had each initiated two-year part-time CNAA-validated Educational Computing Diplomas, starting in 1980 and 1982, respectively. These courses attempted to provide a very broad coverage of the educational computing field and they immediately succeeded in attracting applications from teachers and lecturers across many subject areas, and from the primary, secondary, and tertiary sectors of education.

Certainly, those who comprised the first few cohorts had cause to wonder if they had not been over-rash in submitting themselves to the experience. The inexperience (and, sometimes, ineptitude) of college tutors and their almost complete lack of any IT research and development background made the early Diploma programmes look painfully thin at times. Fortunately, there was immense goodwill amongst participants. The courses survived the early traumas and, after numerous modifications of content, staffing, and approach by the mid-1980s they seemed to be developing reasonably well. In 1986 a third course entered the scene in the shape of the Information Technology Diploma offered by St Andrew's College of Education.

By that time the SED's policy reversal in favour of Computing Studies was already having a growing impact on the Diplomas. LEAs with limited INSET budgets began to view the priority role of the Diplomas as being to provide a route whereby teachers could obtain a qualification enabling GTC[12] registration in Computing. Increasingly they nominated (i.e. sponsored) only teachers who were switching towards, or who had an existing commitment to, the new school subject of Computing Studies. For the Moray House course, for example, Lothian Region received from its teachers forty-four requests for nomination to the 1987 intake:

the region awarded all twelve of its allocated places to secondary teachers, with teachers' involvement in Computing Studies programmes made the prime criterion for selection. Other regions acted similarly, and the twenty teachers who entered the Diploma course in that year included not one primary teacher – the first such occasion since the Moray House Diploma was initiated.

Inevitably the character of the courses changed also. Where the original aim had been to study and promote educational computing in its widest sense, the Diploma programmes more and more were expected to provide support exclusively for the SEB's Computing Studies prescriptions. Cross-curriculum computing did not vanish entirely, particularly since the LEAs typically required computing teachers to accept a cross-curriculum role as part of their remit, but the focus was undoubtedly narrower than it had been previously. There was pressure also to move away from an educational approach to a narrower 'training' style, in which college courses merely echoed SEB syllabus content at a notionally higher level. One (non-CNAA) college course actually appears to have succumbed to this view, switching its teaching of programming to the SEB's sole-approved language, COMAL, for example, but in general this degeneration was resisted by teachers as well as by college staff.

Sadly, the principles which lay behind these tensions were seldom, if ever, openly debated. Plainly, some serious issues were involved, such as the appropriateness of training versus educational approaches to IT INSET, as well as all those other controversial questions about models of staff development which were posed at the start of this chapter. Yet none of the individuals or agencies involved (and clearly these included HMIs, LEAs, and others in addition to the colleges) appears to have produced anything resembling a discussion or strategy paper to illuminate the alternatives. Such debate as did occur stumbled along mainly at the level of surface code, only occasionally emerging onto the largely unread pages of CNAA and other similar documents. In view of what was about to be proposed for award-bearing INSET, this failure to analyse and reflect turned out to be a critical weakness.

THE 'GREEN REPORT' AND THE 'THREE-TIER STRUCTURE'

To a significant extent, the three Diploma programmes had developed apart from one another. There were differences in modes of attendance, in the size, strength, and composition of the respective staff teams, in the structure, content, and assessment of courses, and less tangibly but importantly, in the course ethos. To some extent these differences were reflections of the diversity of Scottish educational computing in the early part of the decade, and of its attempts to grope towards some kind of self-definition.

In 1986, however, the history of the Computing Diplomas began to collide with the plans for INSET which had been devised at a higher level.

By that time the SED had long been committed to a policy which would 'rationalise' INSET within a 'national framework'. The new policy was established by the 1979 'Green Report' (*The Future In-Service Training in Scotland* 1979) of the NCITT,[13] and it was refined in the 1984 'Three-Tier Structure Report' (*The Development of the Three-Tier Structure . . .* 1984). Briefly, the first of these documents argued that INSET provision was patchy, ill-planned, and 'supply-led' (a phrase which was meant to imply that course offerings depended on college whims rather than arising from external demands). It proposed a structure of INSET based on a national framework of modular awards at three levels: Certificate, Diploma, and Masters. The second report specified the modular unit to be one of thirty hours' duration, and it recommended that 'guidelines' should be created for all the main award-bearing INSET areas. Guidelines would be necessary in order that courses with similar titles should be broadly similar: they would facilitate credit transfer between courses, assist employers in recruitment, and generally 'help to create a national system'. The NCITT pointed out that such a system required some form of policing: 'Once guidelines were drawn up, it would be necessary to ensure that course proposals did not deviate from them' (p. 11). The report offered suggestions as to how the enforcement could best be accomplished. It is perhaps hardly surprising that the SED was quick to adopt these 'rationalisation' proposals.

But from some quarters at least there was strong protest. For example, David Hartley (1985) objected that the 'Three-Tier Structure' represented an unprecedented extension of the central control of education, and he went so far as to accuse the SED of seeking to limit the content of INSET to matters of pedagogical competence, 'thereby avoiding any wider analysis of education'. Other, less iconoclastic, criticisms, particularly of the proposal for national INSET guidelines, were fairly widespread. The main objections were certainly anticipated by the writers of the 1984 report, who noted that

> it has been argued that guidelines may be unduly prescriptive. If they take too much responsibility away from course teams, then they may well stifle creativity and discourage innovation. Another concern is that, once established, it may be difficult to change them quickly should circumstances so demand. For these reasons, it has been suggested that guidelines are more likely to be harmful than beneficial and that the quality of courses is better safeguarded by proper validation.

But, having recognised these as 'real concerns' the report proposed to deal with them by 'adequate safeguards'. Guidelines were not to be prescriptive:

> guidelines should normally be concerned only with level, length, target population, aims and outcomes and some aspects of structure (e.g. the proportion of school experience)

Furthermore, guidelines were to be regularly reviewed; they were to emerge from a process of widespread discussion so that they could represent a broad national consensus for a particular award; and they could be dispensed with altogether in the case of 'first initiatives in new fields'. With these safeguards, the argument continued, the advantages of guidelines would outweigh the disadvantages.

There is little evidence that those responsible for IT INSET made any contribution to these discussions. Yet, for them, a great deal was at stake. For example, it was highly questionable whether the 'Three-Tier Structure' was appropriate to an area in which Diploma-level courses were already being widely used to provide what was in effect an *initial* diet of study: only the Master's award would be left to supply all further needs. And the prospect of 'guidelines' for the computing area should surely have seemed fraught with dangers.

THE 'GUIDELINES' IN COMPUTING

The publication, in October 1986, of a document entitled *Guidelines for Computer Related Award Bearing Courses* came as a matter of great surprise to many in educational computing. Few were more than dimly aware of the national trends towards INSET centralisation, but all were soon to realise that the term 'Guidelines' was a kind of Orwellian newspeak for 'inviolate law'. Any future proposal relating to award-bearing INSET in the IT area would have to prove its consistency with this document. The SED had by now set up a new committee, the SCOSDE,[14] which would perform the policing role that had been identified by the NCITT, and it was made clear that SCOSDE would refuse to accredit course proposals which deviated from the 'Guidelines' in any significant way.

Computing had been selected as one of the very first areas for guide-lines-writing. Why this should be so was far from clear: after all, the 'supply-led' criticism of INSET provision which had underpinned the 'Green Report's' proposals was hard to sustain for computing, since IT-related INSET was an official national priority. Furthermore, in three out of five colleges, Diplomas were already in place, and these were generally agreed to be doing good work. Naturally there were problems, but nobody had suggested that these could not be tackled by the normal processes of internal monitoring and evaluation, external examining, and regular review by the CNAA. In reality, the problems which the 'national system' of INSET was supposed to solve simply did not rate as significant issues for computing. There was very little demand for credit transfer arrangements, for example, and 'Guidelines' were hardly necessary to assist Local Authorities with recruitment, since most LEA IT Advisers had personal knowledge of the courses as they stood (indeed, many of them had contributed to their design).

Yet the harm which a premature standardisation could do was obvi-ous. It was plain that the educational computing area was volatile and that it had a long way to go before a mature and stable consensus could be expected: to 'freeze' on some course prescription now would be to risk doing great damage to the maturation process. To an extent the NCITT had recognised the dangers by its proposal that 'first initiatives in new fields' (and the existing Diplomas were all in this category) could dispense with 'Guidelines'.

The 'Computing Guidelines' had been written by a group led by a College Assistant Principal (an ex-geographer with no background in computing). The other membership comprised an HMI representative of the SED plus five college staff, mostly heads of computing departments. There were no teachers, Advisers, or representatives of the education profession more widely. None of the meetings was ever minuted, in spite of repeated protests by one of those present that the absence of minutes made effective consultation with colleagues almost impossible, and no reports of them were published. Open, public discussion was virtually non-existent: as far as can be ascertained, the group generated no discussion papers nor interim proposals, and neither did it make any serious attempt to canvas professional opinion more widely. An indication of the extent of the gap between the reality of the 'Computing Guidelines' and the 'process of widespread discussion' envisaged by the writers of the 'Three-Tier Structure Report' can be gauged from the fact that until the document appeared, none of the (unpromoted) computing staff in the largest College of Education had any idea of its contents: they had not been consulted at any stage.

FREEZING DEVELOPMENT

What did the 'Computing Guidelines' contain? They permitted three classes of award – with the titles Computing, Educational Computing, and Information Technology – while more or less equated to the Diplomas that were already running in the colleges. Superficially, then, it was possible for INSET managers to try to allay fears by arguing that the existence of 'Guidelines' need make little difference. As time went on, it became clear that such a view was naïve at best. Moray House was the first college to be affected by the existence of the new document; the scheduled five-year review of its Diploma became due just after the 'Guidelines' appeared. Course developers at that college quickly realised that the rigidity of the three classes excluded the kind of flexibility which was needed for the development of their Diploma. Forced to select between the Computing award, which was favoured by LEAS but narrowly targeted towards Computing Studies, and the Educational Computing award, which was potentially much broader and more innovative but to which LEA commitment was very uncertain, Moray House opted for the former. The presence of the 'Guidelines' effectively excluded the preferred solution, which would have been for an adaptable course structure containing two or more pathways.

In effect, the 'Computing Guidelines' merely locked into place what was a close approximation to the pattern of course provision that existed at the time they were written. They constrained development to match the 'snapshot' of 1986, and in so doing they *inter alia* perpetuated the INSET distortion which had emerged in favour of Computing Studies and against the broader curriculum uses of computing. And the worth of the NCITT's other 'safeguard', that 'Guidelines' were to be regularly reviewed, must be judged in the light of the fact that no review is planned until 1990 at the earliest.

In passing, the 'Guidelines' are worth reading, if only because this document represents one of the very few occasions on which those involved committed themselves to print. It would be fair to comment that opinions differ as to the document's quality, but that they are not uniformly high. As a sample, the following is a verbatim rendering of the section which stipulates the topics listed under the heading 'Technology: Applications' as prescribed content for the core of the Diploma in Computing:

- pervasive nature of computer usage
- case studies to illustrate processing power, information storage and retrieval, communication, and control including examples from business, industry and education
- artificial intelligence
- ethical, social and moral implications

Another heading for the same Diploma is 'Curriculum and Pedagogy', but it is apparent that the 'Guidelines' writers found this area a vexatious one by comparison to the 'Applications of Technology', for beneath the heading comes only a single topic:

- curriculum development in computing

It should be noted that, in attempting to prescribe *content*, the 'Computing Guidelines' actually went well beyond the NCITT's limits of what guidelines should contain. Fortunately (for course developers), the ineptitude with which it was done made strict enforcement impossible. Even the group of SCOSDE appointees which, in May 1988, scrutinised the Moray House proposals in an effort to detect any possible transgression of the 'Guidelines' found difficulty in interpreting the latter in a suitably solemn and reverent fashion.

Yet the 'Computing Guidelines' group evidently had relished their task. They concluded their report with a recommendation that a 'national advisory committee' (by which they clearly meant themselves) should be set up: its main task would be to 'develop' the 'Guidelines' into a 'national scheme of courses'.

THE OFF-THE-SHELF CURRICULUM

The concept of a national scheme of courses went far beyond the limits of what had been suggested by the 'Green Report' and the 'Three-Tier

Structure Report'. These reports had advocated a national system not of courses but of awards; they insisted that although local course teams would have to abide by national guidelines, a great deal of 'local' influence over the INSET curriculum would remain, and 'safeguards' were supposed to guarantee that this was so. What was now being proposed represented an almost total transfer of curriculum control towards the centre. The national courses would give complete prescriptions, down to the detailed level of individual module descriptors. At 'local' level (i.e. at the level of colleges, teachers, and LEAs) the entire curriculum would merely be lifted 'off-the-shelf', and the only remaining decision-making would concern minor details of delivery. Where 'local' courses (such as Diplomas) already existed, it was assumed that these should be dropped in favour of a cloned version of one of the 'national' courses. But, although the reaction inside the colleges was one of widespread dismay, the proposal to develop a national scheme of courses was enthusiastically endorsed by the SED. The former chairman of the 'Computing Guidelines' group was duly nominated to lead a 'Field Group' on behalf of the SCINSET.[15] It was noticeable that the SED representative, the same HMI who had participated in the 'Guidelines' exercise, increasingly referred to the 'Field Group' as a 'consortium': the term was significant, for the SED was soon to reveal that the computing pattern, in which guidelines represented only a first step towards national courses, could be expected to become the norm for all award-bearing INSET in the future. The SED's use of the term 'consortium' in this context was instantly recognised as another example of newspeak (one wag suggested that 'chain gang' might be a suitable translation).

Under strong SED pressure, the work towards the national scheme of courses pressed ahead. Of course, all the arguments against guidelines applied with double force against the concept of 'national courses'. What arguments were adduced in favour? Unfortunately, there seems to exist no published defence of this remarkable extension of centralisation. However, the SED representative and like-minded individuals on the group advanced arguments along the following lines:

(1) There would be safeguards against an over-prescriptive approach: module descriptors would leave some scope for interpretation, the scheme would be regularly reviewed, and wide consultation would ensure that it represented the best consensus that could be had.

(2) The consortium enabled collaboration in the development of resources, especially open-learning resources which were urgently needed for computing INSET. It was unrealistic to expect the open-learning needs to be met by an individual college acting alone.

(3) By avoiding duplicated efforts the consortium would save public money. The best available expertise and resources could be shared throughout the national system.

Inevitably, the first of these arguments provokes a strong sense of *déjà vu*. The other two represent a logic which is almost insultingly defective. No-one could dispute the desirability either of genuine professional and academic collaboration or of the need for high-quality resources, including 'open learning' resources, but these things neither imply, nor are implied by, a centralised INSET curriculum.

But the emphasis which was now being placed on open learning was new and significant. Certainly, wider and more flexible access to INSET was desirable, and if the development of self-study materials could contribute part of the solution to the INSET crisis, then that would be a cause for celebration. However, the ferocity with which the SED had turned towards open learning was alarming: a rolling programme of distance learning resource development had been unleashed which was intended to cover the proposed national scheme of courses in their entirety. There was no widespread discussion even of the most basic questions, such as: what circumstances justify a style of INSET which is based on teachers studying in isolation rather than in groups? How would distance learning cope with a knowledge base which was volatile and for which college expertise was often thin? Which strategy would make the best use of the available resources?

In October 1988 the proposals for the scheme were presented to SCINSET. A minority report was submitted by Moray House College, which presented a list of objections based on the following:

(1) By prescribing INSET courses at a national level the scheme represented an unprecedented extension of central curriculum prescription. The 'national courses' left very little scope for decision making by course teams and LEAs; the scheme was already outdated, being built on the 1986 'Guidelines', and would quickly become even more so; it would discourage innovation and creativity; it failed to recognise the individual circumstances of distinct regions and colleges.

(2) The scheme was over-complex. It attempted to define the entirety of award-bearing computing INSET within three titles of course across two levels of award covering three modes of delivery and multiple target groups, but this degree of elaboration was premature and it had been achieved only at the expense of consistency, quality, and reliability.

(3) Some highly promising areas (including Expert Systems, Interactive Video and Control Technology) in which Moray House had pioneered INSET provision had been excluded on the grounds that these areas were 'too specialised' for the national scheme.

The Moray House minority report also commented on the nature of the 'consultation' exercises which had been undertaken during the scheme's development:

> We would wish that the Field Group should be much more thorough and broad-ranging in its consultation with the profession. LEA input should go well beyond that which can be provided by one or two senior individuals

and it pointed out that this concept of 'consultation' contrasted badly with established 'local' college practice, which favoured an active involvement in course development of past and present course members, course team tutors, LEA Advisers, and so on. Finally, there was some acid comment on the SED newspeak: 'Collaboration must not come to mean "imposition" or goodwill will rapidly vanish'.

In fact, however, by that stage there was probably very little 'goodwill' left. The college computing staff had never worked particularly well together, and this bureaucratically enforced partnership had done little but harm to relations between them. There was strong resentment against those who were seen as *apparatchiks* and pliant tools of the centralisation policy, and there was a widespread feeling that the management of the open-learning developments in particular had been heavy-handed and clumsy. But as so often, the feelings were generally kept private: in all but one college, open protest was conspicuous only by its absence.

THE COLLEGE MANAGERS CAPITULATE

The SCINSET gave the minority report some sympathy. It ordered that the excluded Moray House modules should be immediately added to the scheme and it instructed that the group which was to take the scheme of courses to the final stage of CNAA validation should pay more attention to the requirements of flexibility. But the main objections were ultimately overruled.

Why did the senior college managers capitulate to the off-the-shelf INSET curriculum for IT? After all, by so doing they were conceding an unprecedented degree of autonomy. Neither did it require a great step of imagination to guess where the bureaucratic thinking might lead: if the courses running in different institutions were to be identical clones then why not just have one big national 'college', centrally organised across local 'sites'? But the colleges were punchdrunk. They had been ten and were now five; the state of embattlement was nothing new. Those college managers who had the will to resist had learnt to choose their moments. At the present time the SED seemed determined to pursue a 'consortium' path for the IT area. This, plus the fact that at least some college computing staff seemed to be volunteering to put their heads in an academic noose, suggested that perhaps this was one to let go.

But in a sense, too, the college managers had hanged themselves. They had initiated (or, at least, had not opposed) the centralisation which was inherent in the 'Green Report' and the 'Three-Tier Structure'. For example, Gordon Kirk, the Principal of Moray House, had robustly defended the 'Three-Tier Structure' against critics such as Walter Humes (Humes 1986) and David Hartley (Hartley 1985). Kirk had claimed that national guidelines would be the product of 'vigorous debate', they would represent imaginative and critical professional standards, and in any case bodies such as the GTC and the CNAA could never connive in any 'deadening effect' which might be produced by an over-centralisation (Kirk 1988). In fairness it must be said that neither Kirk nor any other senior college figure had publicly argued for an extension of the 'Three-Tier Structure' to cover 'national courses'. But the computing experience had shown that the fears expressed by Humes and Hartley were substantially justified; the supposed 'safeguards' which had been written into the 'Three-Tier Structure' had proved far from adequate. As for the GTC and the CNAA, the former had no locus in INSET and the latter was widely regarded among college staff as having been weakened by government action to the point where it could no longer be expected to guarantee the protection of academic standards.

However, there are signs that the battle over the centralised IT INSET curriculum may not yet be settled. This is not because its practical realisation will be bureaucratic, inflexible, and monolithic, although these things are likely. Neither is it because the 'national scheme' enjoys such little commitment among those who will be expected to implement it. It is not even because of a management which has been singularly inept. Rather, the development may founder because the model is so much at odds with the 'free-market', 'demand-driven' philosophy which is supposed to be the hallmark of late 1980s government policy, in Higher Education as elsewhere. Where is the 'INSET customer choice' when all courses are stamped in the same mould? How can 'INSET suppliers' show 'enterprise' when they are locked into a tightly regulated consortium cabal? In a sense, the centralised IT INSET curriculum reflects the ideology (of paternalistic and bureaucratic control) that was *yesterday's* clothing for the Scottish educational leadership class. With 'INSET vouchers' on the horizon, it looks distinctly out of time. The new political regime marches to a different tune and unless the 'free-market' propaganda is mere rhetoric then what was once a fashionable creation may, after all, become viewed as embarrassing garbage.

LOOKING BACK AND LOOKING FORWARD

This chapter began by asking how Scottish education in the 1980s responded to the staff development crisis arising from IT. The analysis presented here suggests that three recurring problems have weakened that response. We shall conclude by recapitulating these problems: in the 1990s the challenge will be to overcome them.

The first problem is one of resources. At a rough guess, it might be estimated that the average Scottish teacher has benefited from less than a single day of IT-related INSET during the entire 1980s. That statistic represents a miserable failing on the 'immense needs' which had been identified by the SCET's 'National Plan'. It shows that the IT staff development crisis has been anything but solved and, indeed, in some areas, such as secondary school Computing Studies, the crisis has steadily deepened. The blame here lies clearly with a government which has been happy to bask in the political kudos that followed the introduction of microcomputers into schools, but which has been unwilling to follow through with adequate funding to support the less glamorous task of staff development. But the lesson of the 1980s is that success in educational IT means an investment not only in machines but above all in *people* – people to work as tutors in colleges and LEA's, people to act as cover staff to support the secondment of teachers from schools, people to undertake the research and development work which is essential to underpin successful INSET, and so on.

The second problem is more serious, and is really a matter of intellectual integrity. The above account has shown that repeatedly there has been a failure on the part of Scottish educational computing to debate honestly and to evaluate openly the needs and experiences of INSET. A search of the available literature will reveal a striking absence of serious attempts – whether by HMI's, college staff, LEA Advisers, for example – to analyse the problems and appraise the alternatives. There is an irony here: these same people would always be keen to urge school pupils undertaking even the most minor project task to act in a manner which is collective, participative, and investigative. Yet their own style of work belies this commitment. The track record suggests that the absence of *glasnost* in particular has been very damaging, and it needs to be rectified.

The third recurring problem is related to the second. Although staff development models for IT INSET have scarcely been discussed, in effect one very unpleasant model has emerged as dominant. This model is best exemplified by the 'national scheme' of computing INSET courses, and its characteristics are those of central government control of the curriculum; remote bureaucratic management of courses; and heavy-handed syllabus prescription. Of course, there is a fundamental contradiction between these attributes and the requirements of a healthy educational computing. The latter seems likely to flourish only within a system which can offer an educational reflection of the vibrancy and diversity which characterises computing itself. It requires an INSET which recognises many different needs, collective and personal; which can secure the commitment and creativity of individuals; which can cope with rapid change; and which accepts the fact that, if only because practically nothing in this area is certain, it would be sensible to tolerate pluralism.

Unfortunately, the 1990s may open with a false contest between the centralist and bureaucratic model of staff development, on the one hand, and the newly fashionable (inside the SED) deregulated ideology of 'free-market competition', on the other. The second of these models is as irrelevant as the first is discredited: Scottish education deserves much better than either can offer. However, to build the alternative will require a willingness on the part of the teaching profession to take much more direct responsibility for INSET, so that INSET becomes something that they control rather than being something that is done to them by others. Are teachers ready for this?

NOTES

1. In-Service Education for Teachers.
2. Department of Trade and Industry.
3. Scotish Education Department.
4. I shall use 'IT INSET' very broadly to imply all kinds of INSET in the computing-related area. Similarly 'IT' should be given a wide interpretation.
5. Technical and Vocational Education Initiative.
6. Scottish Microelectronics Development Programme.
7. The official titles are 'Computing' at O-Grade, 'Computing Studies' at S-Grade and H-Grade.
8. Council for the National Accreditation of Awards.
9. Post-Graduate Certificate of Education.
10. TVEI Related In-Service Training.
11. Scottish Council for Research in Education.
12. General Teaching Council.
13. National Committee for the In-Service Training of Teachers.
14. Scottish Committee for Staff Development in Education.
15. Standing Committee on INSET (a sub-committee of the Committee of Principals of the Education Colleges)

REFERENCES

Butts, D. and Turner, E. (SCRE) (1988). *The National Evaluation of TRIST in Scotland*, TVEI Unit, MSC, London.

Cumming, C., Kidd, J., Wight, J. and McIver, J. (1985). *Becoming a Better Teacher*, Moray House College, Edinburgh.

The Development of the Three-Tier Structure for Award Bearing Courses. (1984). NCITT.

Evaluation of the DTI Micros in Schools Schemes, 1981–84 (1988). Centre for Applied Research in Education, University of East Anglia, May.

The Future of In-Service Training in Scotland (1979). NCITT.

Hartley, D. (1985). 'Bureaucracy and professionalism: the new "hidden curriculum" for teachers in Scotland', *Journal of Education for Teaching*, 11 (2) pp. 107–119.

Humes, W., (1986). *The Leadership Class in Scottish Education*. Edinburgh: John Donald.

In-Service Report of the Central Support Group Computing Studies (1987). Computing Studies CSG, January.

Kirk, G. (1988). *Teacher Education and Professional Development*, Edinburgh: Scottish Academic Press.

Learning and Teaching in Scottish Secondary Schools: The Use of Microcomputers (1987). SED, HMSO.

Microcomputers in Scottish Schools: A National Plan (1985). SCET/SMDP.

8

WHAT DO WESTER HAILES EDUCATION CENTRE STUDENTS NEED FROM COMPUTING?

LAURENCE O'DONNELL

ME AND MY SCHOOL

Let me start off by introducing myself and the school I work in, before I attempt to answer the question set in the title of this chapter. I was in what must have been the first generation of school/college computing courses. When I say 'in' I mean enrolled as a sixth-year school student on 'day release' to what was then Bathgate Tech (now the 'Wild' West Lothian College) to do part of a SCOTEC module. Throughout the course the only computers that my classmates and I saw were the ones on the glossy wall posters which adorned the Computer Science Department. After that I went to the University of Edinburgh to start a degree in Physics, that included one year of computing and finished up as an Honours degree in Politics. Moray House was my next stop and, in order to teach Computing, I had to gain entry to the Mathematics course. Two teaching practices later I arrived at Wester Hailes Education Centre (WHEC) in Edinburgh and having had a telephone stolen during a 'crit' lesson (with a college tutor in the room with me) the Principal decided I was what they needed to become the 'sorcerer's apprentice' in the Computing Department. I finished my training in the summer of 1986 and have worked at WHEC since then. I spent two years on a two-thirds Computing one-third Maths timetable to complete my probation in both subjects and then started this year (1988–9) on a Computing only timetable.

WHEC is a purpose-built community school which has just celebrated its tenth birthday. Once labelled 'the strangest school in Scotland' by the *Sunday Post*, its teachers have gained a reputation amongst educators for curricular and guidance innovation. However, as a result of the twin processes of, on the one hand, a real increase in take-up of adult classes and, on the other, falling rolls and the 'Parents Charter', WHEC now has more adults on its roll than school students. Some parents seem to value the opportunities provided for them by the centre but prefer to send their children out of Wester Hailes for schooling. The school is relatively well resourced. This is the result of a combination of factors: its age, community status, designation as one of Lothian's TVEI pilot scheme schools, and the regional policy of 'positive discrimination' for areas of deprivation.

In attempting to answer the question of what do WHEC students need from computing and information technology, I will, first of all, describe the context in terms of resources and courses. In the second part I will shift the emphasis towards the central figures of this piece – the youngsters themselves – through the results of an informal questionnaire and discussion. In the third part I will lay down some ideas which I argue will help us to understand the needs young people have from computing. What are the needs of school students in general? How are these needs determined? Are school computing courses designed to take these needs into account, or are they considered peripheral to the needs of society? I can only begin to outline a theoretical framework for answering these questions, as any satisfactory answer will inevitably go to the very heart of schooling and its legitimation.

WHAT YOUR TEACHER CAN DO IS WHAT YOU GET

There are several factors which necessarily limit the scope of computing courses for school students. The standard of the software employed is an obvious one, but this has to be considered in the context of both the quality and availability of hardware and the competence and experience of teachers. So what is this context at WHEC, in January 1989?

The hardware
Room A
7 BBC B
4 BBC Masters
1 Modem
3 dot matrix Printers with printer sharer
(plus 1 BBC B and a Master on trolleys owned and much used by the Maths and Learning Support Departments, respectively).

Room B
10 BBC B
1 BBC Master
1 Modem
5 dot matrix printers with printer sharer
(plus 1 trolleyed Master belonging to the Maths Department)

Room C
1 Apple Macintosh SE20 (with 20 mb hard disk built in)
4 Apple Macintosh Plus (1 with 20 mb hard disk)
1 Imagewriter printer
Appletalk printer sharer network

Miscellaneous

4 AMX Mouses
1 Light Pen
1 Bar Code Reader
1 BBC Buggy
1 Big Trak
A part share in some robotics hardware

This is probably above average for a Lothian school, but most computing departments are heading in that direction with the extension to the TVEI footing at least a part of the bill.

The teachers

One of the other major constraints on the quality of courses is the training of teachers. As I have already indicated, I have done the one year post-graduate course, my Principal Teacher has no formal qualifications in computing (as he is very fond of reminding me from time to time), and the third, or should I say second, member of the department (an Assistant Principal Teacher of Guidance) has added to her four years experience the two-week college conversion course. There is also a PT Modern Studies teaching a first-year class along with an evening class in 'desktop publishing' who has no formal computing qualification but a high degree of competence and eight years of experience. This is certainly better than most schools, as headteachers attempt to keep their staff by cobbling together bits of timetables usually including some computing.

THE COURSES
Lower school
S1

The first-year course has recently become an hour a week for all students instead of a ten-week block which involved extraction from Physical Education. Class sizes are around twelve, which is approaching a computer each. In S1 the enthusiasm and genuine interest in what the computer can do is not squandered. Many programs are used which both motivate and stimulate these classes. Some of these programs have been created with the primary school in mind, but as children develop at radically different rates many are still appropriate in lower school. A selection would include making a wordsearch, the robot toy 'Big Trak', using the sound facility on the BBC, making a newspaper page, making Christmas cards, and using a program which digitises video pictures. Adventure games such as 'The Lost Frog' and 'Granny's Garden', and 'Scoop' are included. An as yet unrealised aim of this course is to tie in content from other classes with appropriate software. An example may be a Maths program which teaches co-ordinates used at the time this topic is being taught in Mathematics. Such an innovation will involve not only close interdepartmental co-operation but also careful forward planning.

S2

This is a ten-week ten period course taken by all students. Three of the Acorn CES programs are used: a database, a programmable crane simulation, and a housing scheme simulation (which looks nothing like Wester Hailes), along with a Teletext simulation, and a LOGO-style Turtlegraphics program. The main aim of these courses is to engender a confidence in, and a knowledge of, the uses of computers. They are designed for all and not to fit neatly into a pre-standard grade format.

These courses do capture the imagination of all but a few of the students, although they are in the process of a much-needed review at the moment. The whole area of S1 and S2 computing has been relatively neglected in recent years as the thrust of post-industrial action development was directed at raising the quality of the new middle-school courses, the Standard Grade, and Modules.

Middle school

From here on students are involved in the pursuit of certification, voluntarily or otherwise, and as a result we as teachers become involved in delivering other agencies' (SEB and SCOTVEC) courses. The particular content of any course may be flexible to some extent, but assessment procedures necessitate a uniformity and external control.

S3 module

This is the sixteen-minus 'Introduction to Computers' module. The module descriptor is designed with employers and Further Education in mind, and has little to do with the needs and aspirations of fourteen-and fifteen-year-olds. However, something that meets the module descriptor, satisfies the ever changing Learning Outcomes, and, most importantly, bears some relevance to the students has been put together. The assessment could be satisfied by our S1 and S2 courses though. This is a course done by all those who have not chosen to do the Standard Grade (around fifty from a year group of 120). Content includes such delights as 'Telfax', the teletext suite of programs, speech synthesis, 'Prestel', word processing with Wordwise, and the 'AMX Super Art' program. Short courses are a good idea in as much as they offer a wider choice for students, but are more difficult to assess, and, if they happen to coincide with a spate of Monday holidays, more difficult to complete. However, the majority of students taking this particular course seem to get some reward from it, often making a belated and unsuccessful request to take the oversubscribed Standard Grade.

S3 and S4 Standard Grade

This is, I suppose, the flagship of computing at the moment: in both S3 and S4 we have four classes in each year of between sixteen and nineteen students (the most popular course choice). The course itself has improved greatly over the last year, with more appropriate projects and more experience on the part of the teachers. However, it is still a course dominated, to the point of being positively hijacked, by the assessment. The full critique of Standard Grade Computing Studies will be found elsewhere. It is a course which was designed to be inflexible at a time when it was perceived that teachers of the subject did not feel confident about their chosen subject. Those times have changed, and it is now time to open Standard Grade up to innovation and allow for necessary changes.

To what extent the resources available so far match the range of abilities is unclear. There appears to be very little in the way of genuine Credit materials at the one end, and programming remains a world apart for some at the other end. Compulsory certification for all has its drawbacks, some of which have not been adequately anticipated in the design of courses. The inflexibility of the projects (they do not allow for different levels of working) mean that teachers have to decide too early about working levels. However, the course remains popular even among those who do not gain much in the respect of actual grades from the course. There is some content overlap with the S3 module, but topics are not covered to the same extent. Content includes Electronic Document Processing, with the compulsory case study in word processing making use of 'Wordwise' and its 'wysnyme' (the whec motto) format. The central software packages in the Information Systems case studies are the database 'Quest' and 'Telfax' teletext programs. For Automated Systems a robot arm, cnc Lathe simulation, and the odd logic board are combined with a hotchpotch of software and hardware. Commercial data processing involves the now almost infamous and still compulsory 'Mail Order' package which, when run on 40-track disk, involves enough in the way of inserting and removing disks to constitute a workout. This is supplemented by a program which simulates a subset of the data processes carried out by the dvlc computer system. Comal is the prescribed language, which is now taught in a way that leaves the library of sub-programs (with the mystifyingly named 'Demons') approach until S4. Projects play a big part in the course, especially when it comes to tying up loose ends for those who have been absent (which can result from illness, work experience placements, and term-time holidays). These projects are what divide the classes into levels (as intended), however, the progrmaming projects in my experience are the crucial ones in this respect.

Upper school

S5 Pascal programming and Information Studies

The scotvec module 'An Introduction to Computer Programming (Pascal)' makes use of the Macintoshes and Turbo Pascal. This has proved very popular amongst a small fifth year and possibly points to Higher Computing sometime in the future. The module 'Information Studies' is being taken by a small number of fifth years, and involves looking at a number of relevant packages on the BBC and on the Apple Macintosh.

Computers across the curriculum

Students also have access to computers in other subjects, especially in the Business Studies Department (a room of BBCs and one of Amstrad PCs), and including Maths (two BBCs), Social subjects, Science, Technical, Home Economics, and Learning Support. Despite the emphasis on computing courses, there has been little conflict between departments wanting to make 'curriculum computing' innovation and those delivering information technology (IT) courses (Computing and Business Studies departments). The fact that there has not been much in the way of tension until now was highlighted by a dispute on the placement of the school's six Apple Macintoshes. The first one was placed in the Computing Department and then the next four (all funded from TVEI) were distributed around the school. When a third computer room was fitted out, the argument that ensued was not between those who argued for curriculum computing against those who supported IT courses. Rather it was between those who saw Apples as teachers' resource preparation machines and those who saw their primary function in the classroom (a Computing Department classroom, admittedly).

WHEC computing report

There has been little in the way of evaluation for WHEC computing. This reflects its unplanned birth and the pace of its development. The extent of funding for more computers or extra accommodation has not been matched by consultation with the staff as a whole on the future of computing as a subject or as an aid to learning in other subjects. The questions raised by vocationally oriented courses have not been properly discussed, and despite many teachers becoming actively involved as software users very few have raised questions about computing's place in the curriculum. For the record, my evaluation of computing at WHEC is largely a positive one, with only a few reservations. The development of 'curricular computing' has been speeded up by the presence of IT courses and specialist departments. This may be a product of the 'little empires' nature of schools departments as the focus for the division of resources. There was a need for someone in the school to prioritise the argument for computing resources. One of my reservations is that much more energy (involving time that was not made available) should have been spent working out a coherently planned and deliberately executed IT strategy for the whole school with the quality of educational provision as the determining influence.

PLAY GAMES AND GET A JOB (A QUESTIONNAIRE)

The overall impression of student perceptions of the computing provision at WHEC, that I have given so far is a positive one. This is reinforced by the results of an informal questionnaire I carried out for this piece. This section will take the form of a summary and analysis of that survey. Thirty students were involved: fifteen from S3 and fifteen from S4. All were taking Standard Grade Computing, and the questions concentrated on that course. The questionnaire was completed question by question, the students writing something down first, then discussing their answers as a class. This method allowed me to get genuine responses on paper and encourage debate and an opportunity to expand on some of the answers orally. All the quotations used below are from the paper responses, but many of my comments derive from the discussion.

Primary school

All but one of the students claimed to have used computers in their primary schools, and that was four and five years ago. The time spent varied from 'five minutes a month' to 'every Tuesday until dinner time'. Group work seemed to dominate. The programs which made a lasting impression were 'Granny's Garden' and 'The Lost Frog', used again in S1 and S2, with only three students naming mathematical computer-aided instruction programs.

Why Standard Grade?

The reasons given for choosing Standard Grade Computing Studies fell into four main categories. First, those who thought it would enhance their job prospects in general. The subject for them provided 'a skill I need for a job', on the one hand, and also reflected the notion that 'computers are used in most jobs', or, more bluntly, 'because everything will soon be all computers'. When asked later in the questionnaire whether they thought a pass in Standard Grade would help them to get a job, two-thirds considered that it would help, with one-third considering that it might: 'depends on what job you want', and significantly none answered with a direct 'no'. The second group reflected a more specific vocationalism, that is they wanted jobs in the computer-related industries. Typical of these responses were 'I want to work with computers' and 'I wanted to be a programmer when I was older'. The third group were those who claimed to have 'enjoyed it since primary' and, of course, in S1 and S2. A fourth group (involving only two students) claimed that the major influence was that computing was 'a better choice than history', and what is more there was 'nothing else to choose of interest'. It is clearly unfair to look at simple responses to a questionnaire with a view to uncovering the complex processes which lead a youngster to choose any particular course. Most students when asked directly did

admit to having a combination of influences. The strength of the vocational factor was not based in their own experience (brothers and
sisters with computing qualifications did not step easily into IT jobs) but
rather to the hype computers have been given in the retraining and skills
shortages discourses. The extent to which false hopes have been raised
in this respect is unclear, but the responsibility teachers have for defus-
ing the myths about the IT job market, both with parents and school
students, is considerable and undeniable.

Standard Grade by the 'consumers'

When asked if they thought the course had turned out to be as they
expected, there was a clear divide between S3 and S4; the majority in S4
who answered 'yes' were matched by an equally significant majority of
S3 students who claimed the answer was 'no'. This may reflect the time
lapse; for some students in S4 expectations of two years ago are ancient
history. Some had expectations of 'lots of programming' and 'lots of
work', another 'thought we would have played some games', but a
classmate was more in touch, she 'knew we wouldn't get games'. So the
pre-choice description of the course (that it was something quite unlike
the experience of primary and much of S1 and S2) seemed to have hit
home. In the S3 sample fourteen said they had 'enjoyed' the course so
far, with only one against. The S4 response was nine for, and one
'against', but with a definite five abstentions. This could mean that at
least five have become disillusioned with computing, or, more likely,
with school and certification in general.

When asked to identify the aspects of the course that they liked, there
were no clear trends either 'for' or 'against' any of the 'applications' –
word processing, databases etc. Although in S4 some of the projects
were generally popular, and programming had become more unpopu-
lar. This unpopularity might stem from the reality of placing students in
levels. The determining factor is, as I have already mentioned, more
often than not whether a student can cope with a general or credit level
programming project. Some can; others, who, in using some of the
applications might consider themselves to be doing well, cannot manage
the programming projects aimed at that level. One student's answer to
what parts of the course s/he particularly liked was as follows: 'I like
some of the people in the class and the teacher is a good guy ...
sometimes.' Back to earth with a crash, let us not forget the power of peer
pressure in swaying opinion, and, even more dangerous, the favourite-
teacher-favourite-subject effect.

One of the questions asked students what they thought should be
incorporated into the course that is not present at the moment. As
expected, a majority opted for 'games'. A couple even wanted to learn
how to 'program games' and their 'graphics'. Other responses ranged
from a call to use 'different computers' to a class visit to 'the computer

place' (which one you may ask?). The games lobby should be no surprise, as many of the students (predominantly boys) own or have access
to a home computer and have derived much pleasure from an almost
unlimited range of of very similar arcade-style games. While we have no
problem including spreadsheets, databases, and word processors with
clearly acknowledged business orientations, we systematically ignore
the one area where computing is dominated by the youth market:
computer games. I am not suggesting that we collapse Standard Grade
into a classroom arcade game show. What I am suggesting is that we
need to take home computing seriously, study some of these games, and
try to encourage different approaches. We are still suffering from the
early 'Space Invaders' days of computing. We have nothing to fear now,
and can only gain by drawing on an area of expertise amongst students
which is unparalleled in other subjects. As usual, teachers are seen to be
writing off what happens in the out-of-school life of students without
due consideration. (How about a secondment to write an optional case
study on 'computer games' or 'computer aided leisure' to add to the
existing one in 'computer simulations'?)

Summary

So what can we conclude from this the questionnaire? First of all, that
there are many other questions that could and should have been asked –
not to mention a comparative study between those taking the Standard
Grade and those who opted for other subjects. Secondly, computing
courses at WHEC have generated and maintained a popularity with
young learners. Thirdly, many of the students are taking the subject with
what could be construed as the false hopes of a passport to a job. The
fourth and final point I would draw out of the questionnaire is that
student expectations are vague and evaluations limited. This is only to be
expected from young people who are rarely consulted in the provision of
their education amongst almost everything else in their lives.

WHAT DO THEY NEED FROM COMPUTING?

What do students need from IT, in general, and computing in particular.
Qualifications I suppose must appear somewhere (for some?) in any list
of needs. Expertise, or at least confidence, in using the technology and its
vocabulary (an initiation into the 'world of computing') must be considered as well. The question then is what type of qualification and what
degree of competence should be facilitated by schools? Computing has
presently a business orientation and, therefore, business applications
dominate. Do our students need computing vocational courses from the
age of fourteen? Could we deliver these vocational courses with the BBC
micro at the heart of our work even if we wanted to? This is a question I
will dodge for the moment, leaving it to other contributors to thrash out.
I want to concentrate more on the style of courses and their sources and

influences. Self (1987), on the subject of what he called 'the institutional-isation of mediocrity' in computer-aided instruction bemoaned the present standard of software. This verdict, he claims, is not unproblematic; the fact that students actually like using the programs can beguile teachers into a false sense of the value of the experience they are providing:

> It may be thought a desirable, even necessary, condition to be met by good educational software that students find it enjoyable to use, but it is not a sufficient condition. In short, we should reject 'market forces' as a judgement of quality, and ask bluntly, do computers aid cost-effective learning?

However, 'cost-effective' educationally sound courses and software packages would be more effective if they were also enjoyable and able to motivate and enthuse students. A 'consumer' led approach to course design would almost certainly lead up the blind alleys of arcade games and narrow vocationalism. Computing must take its place within a schooling which is predicated on a restriction of freedom for the under sixteens. A restriction which is based in law and in theory at least is enforceable. To justify this denial of freedom, school must meet the needs and expectations of youngsters not passively but head on, and in the process challenge and transform them. Needs have to be understood as socially produced and, as such, neither inherent in any particular person nor, for that matter, immutable. However, this does not mean that the subjective desires and aspirations of youngsters should be ignored, rather they have to be taken seriously if statements such as the one which opens WHECs *The Centre Ethos* (1986): 'We would like every youngster to feel valued as a person', are to move beyond well-motivated rhetoric free from actual practice.

The long-standing weakness that penetrates all of the Scottish education system is the lack of a democratic tradition extended to those who are taught to understand, adapt, and learn to cope but rarely to decide. From the point of view of the teacher, this must mean that the minimum they can do is to provide varied, flexible, and student-sensitive courses. The variety should not be apparent only in the content but also in the teaching methodologies employed. Students learn in different ways, and, as Entwhistle (1981) points out, if practitioners are to be effective, they need to 'provide opportunities for students to learn in a way which suits their preferred style of learning'. In computing this could mean that sometimes a 'workstations', approach may be employed; at other times perhaps a more didactic formal teaching approach should be used. The latter may be difficult to institute in a subject which has 'hands-on experience' as one of its not so long dead ancestors. Much work needs to be done on the development of the 'new technology' of pedagogy in general with a particular subset of that technology applied to the teaching of computing. I have used the term 'student-sensitive' rather than 'student-centred' because the latter can be construed as an approach which concentrates on resources and devalues the role of the teacher; a role which in the light of technological innovations such as 'interactive video' admittedly will need to be reconsidered if it is not to be relegated to that of a 'hi-tech' resources deployment manager.

What should be the aims and objectives of a popular, democratic, but still compulsory schooling? Could they be adequately satisfied with the production of 'electronic office fodder'. Surely not, if our aim is to foster understanding in the context of a realisation and development of powers. Computing courses and 'curricular computing' must have the interests of our students, broadly understood, at their heart rather than the 'mastery' of particular computer applications. Learning for youngsters can, and should, be a rich process which involves, according to Simon (1985):

> the child's own self activity through which he or she masters and transforms the surrounding world, and in doing so transforms him/herself – in short learns, develops, acquires skills, abilities, an outlook, character, attitudes, autonomy – and all the better with systematic aid from adults in the family, the school and elsewhere.

Much of this happens anyway, often despite schooling, but it is only by including such a view of the young learner that the theory and practice of computing in schools can even begin to meet the needs of youngsters. The problem is that teachers are constrained by, amongst a host of other things, agencies such as the SEB and the MSC, which often do not imbue their courses with such a vision.

REFERENCES

The Centre Ethos (1986). Wester Hailes Education Centre, Edinburgh.

Entwhistle, (1981). Styles of Learning and Teaching, Wiley.

Self, J. (1987). The Institutionalisation of Mediocrity and the Influence of Outsiders' in E. Scanlon and T. O'Shea (eds) *Educational Computing*, Open University, Wiley.

Simon, B. (1985). 'Education in Theory, Schooling in Practice' in *Does Education Matter?*, London: Lawrence & Wishart.

9

INFORMATION TECHNOLOGY AND THE SOCIAL
SUBJECTS

BOB MUNRO

This contribution to the wider educational debate concerning the impact of information technology (IT) on education comes at a critical stage in the acceptance, uptake, and integration of the many facets of IT in the social subjects curriculum. The social subjects were early identified as fruitful areas for IT-oriented development but, twenty years on, the widespread application and general curricular integration of IT within the social subjects has not occurred. This could be regarded as a spectacular failure or as a necessary consequence of a period of experimentation and exploration, where a great many educational possibilities were tried, tested, proved, or rejected. Certainly, we now have a much clearer perception of how IT can contribute to the learning and teaching process, and of which applications are the most educationally valuable within the social subjects. These are positive products of a realistic and rigorous educational appraisal of a most seductive technology, which has promised much more than it has been found able to deliver.

Can the social subjects realise the potential of IT in the future? Previous technical constraints imposed by hardware and software limitations have been swept dramatically aside. The availability of low-priced microcomputers of considerable sophistication and vastly increased memory capacity (with excellent screen resolutions and quality graphic input and output facilities), the advance of videodisc and compact disk technology, and the development of a comprehensive range of peripheral devices have opened up a new hardware scenario. The creation of complex software, ranging through generic packages concerned with word processing, data handling, desktop publishing, expert systems, and object-oriented manipulation to integrated multipurpose software, has expanded the range of applications of the technology. Throw in the advantages offered by parallel processing and a communications revolution which provides microcomputers with access to mainframes and memory stores crammed with global information, and you have technology in the fast lane – and accelerating. The possibilities now open to the social subjects to deploy IT to enhance the learning and teaching process are both more numerous and vastly more important and power-ful than ever before. To fail this time would irrevocably divorce edu-cation from the benefits of the information revolution – but we should not contemplate failure!

During the 1970s pioneers of educational computing in the social subjects, such as Deryn Watson at Chelsea College, Dr Bill Tagg at the Advisory Unit for Computer Based Learning, David Walker at Lough-borough University, and Dr Richard Jennings at Aberdeen College of Education, identified a range of applications of the computer in social subjects work, and tried both to create appropriate software to stimulate the use of the computer and to advise on the curricular integration of computer-related activity. Their work was mainframe-oriented and in-volved 'batch' processing, often at a distant location, of pupil data and pupil decisions related to specific software packages. The teacher, there-fore, was required only to organise data collection and promote dis-cussion in the classroom. The technology was largely divorced from the educational process.

Simulations, especially those associated with mathematical models so beloved of physical and urban geographers, allowed the exploration of topics such as industrial location, industrial change over time, physical geography processes, factors controlling retail gravitation, and aspects of urban morphology. Such activity was valuable to the aspiring uni-versity student in the fifth or sixth year, but hardly meat and drink for the masses. Other simulations, allowing the user to fight the Civil War or the Battle of Waterloo, to manage a Prairie farm or the American energy budget, or to sell deep freeze cabinets over the whole of the UK, widened the scope of computer oriented activity but were tedious and, because of the time delay associated with the 'batch' processing of information, held pupil interest and enthusiasm for only a very short time.

The microcomputer, theoretically, brought IT into the ambit of use of all teachers, although precious little educational justification for the use of a microcomputer was ever advanced. A variety of widely different systems proliferated in Scottish secondary schools, until the BBC micro-computer assumed a dominance which was due to political rather than educational reasons. With such a range of equipment, it was hardly surprising that social subjects teachers, who in the past had no need to manage the technology and who were concerned about their limited technical expertise, drew back from involvement with IT. This 'tech-nofear' still exists and, over the past decade, has been a very real inhibiting factor influencing the uptake and use of all forms of IT in the social subjects. In retrospect, staff in Colleges of Education and Local Authority Advisers have failed to provide sufficient, appropriate pre-service and in-service training, and assistance to counteract this technofear.

Since the introduction of the microcomputer, the range of software available for use has burgeoned, and today a considerable number of packages for use in History, Geography, and Modern Studies exists. The software has come from many different sources. These include individuals (both teachers and non-teachers) with an interest in programming; educational publishers who have perceived a market sector; LEA initiatives; and through the activities of specific educational support bodies such as the Scottish Microelectronics Development Project, SMDP (now an arm of the Scottish Council for Educational Technology, SCET) and the Microelectronics in Education Project, MEP (now Microelectronics Education Support Unit, MESU, within the Council for Educational Technology, CET). Both the SMDP and MEP had a software development remit when they were set up, and their policy of marrying teacher expertise to programming expertise has often proved most effective. Some of the software produced by them in their early years still makes an important contribution to curricular activity in the social subjects. Recently, however, their output of subject-specific materials has diminished because their scarce resources have been devoted to the development of generic software which has more general application.

Not all of the software developed through these different sources can be commended. Only a tiny percentage is built on sound pedagogic principles and is truly acceptable educationally. The uncoordinated, non-standardised software generation process has resulted in the production of a large quantity of educational dross which has certainly damped down the fires of enthusiasm for the microcomputer in the classroom. Regrettably, in the absence of systematic appraisal of educational software and of an information dissemination system which informs teachers of the quality of the software, many teachers have purchased software blind, or have acquired 'pirate' copies of the programs and have frequently found them disappointing. Once bitten, twice shy has been the rule, and the inadequacies of the software and its inapplicability to the learning and teaching process have soured the attitudes of many teachers to the potential of IT.

Equally, some teachers use software quite happily but wholly inappropriately. The use of commonly available drill and practice software, which can be simply integrated into classroom activity, is frequently justified by the stated need for pupils to have a body of factual knowledge on which they can develop higher order thinking skills. Some testing packages, supported by print materials such as maps and atlases (e.g. 'Target Scotland' by the SMDP), can be used effectively with, in particular, less-able pupils, but there is little justification for using such software with all pupils. I do not think that the use of a microcomputer with drill and practice software is the best way to establish any body of knowledge, and it has been my experience that there are more valuable educational uses for the computer in the areas of simulation, data-handling, and reporting.

The more sophisticated testing, concept-establishing, or skill-enhancing software (usually known as tutorial software), which can help children to gain an understanding of processes and concepts, or which can sensitively identify learning problems and assist in their rectification, has not made much impression on the social subjects. Such software is best developed to provide individualised learning materials for small group use, or for a particular pupil. The time required to produce such user-sensitive software is enormous, and the author systems which purport to make the software production process simple are actually quite difficult to use at anything beyond the level of producing the most elementary teaching and learning material. Some LEA working parties, in conjunction with Jordanhill College staff, have produced tutorial software for the S1/S2 area of the geography curriculum ('Coalfield Model', 'Iron and Steel Game', 'Farm Model', 'Urban Models'). This is old teaching material offered on a new medium and there is little in-built diagnostic or remedial assistance, but teachers who have used it are favourably disposed towards it. Other tutorial material is very thin on the ground.

There are, however, some available software resources which can and have made a very positive contribution to work in the social subjects curriculum. These have enhanced the learning and teaching process, have helped establish, most effectively, certain concepts and skills, have stimulated discussion and off-computer activity, and have provided a means whereby pupils can complete mundane or technically difficult tasks speedily and so free time for deeper analysis of data or examination of results and relationships.

Data handling has proved to be the most successful use for the microcomputer and developments have been particularly interesting and impressive in the History sphere. Here the analysis of population census data has been the main focus since Dr Tagg developed the sophisticated query language, commonly available as 'Quest'. This permitted the investigation of computer datafiles and the speedy identification of facts, relationships, and patterns in the data. Early use of 1851 census data for two English villages, Somerleyton and Datchworth, led to a growth in the exploration of real historical evidence, frequently home-area based, from the upper primary school classroom right up to the undergraduate and post-graduate research activity promoted through the 'DISH Project' (Design and Implementation of Software in History) at the University of Glasgow.

The last few years have seen the proliferation of data handling packages such as 'Inform', 'Grass', 'Find', and 'Key'. These are all used within the social subjects and, indeed, it is in the social subjects area that they are most used! Each has its devotees, partly as a result of the facilities the packages offer, but the recent decision of the Central Support Group for Geography to provide 'Key' to all schools as part of a Standard Grade resource pack will undoubtedly mean that activity within the geography curriculum will be biased towards the facilities it offers. Using these data handling packages, many pupils have conducted historical investigations into the earlier residents of their home area, of the first settlers sent to Australia, of members of a whaling boat sailing for Antarctica from Dundee, and of victims of the mining disasters. In Modern Studies and Geography the availability of the 1981 Census data for their home area and the specific samples provided by the Economic and Social Research Council (ESRC) in their 'Census Data Pack' has allowed pupils to explore simple housing conditions or population structures as well as more complex socio-economic relationships. Other datafiles on Europe, Japan, the USA, and even the whole world on weather or agricultural commodities, and even on the superpowers' ownership of weaponry, enhance the inquiry skills and the development of hypotheses.

Until very recently, the advantage offered by the technology for such data processing was simply that of speed. While considerably more information could be processed on a microcomputer than could be analysed manually by pupils, the datafiles were relatively trivial, the conclusions rather superficial, and the spatial relationships of the data impossible to discern without considerable off-computer mapping. New software, such as 'Place and People', allows the data to be mapped very quickly, perhaps as a choropleth map or perhaps as a located symbolic map. The screen display and the printout facility afford pupils a revealing insight into spatial relationships and open up new investigative possibilities. In a more sophisticated form this facility is also provided on the Domesday videodisc.

A major stumbling block to the widespread use of data handling in the social subjects has been the relative paucity of appropriate datafiles for classroom use. This is a matter of some concern and requires a response from LEA or from national educational software development bodies. Unfortunately, their role has been seen as the production of software rather than the production of resources to support software. Once again, there has been the expectation that teachers would respond to the availability of data handling software by creating their own datafiles. However, data accumulation and organisation is time-consuming and the business of file creation is extremely onerous. None the less initiatives associated with datafile provision are essential if the potential of the data handling software is to be realised in the near future.

Simulations of real life events and processes are resources which are used in all of the social subjects to foster decision-making, to allow pupils to explore relationships, to encourage the formulation of alternative strategies, and to stimulate discussion and reporting skills. Many simulations are now computer-based, and a large number of History departments make use of packages such as 'Into the Unknown', 'Battle of the Somme', 'How we Used to Live', 'The Vikings', or '1914'. In Geography departments the software may include 'Slick', 'Sand Harvest', 'Farm-ing', or 'Nomad', or may be concerned with the passage of a weather depression or the locational decision-making processes behind a pre-sent-day industry. Modern Studies may use 'Election Simulation', 'East–West', or the 'Arab–Israeli Crisis'.

While these packages have undoubtedly made a contribution to the pupils' understanding of process and decision-making, it should be remembered that many of these computer simulations are simply the microcomputer update of an old mainframe package, or a computer version of a board (even blackboard)-based game which was used effec-tively in the non-computer form many years ago. Both 'Slick' and the recently marketed Coca-Cola 'Man in his Environment' packages are microcomputer versions of simulations I used most effectively in class-rooms in 1973! I do not believe that the computer versions have advanced the educational process, and I consider that most of the simulations currently in use are very superficial; they do little to enhance children's understanding and, unlike teachers, are unable to respond to the needs of individual pupils.

These inadequacies of what should be a powerful teaching tool are due principally to the fact that computers used regularly by social subjects teachers, or even made available to them, have extremely limited memory capacity and, therefore, can handle only relatively trivial simu-lation software. Additionally, of course, they reflect a lack of intelligent forward thinking on the part of educational software designers. It is to be hoped that future simulation development will allow for various entry levels to reflect the range of abilities of the users; that they will capitalise on the evolving technological facilities (notably the graphics and the memory capacity) to enhance the quality and veracity of the simulation; and attempt to interface with other media sources. A commendable step in this direction is the 'Balance of Power', which is a most sophisticated version of the 'East–West' conflict.

The three areas of drill and practice (despite my reservations), data handling, and simulation are the foundations on which IT use in the social subjects has been built. Some teachers have integrated these software applications very effectively into their classroom work, even though they may have only one microcomputer in the room. This is largely a reflection of the successful adoption of the stations approach within a teaching strategy committed to differentiated learning. The implementation of Standard Grade, which favours process-based and investigative learning, will reinforce the role of the stations approach and should foster the increased use of IT in the classroom.

While there is evidence of satisfactory development, it is, however, imperfectly formed and poorly distributed. Many teachers of social subjects still require encouragement, coercion, in-service training, guid-ance, and support before they will even contemplate the introduction of any aspect of IT to their curriculum planning, far less their actual class-room. Such teachers must be convinced of the worth of the technology. This can be done only by showing them relevant, quality software examples which they can see being used in an appropriate context. They will not be swayed by, and indeed they will no longer even listen to, the computer enthusiast who cannot perceive how difficult even simple aspects of technology are to the naïve user. We have failed to convince the majority of social subjects teachers of the worth of the resource because we have shown them packages and facilities rather than how to use these in context. We have swept the technofear problem aside, and, indeed, have added to the technofear by developing networks in computer rooms, instead of helping teachers to overcome it.

Once persuaded of the worth of the technology, there must be time to become familiar with the software so that the curricular application can be fully discerned and planned. Again this opportunity is frequently denied to teachers. Information on social subjects software does not percolate down from Computing Studies departments; software companies seldom issue inspection software to individuals; teacher resource centres are often distant and hold only a limited stock of software; and there is little planned development time for teachers to appraise materials. Most importantly, the teacher must have the technology to hand in the classroom or at least have it easily accessible. The emergence of Computing Studies, with its growing importance as a mainline examination subject and as a vehicle for post-sixteen modules, has been a major factor inhibiting the development of the use of IT across the curriculum. Computer resources, as well as associated devices such as modems, printers, digitisers, and videodisc resources have been concentrated in these departments, and there has been only a token diffusion of hardware throughout schools. The future appears to offer little prospect of change, as already the new sophisticated computers, such as the Nimbus, Archimedes, and Macintosh, are being located centrally. They are being used either to support the new demands of the Higher Grade in Computing Studies or the various new syllabuses in the Business Studies departments. I suspect these departments will make little all-round use of such sophisticated hardware. As almost all aspects of Computing Studies can be taught most effectively using the humble BBC and BBC Master, and many of the Standard Grade Computing Studies aims can be most adequately met through IT experiences throughout the school curriculum, I suggest that the newer 16/32–bit technology, with its attendant peripheral devices, should be located in departments such as the social subjects. Here the facilities offered by the new hardware could be most effectively utilised.

Following my earlier remarks on the failure of social subjects to exploit IT so far, the suggestion that the newest and most sophisticated technological resources should be located in these departments may seem incongruous. However, two major reasons for the earlier failure were that the hardware was not provided to social subjects departments, and that the installed hardware was so limited that it could not perform the tasks which social subjects teachers wished it to do.

Today the social subjects stand at the crossroads in terms of the future development of IT. Teachers can choose to accept the handout of clapped-out BBC machines rendered redundant by Computing Studies departments, realise that they are adopting outdated technology, accept the severe software limitations, and try to create resource materials for use with generic software. They will have a resource which is capable of releasing only a fraction of the potential which IT holds for the social subjects. Alternatively, teachers can push and cajole through subject associations, through Advisers and HMI, and through school committees charged with the formulation of IT policy for the powerful 16/32-bit hardware, which, with its sophisticated software (both subject-specific and generic) and advanced peripherals could transform the educational experience of pupils with respect to the social subjects curriculum. Both routes enhance the curriculum, but I know which one I would go down!

For the teacher choosing the first route, the way ahead is straight and clear with a discernible dead end, but many teachers will prefer the certainly it offers. They will be able to use the computer in the ways it has been used so far, and will be able to do more of the same. It is hoped that they will progressively reject or discard the tedious and educationally worthless activities together with their associated software, and will sharpen the focus of their work related to simulation and data handling. They will be able to make use of simple spreadsheets and develop the possibilities of electronic mail if they can prise a modem and communications software from the centralised resource pool. At a time of educational upheaval, where IT is but one facet of their work, and a facet which has been inexpertly and inadequately explained to them let alone resourced, the BBC route may be all teachers wish to cope with.

The alternative path seems to be a tortuous, uphill, climb, shrouded in uncertainty but with the promise of lush green pastures on the other side. There are many obstacles on the way, but there are equally many markers which augur well for the journey. What are these exciting uses of IT within the social subjects which would encourage us to strike out on this more difficult route?

Word processing is a prime area for exploitation. Teaching staff have a valuable tool which they can use for the preparation of their notes, handouts, and overhead transparencies. These can be modified or updated easily as required. Desktop publishing packages, which can be satisfactorily used only on the 16/32-bit microcomputers, will permit the production of these materials to the very highest quality, and this facility will be invaluable to teachers. Pupil use of word processing facilities is to be encouraged, but it is very hardware intensive and is a nonsense with only one machine in a classroom. The use of elementary packages such as 'Front Page Extra' for reporting on group investigations and for stimulating creative writing on a variety of contentious issues has proved to be extremely motivating for pupils, and has enhanced their learning considerably. It is particularly useful with less-able pupils, but is a slow process. The more sophisticated systems, with their user-friendly and more flexible software, which contain mouse-driven pull-down menus, will ease the demands made on the pupils by the package and should result in the production of more material of a higher quality in a shorter time. More-able pupils should be encouraged to use word processing for group reports and summaries, and there is tremendous scope for use within the investigative activities at Standard Grade, and for practical exercise and project work carried out by fifth-and sixth-year pupils.

IT has a massive contribution to make to the social subjects in the area of data handling. The increasing range of facilities for accessing and processing data make this the critical development area, and it is vital that sophisticated microcomputer hardware should be deployed to ensure that the potential is exploited carefully and effectively.

Earlier mention was made of the fact that, until recently, the spatial distribution of data was difficult to effect on microcomputers. The high definition of new computer screens and the development of various graphics and mapping packages (including 'Cricket Graph', 'Business Filevision' and 'Hypercard') have solved this problem. The greatly increased memory capacity of microcomputers and the use of hard disks permits the use of these complex packages and allows the fast processing of large amounts of data. Geographic information systems allow us to organise data into enormous datasets and display the information in a variety of differing map formats.

Many types of information can now be stored digitally and accessed by computer, analysed, and the results displayed in a range of formats. New technologies such as videodisc and compact disk offer storage of the most comprehensive data on a scale which many people are unable to believe. The 'Domesday' videodisc, containing a full coverage of Ordnance Survey maps at a number of levels and a comprehensive gazetteer, thousands of colour pictures and aerial views, a quarter of a million text pages, half an hour of video film illustrating significant events of the 1980s, surrogate walks, and thousands of datasets, including detailed coverage of 1981 census data, is the classic example of a quantum leap in information provision which has caught education flat-footed. For years, Geography and Modern Studies teachers bemoaned the lack of comprehensive datasets, the scarcity of map resources in the average school, and the costs associated with the provision of all sorts of photographic record. Suddenly they have it all encapsulated on two vitreous discs the size of two long playing records, and each item retrievable within seven seconds. Now transformed from beggar to millionaire in information terms, they are unable to grasp this resource and exploit it for curricular purposes. Teachers are placed in the position of a 'terracing know-all' who is suddenly put in a Scotland number nine strip and told to score the winner in the World Cup final! This is more technology, more sophistication, and makes more demands, both practical and imaginative, on the teachers. They need to be shown how to exploit such a powerful resource and must be given time to investigate its teaching and learning possibilities.

This dichotomy must be solved quickly because all the indications are that the social subjects is one of the most suitable areas for videodisc application. Many of the discs already on the market are social subjects-based: 'Domesday', 'Volcanoes', 'Ecodisc', 'The Arctic', 'The Countryside', 'Water', and 'Energy'. To ensure that these vast information stores, with their impressive photographic resource, are integrated into the curriculum activity of the social subjects requires a commitment of hardware to the departments and an in-service development to help teachers explore the resource and experiment with the necessary authoring software to create teaching exemplars and pupil tasks and investigations. The expense of advanced interactive videodisc equipment (normally about £3300), and the tendency to isolate it in a library or to send it like a museum piece round schools on a short-term basis, have so far constrained the educational use made of videodisc resources. Work at Moray House College and at the MESU has addressed the video disk and social subjects relationship and it is to be hoped that these developments will be supported and advanced.

Following hard on the heels of the videodisc and showing every sign of dominating the information storage sector is the compact disc (CD-ROM). This lower price technology (about £800 for a player) is capable of massive storage, particularly of print materials, and is a powerful resource for all social subjects teachers. The prospect of rich and varied, yet wholly comprehensive textual resources, complete diaries, newspapers, and shoals of correspondence, all instantly accessible through keyword searching and supported by a range of graphical and photographic materials is extremely attractive to teachers who, to date, have felt that true investigation has been constrained by the limitation on information imposed by the technology. In broader curricular terms, the day is not far away when the entire syllabus, together with all of the appropriate texts and worksheet materials, will be stored on one CD-ROM which could be copied and distributed to schools. This could be updated on an annual basis. Teachers could then access any curricular material they wished to use to support classroom work.

While such a scenario paints a picture of a self-contained technology resource, we must not forget the communications revolution, which offers the social subjects even more possibilities. On-line data sources such as Prestel and Campus 2000 (formerly TTNs) are used in schools, but to little effect. Again, this is partly due to the unwillingness of education to finance the costs of data access, and partly because the communication link and modem is located in computer departments or libraries. For Geography and Modern Studies work, the burgeoning resource of on-line data in the form of full text newspapers and magazines is an essential investigative component, and educators involved in the social subjects will have to argue for the inclusion of on-line data access facilities, together with necessary financing, within the social subjects departments.

The immediacy of data provision is also available through access to satellite. Weather information from Noah 9 and Meteosat is already being used in a small number of schools, and this information is communicated via Campus 2000 or stored on disk and posted to various interested educational establishments. Such a system appears to me to be perfectly adequate and very satisfactory, and I would not advocate the purchase of satellite equipment for every school. However, I would suggest that the enhanced graphic facilities of the more sophisticated hardware and its attendant software will make the processed data much more meaningful and consequently more valuable to education.

The communications facility which permits access to on-line data should not be thought of as simply providing one-way data flow. The interactive possibilities it offers are presently grossly under-utilised, although their educational value is well established. Communication using electronic mail between pupils who live in sharply contrasting environments, or who are engaged in the exploration of similar topics can only be beneficial. Within Geography and Modern Studies, postal communication between children in different countries was always possible but lacked immediacy. Microcomputers, through communication links, offer this immediacy, and recently Scottish pupils in an S1 class in a Dumbarton school were able to enhance their investigation of the 'empty lands' by communicating directly with the pupils of an Alaskan school. Other pupils in an Inverness primary school supplied information on Culloden to primary pupils in Stratford-upon-Avon in return for material on Shakespeare. There are few areas of the social subjects curriculum which would not benefit from such interaction, and while initiatives exist they need to be expanded; the recent SCET project linking Scottish and American schools is to be commended.

Thus, the comprehensive data which could transform social subjects teaching is accessible and the 16/32-bit route offers the facilities with which to effect the transformation. The stumbling blocks are access to equipment, provision of communications facilities, staff development time, ongoing finance, and the production of curriculum integration models which would ease teachers into utilising the resources in their teaching strategies. The push to investigation and process-based learning must be matched by the provision of appropriate IT resources.

Once accessed, the data can then be manipulated using the sophisticated software which has been best developed for 16/32-bit microcomputers. Spreadsheets, Prolog shells, and expert systems do exist for the 8-bit machines, but they are trivial and have been little used in the social subjects except within History, where Ennals, Briggs, Nicol, and Wild have created and trialled material in England. Spreadsheets hold great potential for geography; Prolog for History; and expert systems will be of particular relevance to Geography. The acquisition of sophisticated hardware in the social studies will allow the facilities of these software tools to be effectively deployed.

Simulations on the advanced 16/32-bit systems are much more powerful, allow the interaction of a greater number of variables, and can incorporate other media devices. There is a quantum leap possible in the educational potential of such software best exemplified by 'The Would-be Gentleman', which provides a fascinating study of a strata of French society at the time of Louis XIV, and 'Balance of Power', which explores aspects of global political interaction. The latter incorporates detailed graphics, complex and varied datasets, and is underpinned by a sophisticated model. However, it presents data and scenarios to users in a form which is easy to understand and allows them to explore and develop important concepts at their own pace.

The production of the 'Ecodisc' which simulates the management tasks of a nature reserve in Devon, has further developed the educational possibilities of simulations. The CD-ROM version, which offers even more sophisticated environmental modelling and visual materials, now offers the most sophisticated resource which can, paradoxically, be used with the widest range of abilities. The future for the production of such multi-media resources, directly applicable for use in the social subjects, is bright.

Thus, while we have so far failed to integrate IT effectively into the social subjects curriculum to any widespread degree, I would submit that there are several understandable reasons for this. In spite of the difficulties over the past decade, some progress, even though it has often been concerned with finding that the promises of the technology were false, has been made. My own preference would be for the immediate adoption of sophisticated hardware, appropriate software, peripheral equipment, and communications facilities for the social subjects department of every secondary school, accompanied by comprehensive in-service training to exemplify curriculum possibilities of, and integrative approaches to, the new IT resource. Teachers would have to be prepared to support this initiative by developing a resource base of curricular related materials which would effectively utilise this hardware and software input in their individual classrooms.

With such an input of equipment married to the educational expertise of the teaching force in the social subjects, a curriculum could be developed which would give pupils a set of IT experiences which would develop understanding, conceptual awareness, and specific skills. They would soon use IT so naturally that they would turn to it at many stages of their school career to assist in the explanation of problems and to test hypotheses, as well as using it as a labour-saving tool for reference information-gathering, or for the production of reports and for graphic communication. Additionally, of course, the social subjects and not Computing Studies should be where pupils investigate and discuss the implications for society of the applications of the technological revolution! In so doing, they would gain a heightened appreciation of the technology with which they are dealing, and would acquire sufficient computer literacy to render many current computing courses redundant.

With guidance, IT will greatly enhance learning and teaching in the social subjects. It will open doors to a range of strategies which will become even more valuable as the technology advances. The successful realisation of the potential which all aspects of IT afford education, in general, and the social subjects, in particular, requires a commitment from educational administrators or policy-shapers to the resourcing of technology in a different way and to a higher level than previously. They must adopt a policy of investing across the curriculum rather than investing in centralised resources. The technology resource is as vital to the education of the pupil in the social subjects classroom as it is to the pupil in the computing classroom. If this commitment is forthcoming and is matched by a professional commitment from teacher trainers, Advisers, and teachers to deploy these resources as effectively as possible, then the successful integration of IT into the learning and teaching associated with the social subjects is assured. Any deviation from such commitment will see us fail again, and the most important components of the educational process, the pupils, will be the losers.

10

THE INTRODUCTION OF INFORMATION TECHNOLOGY INTO SCIENCE AND TECHNOLOGY

BOB SPARKES

Information Technology (IT) includes computers, communications, electronics, and control. At school level, there has been a tendency to ignore all except the first of these, but this chapter adopts the wider meaning of the term. It is useful to consider electronics first, since it has the longer history and demonstrates so clearly the issues raised in this book.

ELETRONICS AND MICROELECTRONICS IN THE CURRICULM

Electronics itself is a century old and had its first real impact on everyday life decades ago through the provision of public broadcasting. Television in the 1940s enhanced its importance, but it was the invention of the transistor, and its subsequent development via microelectronics, that really established it. In 1977 the BBC Horizon programme *Now the Chips are Down* awakened many to the potential and the problems of the microelectronics revolution, and the implications for education were quickly recognised. The plans of the Labour government to bring microelectronics into the classroom were postponed when they lost the election in 1979, but by the following year, the plan had been revived by the new government. This resulted in Scotland, in the launch of the Scottish Microelectronics Development Programme (SMDP) and the similar Microelectronics in Education Programme (MEP) for the rest of the UK.

Unfortunately, from an educational point of view, the arguments advanced by the government for introducing electronics and microelectronics into the curriculum tended to be vocational, based upon the country's need for more electronics engineers and technicians. This, while perfectly true, has tended to obscure the other more fundamental arguments: one based on 'awareness'; and the other on 'personal development'. For the former, it is argued that electronics and microelectronics are an essential part of modern life, and that people should be aware of the basic principles on which they work and the economic and social consequences of using them. The MEP, particularly, made one of its main aims 'to prepare children for a life in a society in which devices and systems based on microelectronics are commonplace' (NEMEC 1988).

The persuasiveness of the second argument depends upon one's personal philosophy of education. Electronics, it is claimed, involves aspects of learning not reached by other parts of the curriculum. It is readily accessible by pupils of all ability levels and has an intrinsic capacity for motivating them – it appears to be the one technology that appeals as much to girls as to boys. It brings together a whole host of different abilities, only too often 'compartmentalised' by pupils – mathematics, science, design, problem-solving, and craft skills. Electronics integrates hand, eye, and brain in a way unmatched by any other subject.

These arguments were well known, even in the 1960s, and there were many teachers then who championed the cause of electronics in the curriculum. The most fertile soil was in England, where 'Project Technology' (a Schools Council project) encouraged technical teachers to include electronics in Craft, Design and Technology (CDT) as a better example of 'technology' than traditional technical subjects provided. By the mid 1970s, an A-Level in Electronic Systems had been established and an O-Level was in preparation; its place in the English curriculum seemed assured.

In Scotland, there was clearly confusion over what constituted 'microelectronics' – for most it meant no more than 'microcomputers'. In the rest of the UK, an Electronics and Control Technology (ECT) domain was established within the MEP specifically to look after this area. Within a short time, this domain received the larger share of the funding, and centres for research and development were set up to promote the teaching of microelectronics throughout England, Wales, and Northern Ireland. In contrast, electronics had not then taken root in Scotland, and those chosen to lead the SMDP had little sympathy with it, assuming their role to be the promotion of microcomputers only.

Having been closely connected with 'Project Technology' in the 1960s, I considered their emphasis to be misplaced. In a letter to the Scottish Education Department (SED) in 1982, I protested that the SMDP was not giving sufficient attention to electronics and microelectronics, instead their whole programme was being devoted to microcomputers in education. The SED replied that, as nobody shared my conviction, there was not much point in changing the remit of SMDP to include microelectronics, but that, if I were to submit a research plan, it would be considered. Accordingly, I made a request via the National Inter-College Committee for Educational Research for funding to develop general level short courses in electronics and microelectronics for fourteen to sixteen-year-olds. This was rejected by the committee, who claimed that not only was electronics too specialised for general education but that also working

parties had already been set up to develop such courses. Correspondence with the Scottish Curriculum Development Service (SCDS) and
the Consultative Committee on the Curriculum (CCC) did not reveal
what these working parties were actually doing or who was serving on
them.

Early in 1983, the ECT domain of the MEP held a big exhibition in
Birmingham, at which the minister announced that its funding would be
extended for a further two years. Around fifty projects were on display,
demonstrating the great strides being made. This exhibition attracted the
particular attention of the *Scotsman*, which, under the heading 'English
Lead in Electronics and Control Technology' commented:

> coordinated development north of the Border in the domain of
> electronics and control technology, (with the notable exception of an
> investigation by the Consultative Committee on the Curriculum
> into the possible uses of computer numerical control of machine
> tools in schools) appears to be notable by its absence.

Exactly whom the reporter contacted about her comments is unknown,
but she did obtain reassurance from someone, since the article ends:

> A considerable lead has apparently been built up in this domain of
> electronics and control technology south of the Border. We may
> confidently expect, however, that Scottish schools will also soon
> become involved to a much greater extent in this domain which is
> already beginning to affect our daily lives significantly. [The *Scots-*
> *man* 1983]

Some of us were not so confident, still wondering what she knew that
nobody else seemed to, but pressure was mounting from other places
too. For example, in May, Occasional Paper No. 7 was published, arguing that electronics should have more curricular status. In June, I was
asked to resubmit my research application and this time it was accepted,
but by February 1984, for some unspecified reason, this decision had
been reversed. In response, I emphasised the importance of the research, protesting that Scotland was falling behind in an important area
of curriculum development. In reply, the SED wrote:

> Your contention that no development project in the electronic field
> has been established in Scotland is not correct. As part of the
> implementation of the 14–16 programme a number of initiatives
> have been taken with regard to the development of suitable courses.

I challenged this assertion, requesting more details: the SED backed
down and apologised

> for the quite misleading impression given by the penultimate para-
> graph of . . .'s letter of 3 May that microelectronics projects had
> already been established. This stemmed from a misunderstanding
> here . . .

Throughout this whole SMDP period, the impression given by the SED
was that everything was under control and that criticism of what was

going on was unwelcome. However, it is quite clear that, up to 1984, nothing whatever had been done about electronics and microelectronics. Fortunately, the demands of the subject to be included in the curriculum could be ignored no longer, and plans for electronics short courses for the fourteen to sixteen programme were quickly brought forward. Two options in electronics for students of Higher Grade Physics were already under development, although these could affect only a small fraction of the age cohort and reinforced the view that Electronics was 'specialised'. More importantly, the '16–18 Action Plan' was producing a number of Electronics modules that could be offered to post-sixteen pupils (were these the origin of the SED's 'misunderstanding'?). There was, though, no co-ordination between these plans; they were allowed to develop in isolation from one another.

Early in 1984 the SMDP became part of the new national Microelectronics in Education Committee (MEC) and the issue of the place of microelectronics (as distinct from microcomputing) within it was once again raised. The Project Steering Committee of the Microelectronics, Computing in the Curriculum Project (MCC 1984) felt the need to express concern that 'the whole thrust of the new Committee appears to be towards 'computing' and that electronics (including microelectronics) may not be given the importance it deserves'. The MEC took little notice, although this mattered little, microelectronics continued to make progress without its aid. On 1 March 1984, the MCC project held a forum on 'Electronics in the School Curriculum', at which there was widespread support for courses in electronics. Their 'Final Report' in June 1984 gave particular attention to this conference, but displayed no sense of urgency – the main request being for more research and further working parties to be set up. St Andrew's College of Education ran a 'National Course on Electronics and Microelectronics' in July 1984, at which participants expressed shock at how far behind the rest of the UK Scotland had fallen. (Most of the principal speakers and all the major curriculum developments were from the MEP. There were no contributions from the SMDP at all!)

Since then, progress has been slow but steady. Standard Grade Technological Studies contains some measure of electronics and microcomputer control, and the Higher Grade course considerably more. More than one-quarter of Standard Grade Physics is electronics and twelve Scottish Examinations Board (SEB) short courses in Electronics have been developed for fourteen to sixteen-year-olds. The Technical and Vocational Educational Initiative (TVEI) is up and running in all regions, with electronics an important element in many of them. Unfortunately, the lack of co-ordination between these developments has resulted in considerable overlap and consequent friction between Physics, Technical, and Computing teachers. Those chosen to lead these developments had limited knowledge of the wider aspects of school technology, no involvement with the ECT domain of the MEP, and little experience beyond the narrow topics in which they were involved. Those with wider interests and greater expertise, who could have avoided overlap and conflict, paid the penalty for previous protests – they were not invited to contribute!

To demonstrate the errors that were made, one particular instance will suffice. The initial choice of equipment for the electronics modules in Standard Grade Technological Studies was the E & L kit. The majority of Physics teachers (and others subsequently developing the SEB short course modules) chose the Alpha kit. Although the two systems work in a similar way, they are incompatible with each other. But the E & L system is not compatible with other important electronic equipment either, particularly that of the Microtechnology Resources programme (which allows printed circuit boards to be more easily developed) and the 'Microelectronics for All' programme (developed for eleven to thir-teen-year-olds). The Alpha equipment is not only compatible with these but also has an extension range specifically for the new Standard Grade Physics course. Most importantly, the quantity and range of curriculum resource material to support Alpha is far greater than that to support E & L. The E & L kit is not even compatible with the equipment chosen for the rest of the Standard Grade Technological Studies course, nor will it suffice for any Higher Grade course. Yet, despite this evidence against it, the original decision is adhered to almost everywhere. It is a clear example of decisions being taken by people with insufficient knowledge themselves and who did not consult the acknowledged experts in the field.

This situation is mostly the result of the failure of the SMDP/MEC to take electronics and microelectronics seriously. Another effect has been that very few Scottish schoolchildren, by comparison with England, currently have much chance of studying these topics in school. How serious is this? From the point of view that electronics contributes to education dimensions not provided by other subjects, the outcome has resulted in an impoverished education for the pupils. From the view-point of the Scottish economy, the effects could be much more import-ant. The electronics industry is Scotland's largest employer, and there is evidence that its further expansion is inhibited by the lack of interest amongst school leavers in taking up careers in electronics. Good teach-ing of electronics at school might directly increase the number of such people (in the same way that inspired teaching of History and English produces large numbers of such students in Higher Education). If the Scottish electronics industry is affected adversely, schools will doubtless get the blame, yet Scotland's backwardness at teaching electronics in schools is not the fault of its teachers, it is because its educational leaders lacked vision and effectively put the brake on development throughout the early 1980s.

MICROCOMPUTERS IN SCIENCE AND TECHNOLOGY

From the very beginning, when microprocessor kits appeared in the mid-1970s, some Scottish teachers saw their possibilities and set about exploiting them. In 1979 the School Science Review carried an article on the possibilities for such equipment in the laboratory. In 1982 books on microcomputers in science teaching started to appear which described the main applications – calculations, simulations, modelling, graphical presentations, computer-assisted learning, and, above all, laboratory measurement and experimental control. Even the SMDP concerned itself with some of these applications and a large amount of their initial software was developed for the science area.

It is in the laboratory that a microcomputer really finds its place in science teaching. With an interface and appropriate sensors, the measurement of almost any physical quantity is possible, to an accuracy exceeding most existing school instruments and with the added facility for manipulating and displaying the data captured. Data logging over very short (less than 10 microseconds) or very long (several days) periods is quite feasible, and this allows for the investigation of phenomena hitherto unavailable to the science teacher. Even better, with suitable software, the microcomputer puts the pupil in charge of the experiment, with the ability to select the appropriate sensors and decide on the best ways of gathering the data and analysing it. Through a microcomputer, a pupil can also be provided with a very much bigger range of instruments than is normally available in a school laboratory, including such items as four-channel, storage oscilloscopes, microsecond timers, and accelerometers.

As early as April 1982, Dundee College of Education mounted a 'National Course on Microcomputers in Science', where workshops and demonstrations on most aspects of interfacing were shown. Several ideas were novel, such as the simulation interface of M. Ryan and J. Stewart which allowed simulations to be made more realistic by rotating knobs to produce a varying voltage rather than entering numbers at the keyboard. Home-made interfaces for the Apple II and PET microcomputers were on display. A. F. Pirie gave an impressive demonstration of the ZX81, which he later developed into a network system run from a ZX Spectrum microdrive. It cannot, therefore, be claimed that Scottish teachers lagged behind their English colleagues either in ideas or ability. Despite this early lead that some Scottish teachers had built up, however, the development of microcomputer interfacing and control in Scotland followed a similar route to that of microelectronics – outwith the concern of SMDP. Yet this was, above all, a time when clear advice was needed.

Some of the early equipment and software was too complicated. One of the first laboratory interfaces, from Unilab, had a large array of sockets which must have appeared daunting to the uninitiated. However, there were manuals which told the user exactly what to do and a few hours of hands-on experience under the guidance of an experienced tutor would have overcome most problems. Unfortunately, science teachers did not have the money to buy the computers or the interfaces; they did not have the time to study the manuals; and they were not given time off to attend in-service courses! In an attempt to get something going nationally, the Department of Trade and Industry (DTI) announced a scheme whereby schools could obtain an interface at half-price. However, they did not know the best sort of interface to use and the only equipment offered was the VELA, from Educational Electronics. Unfortunately, the VELA is not an interface at all, but a stand-alone device intended to *replace* the microcomputer! Since the point of using new technology in the laboratory is not just the collection of data from an experiment but also to manipulate and present that data graphically on the screen, this choice was a disaster. Its selection set back the use of proper laboratory interfaces by several years.

Recognising the problem, a large number of individual teachers went back to primitive microcomputer interfacing and developed their own easy-to-use software, requiring only simple home-made sensors plugged into the Analogue Port of the BBC microcomputer. Much material was published by the Association for Science Education (ASE) or, in some cases, by the teachers themselves, who set up their own companies to market their products. It was through efforts like these that Central Support Groups finally accepted the need to encourage the use of microcomputers in the new Standard Grade courses and commissioned people to collect and disseminate suitable software and support materials. This has given teachers and Advisers the lever they needed to persuade Regional Authorities to provide science rooms with computers and interfaces, and even, in a few cases, in-service training. Even so, the use of microcomputers in the science laboratory is still uncommon.

ROBOTICS AND CONTROL

Throughout the development of O-Grade Computing Studies, there was widespread antipathy towards any hardware orientation. In part, this was to avoid the narrowness of English syllabuses, which set great store by binary codes, digital logic, and computer architecture, but this attitude spilt over into computer control, too. Only with S-Grade was this area given recognition, but there was still anxiety about connecting control interfaces to a computer. An attempt was made to produce a 'Scottish' interface for the BBC microcomputer, but those chosen to lead this development had insufficient experience and work on it was halted fairly quickly. To plug the gap, the Central Support Group for Computing Studies looked south again, and recommended 'Trekker' (a product of TVEI enterprise in Clwyd). At the Higher Grade, Control Pathways has been chosen as the recommended equipment (yet another ECT development).

Technological Studies also contains a robotics section, but here a variety of systems and languages is being tried out – 'PROF' with the Unilab Fischertechnic interface, 'Control Logo' with the MFA interface, and 'Control-IT' with the Control-IT interface (all developments that took place in England). For Higher Grade Technology (and also Computing), the favoured system at present seems to be 'Three-Chip Plus', and here, at least, Scotland can claim to have had a hand in its development. In general, though, the story is the same as for electronics and interfacing: Scotland's educational leaders reacted too slowly and gave insufficient attention to the problem, resulting in almost complete dependence upon educational developments south of the border, just as the *Scotsman* had warned.

IN-SERVICE TRAINING IN IT

Alongside Scotland's failure to invest in research and curriculum development of IT (·as distinct from Computing Studies), a more serious barrier to greater penetration of IT into the science curriculum is the lack of trained teachers. This was obvious from the start, but the problem is still not being tackled. Throughout the 1980s, in-service training has been a haphazard affair, with individual lecturers in Colleges of Education offering the courses they considered to be necessary and teachers who showed an interest attending them. Payment for such courses was made indirectly by the SED, so they were provided 'free' to teachers. While this system was satisfactory for short up-dating courses within a teacher's own specialism, for example to cover new topics introduced into the O-Grade, it was totally inadequate for retraining in new subjects like Technological Studies – an entirely new field for most technical teachers (equivalent to requiring a teacher of French to begin teaching Russian!).

Yet, despite the obvious need for a national plan of in-service updating and retraining, only very recently has a structure (SCOSDE) been set up to deal with it. The Scottish Committee on Staff Development in Education establishes national priorities each year, and institutions are encouraged to develop courses to satisfy them. Where there is thought to be a need for longer programmes of study, such as in computing, technology, and electronics, then guidelines for nationally co-ordinated award-bearing courses are produced.

The delay in setting up this structure has had unfortunate consequences for new subjects, which have been slow to get started even after SEB 'Arrangements' documents have been published. Technological Studies has been particularly seriously affected. At the time of writing, January 1989, nearly five years after the decision to introduce the subject, no in-service training plan to prepare teachers for Technological Studies has been produced. (The SED withheld approval from the University of Stirling Diploma in Technological Education, because their own plans had not been developed!) As we have seen, SEB short course in electronics were contemplated in 1984, but plans to train teachers to teach them have still to be announced. As far as I am aware, there are no national plans at all to train science teachers in the area of microcomputer interfacing and measurement.

At the moment, in-service training, the choice of equipment, and the production of teaching resources are based upon ignorance of alternatives. It is quite common for a Regional Authority to ask an individual teacher who has obtained a particular system and learnt to use it to develop curriculum materials for the whole Region based upon that limited experience. (It would be interesting to count the number of teachers seconded to write curriculum materials for systems electronics and how many of these knew what the others were doing!) Once curriculum materials are ready, it is just a matter of giving schools the equipment and offering a few days of in-service training. The effect has been to turn teachers into automatic dispensers of a centrally controlled curriculum (a job which computers could readily take over!).

If the SCOSDE is properly funded and allowed to develop without interference, it could lead to more professional in-service training for all teachers, by which I mean giving them a deep knowledge, wide experience, and the ability to choose between alternatives. But, despite this promise of better things, if only SCOSDE approved courses receive funding in the future, then control of IT in the curriculum will pass totally into the hands of the administrators (and, as we have seen, their performance in this area so far is hardly inspiring).

FUTURE SHOCK

Has anyone learnt the lessons of past failures? The impact of IT on science and technological education has been minimal so far, but it is accelerating. The modern microcomputer can be turned into a complete science laboratory with access to any number of laboratory instruments, such as multi-channel storage oscilloscopes, voltmeters, pH probes and accelerometers – how will science teaching be affected? Powerful mathematical modelling tools are now available – will they render traditional mathematics unnecessary for future scientists and engineers? New teaching systems such as interactive video are already here, and intelligent authoring languages for CAL software, desktop publishing for pupil worksheets, presentation managers for lectures, and on-line databases of assessment tools are just around the corner. How will the classroom be affected? IT also has cross-curricular applications, with Computer-Aided Design (CAD) as likely to be found in Art and Home Economics as in Technical departments. Desktop publishing is just as useful in Business Studies as in English departments, and which department will deal with satellite communication systems – Geography, Technology, Science, or Computing? Is anyone investigating such issues, or will we, as in the past, wait until these innovations are already in the classroom before their educational implications are considered?

In future, it will be even more important to look ahead and prevent past mistakes from recurring. The amateurs have had their day, Scottish education now needs a 'think-tank' of people with an up-to-date knowledge of IT and microelectronic developments, and with the remit to make realistic suggestions about what to do next. There is evidence that the MEC is, at long last, beginning to assume this responsibility. A report 'Microelectronics in Schools: A Plan for Scotland' is now in preparation and this, if implemented, should radically affect the position of microelectronics and interfacing in our schools.

REFERENCES

MCC (Microelectronics, Computing and the Curriculum Project) 11984). *Newsletter*, February.
NEMEC (National Electronics Microtechnology Education Centre) *CHIP* (and any similar publication) Southampton (frontispiece).
Occasional Paper No. 7, May 1983, S.C.D.S., Dundee.
The *Scotsman* 17 May 1983, p. 14.

11

COMPUTERS IN THE CURRICULUM, THE PRIMARY EXPERIENCE: A VIEW FROM WEST LOTHIAN

IAN SINGER

ON THE WESTERN FRONT

This view of educational computing is necessarily based on my experiences in Lothian's Western Division primary schools. There seem to be such large differences between Regions and, indeed, Divisions that I cannot presume to speak for elsewhere. There are seventy-eight schools in the Division and, since 1984, they have received support from two specialists who visit about five schools at a time, one day per week, for an eight-week block. The specialist's duties involve distribution of software acquired on a regional basis, training, and general support. They work with all the teachers in the Division on an individual or very small group basis. They are also available, to a limited extent, for support outside normal visits if required. There is also a regional programme of in-service training run by primary school staff under the aegis of the Advisory Service. If the reader finds that the views expressed here seem optimistic compared with experiences in a different area, the level of support available in that area should be examined.

THE PRIMARY ETHOS

By and large, computing in primary schools is seen as being a part of the existing curriculum, although it will, by its presence, inevitably affect it. The computer is perceived as a tool to assist in learning and teaching rather than as an object for study in itself. By using the computer from the age of five (or earlier), it is anticipated that children will adopt positive and realistic attitudes towards its use in appropriate situations.

IN THE BEGINNING

In the beginning was the BBC Microcomputer – well, that is not quite true. In a number of Scottish schools the use of the micro was pioneered on Commodore PETS and Apple IIs (and I daresay others), but the real impact did not come about until the Department of Trade and Industry (DTI) scheme of 1982. The scheme met half the cost of a system (computer, monitor, and cassette recorder) to be selected from the three types offered – all of British manufacture. There was a limit of one system per school, no matter whether there were seven or 700 pupils. It was an offer which all but a few schools felt unable to refuse. It is worth noting that the money came from industrial rather than educational sources – an effort to boost British microcomputer firms and to improve the technological awareness of the nascent workforce. The question of vocational influences in education is addressed elsewhere in this volume and the same arguments may yet come to apply to primary schools.

Decisions regarding which system to use were made at a regional level with most opting for the BBC. Two regions chose Sinclair's Spectrum (mainly because of its lower cost and larger memory) with the RML machine failing to make any Scottish impact at that time. Whilst there were many battles between supporters of both camps, it is generally recognised that the work done on a computer is rather more important than its maker. That said, it turned out that the Spectrum was never to be as well supported in software and hardware terms as the BBC, which could make use of standard connectors and protocols.

SHINING BRIGHTLY?

So what did all these schools do with their shiny new computers? Well, first they had to work out how to put them together and run the software which came with them. All the systems were cassette-based, so the process was rather more traumatic than might be imagined by those used only to disk drives! If disk drives had been available from the start, many bad experiences could have been avoided at the paltry cost of a few months. Even six years on, there are teachers who were put off by their first encounters. Certainly, in my region at least, the transition from tape to disk was made fairly quickly and the problems eased. The software supplied with the systems came from the Microelectronics Education Programme (MEP), which was set up to support English and Welsh schools. This task was undertaken in Scotland by the SMDP – the Scottish Microelectronics Development Programme. The SMDP quite rapidly produced numerous programs, based on specifications from practising teachers, which schools could obtain, at no cost, from Regional Distribution Centres. A number of programs, notably from Anita Straker and the MEP, were licensed for their schools by the regions. Many schools bought some commercially produced software and rapidly realised that 'try before you buy' was no empty catch phrase! In fact, the quality of much of the early software nowadays makes it unacceptable, and much has since been rejected. To some extent, this could be seen as the fault of the teachers who wrote the specifications, but, given their inexperience with computers in education, it was perhaps unfair to expect too much. If less had been done, more slowly, perhaps there would have been fewer failures. However, it must be remembered that, at the time, schools were screaming for software. It is at least unfortunate that, just

when many lessons had been learnt, most of the specifying groups were disbanded as funding evaporated. The SMDP's simulation package, 'Apprentice', specified by one of its surviving groups, is an excellent example of what could have become the norm. Unfortunately, without more funds, it seems unlikely that the Scottish Council for Educational Technology (SCET, the now defunct SMDP's parent organisation) will be able to produce such software very often. The original idea was that an educational software industry would spring up from the ashes of the government-funded organisations but, as ever, no one worked out that schools are too poor to support much more than a cottage industry.

It is worthy of note that, from the very beginning, the computer was seen by the overwhelming majority as appropriate to the whole school rather than just the older pupils, although software for the younger children has not been as plentiful.

LICENSED TO COMPUTE?

Some mandatory training was included in the DTI package. This mainly covered setting up and running the machine, with some consideration of software evalution techniques. Quite often the trainers were not far ahead of their students, so perhaps more was not possible – if we had waited until everything was cut and dried, we would probably still be waiting! At the time, the changing of DATA statements in BASIC programs was seen as a 'good thing'. Fortunately, most teachers had the good sense to ignore all the mumbo-jumbo associated with editing data and waited until the same facilities were provided from within the program. Those who did not, either experienced a deep sense of failure or coped admirably. The 'trained teachers' were expected to pass on the modest knowledge they had acquired to their colleagues and, by and large, this happened. Unfortunately, these early training sessions were not extended and continued on a national basis, with the result that training has since varied wildly depending on Regions, Divisions, and proximity to Colleges of Education. Typically, in a Region, there has been a small budget available for the newly arrived and hungry infant that is educational computing. Most, if not all, Authorities have been unable to provide sufficient nurture in the form of training, software, and hardware in the correct balance to promote its growth. Since training is the most abstract element, it has tended to be the most neglected part of an already sparse diet.

Whilst I believe that training provision in Lothian's Western Division is much better than in many other areas, I still do not think that it is adequate. If educational computing is to succeed, primary school teachers will require constant support. A technology support teacher for every twenty schools does not seem to me to be unreasonable. The diverse and dynamic nature of teaching in primary schools places great pressures on teachers, and, if we wish to add more to their workload, we must give them support. The number of specialists should not be so great as to allow responsibility for 'doing technology' to be devolved solely into their hands, but it should be such that a partnership with schools and teachers is possible. The specialist would be responsible for facilitating the involvement of children in technology (not just information technology) by advising on and providing resources, and making sure that the teachers and children are able to use them effectively. There are similarities with modern ideas on the role of the learning support teacher. There is, however, no point in putting such ideas into operation if other components of the equation, such as software and hardware, are not to be maintained in equilibrium.

GREAT EXPECTATIONS

Inevitably, far too much was expected of the computer at the outset. Media presentation of the power of the computer meant that teachers throught of it as the universal panacea, whereas, in fact, they were not even sure of the problems that they wanted it to solve. I frequently hear the complaint that computers 'were just shoved into schools'. At the time, although general areas of use had been identified by the pioneers, no one was really sure which would prove successful; the fact that it all seemed rather vague has, I feel, turned out to be something of a blessing. Teachers experimented with many areas and from this has been distilled a pattern of usage. This is becoming an essential tool in delivering the curriculum, albeit in a limited way, given current resourcing levels. Nowadays, the microcomputer in the classroom is more likely to be seen as a tool for use by pupils and teachers: able to do some things very well and others equally badly. The majority of the teachers I meet are now much more in command. Many no longer feel the need to use a piece of software simply because it involves using the computer, especially when they can think of better ways of achieving the same end without it!

LINE UP FOR YOUR WEEKLY DOSE

Many teachers, when the micro first appeared in their classrooms, found themselves the victim of certain constraints. With the slow cassettes discouraging the loading of different programs for different ability levels, the software had to cater for a wide audience – programs with a choice of levels were particularly appreciated. The program had to be easy to use, and ideally lasted for about ten minutes because it was seen as important that everyone had a turn before the machine was wheeled off to do battle elsewhere. In order to achieve this, children typically used the machine in groups, so that they could all have their 'hands-on experience'. This 'group use' has turned out to be very successful in promoting discussion in many different types of program, from adventures to word processing. Given that there was an early recognition of the need for currricular integration, initially, drill and practice was very popular and there was a constant cry from teachers of 'Have you got anything to fit in with angles in R2D2 Maths?' or whatever. With disk drives, more systems, and more attractive alternatives thinking teachers have been able to restrict drill and practice to those in need of it, and to target it more closely to the needs of the individual.

THE GREAT ADVENTURE

It may seem absurd today, but the computer-to-pupil ratio was again a factor in the growth of the adventure-type program where there was obvious merit in children working together to solve problems. The ubiquitous 'Granny's Garden' by Mike Matson of 4Mation Software was not the first adventure to be used in an educational context, but it must certainly have been the most popular. All over the country, pupils from five to twelve were receiving assistance from the Blue Raven whilst their teachers began to see how the computer could be integrated into the existing curriculum in a more creative sense than drill and practice. Once children had used the program, they did work associated with it and teachers vied to see who could involve the most curricular areas.

Initially things got a bit out of hand, but, given the development of ideas about curricular balance being spread across longer periods, the adventure program has found a somewhat less frantic niche. Attempts to involve children in creating their own adventure scenarios have not been very successful – probably because the software used has been too complex to allow adequate return for the teachers' and pupils' efforts. It is probable that the use of more powerful systems, with better user interfaces and graphic facilities, will allow children opportunities to set and solve problems in a creative manner.

DON'T DO IT WHEN YOU CAN SIMULATE IT?

A very early simulation program allowed pupils to see how lock gates worked. Others allowed children to 'go deep-sea fishing' off Scotland's northern coasts, or to play the role of an eighteenth-century cattle drover. Such small-scale simulations tend to be used merely as an adjunct to a project, whereas more 'heavyweight' ones can be used as the basis for a cross-curricular study of a subject, such as exploration in the fifteenth century. The most successful simulations have been those which enable pupils to have experiences which are otherwise unavailable to them, or where the simulation has allowed them to understand, more fully, something they have experienced in reality. Where possible, there is no substitute for the real thing!

There are times when the distinction between simulation and adventure program can become blurred, especially since the cross-curricular manner in which they are usually employed is often similar. Efforts to make simulations fuller and more realistic will succeed when the computers used in schools allow better quality graphics and more options.

Simulations currently available to, for example, the oil extraction industry, demonstrate the power of interactive video to show detail and to react to the participant's decision.

WORD PROCESSING

As schools acquired more systems, and printers became more common, word processing became attractive. The view that children should produce several drafts of their work before a final copy and write in a more extended manner was a stimulus to the development of educational word processing. A number of word processing programs, originally intended for business use, were pressed into service, but their often obscure ways of achieving effects on screen and paper led to the design of simpler ones, targeted at the primary child. As an aside, it is interesting to note that at least one of these has been given so many enhancements that it is in danger of becoming more confusing to use than the originals! The underlying principles which allow children happily to refine and extend their work many times, whilst presenting it neatly, remain a powerful motivation in children's writing.

Group use of the word processor for co-operative writing on a 'public' screen, as opposed to the relative privacy of a sheet of paper, encourages positive attitudes towards discussion of work in progress. There are, nevertheless, many who proudly imagine that they are word processing with their children when all they are really doing is using the computer as an expensive typewriter in order to achieve neat presentation. The use of the Concept Keyboard (a programmable pressure sensitive pad) in conjunction with word processing allows even the youngest of children to 'write' by pressing words, phrases, and pictures with the results being printed out for them. With the introduction of more powerful equipment, there will be considerable opportunities for speech to be used with the younger child. For example, pointing to a word (or picture) might cause it to be spoken before the child selects it for inclusion in a story. The computer will be able to read the story back to the child for checking before printing it out. The computer is likely to reinforce trends towards the fusion of the reading and writing learning processes. It does, however, seem unlikely that the word processor will completely supplant the pencil!

PLUG ME IN, SCOTTIE!

Computer Aided Learning (CAL) is a term which I feel is seldom used precisely, but rather to encompass educational software that does not easily fit in anywhere else! It is, perhaps, here that the most was expected of the computer, and here that the least has been achieved. Myriad programs were produced by commercial, amateur, and government agencies to assist learning in, it seems, just about every area of the curriculum. As in drill and practice, the call from teachers was for a program to go with every subject they tackled. There are many good programs in this category (and many more indifferent ones), but, because of their variety, it is impossible to discuss them in general terms. It is this diversity which has been their greatest problem; even in one school, it is very difficult to be familiar with all the CAL programs available at one stage alone. If a teacher moves from one year group to another, as is nowadays considered desirable, there is a completely different set of programs to be considered. Small wonder then, that most teachers have stuck to a small number of good CAL packages – perhaps it will be a case of the survival of the fittest. There may well be some justification for the view that the best CAL software is the simulation in which the child learns by his or her experience. Perhaps the distinction between computer-aided *learning* and computer-aided *teaching* should be more clearly appreciated.

WE COULD STORE IT IN THE COMPUTER BUT . . .

From very early on there were databases available. Unfortunately, most had poor user-interfaces and required constant use of the manual – one thing teachers do not like doing is reading manuals! Entering enough data to be worthwhile often became such a hurdle that actually using it became of secondary importance. Most teachers, in the early days at least, found that even when the data had been entered, they were at a loss to know what to do with it! Some pre-prepared files are available for at least one of the databases, but its abysmal user-interface has largely precluded its use in primary schools. The use of a database with built-in graph-making facilities allows for easier interpretation of information collected.

The main problems now lie not so much in the software but in the formulation of the questions required to extract the answers, and in the time taken to enter the data. This might be alleviated by providing, either on a regional or a national basis, banks of information on diverse subjects, together with samples to show how they might be used. The SMDP did this quite successfully with a file containing information about cars. The children were then given scenarios which required them to solve certain crimes by searching the database. This needs to be done on a far larger scale, with real information relevant to environmental studies in primary schools.

'Hypercard', which runs on the Apple Macintosh (although its principles are being copied on other machines), allows a screen to have text, speech, and still or animated illustrations. It allows easy access to information in a way which is more akin to using a book than a database. This is not the place to describe 'Hypercard' but the concepts which it embodies are applicable to virtually any of the primary applications, not just databases. The prospect of replacing most of the existing software on the current low-power systems with just one program, albeit used in different ways, is enticing.

REMAINING INCOMMUNICADO?

Communication between schools and the accessing of information using computers connected to the telephone system is an area which has been held to offer much to the educational user. A few schools have participated in electronic newspapers and link-ups with other countries, and there is no doubt in my mind that computer communication is a very important aspect of IT. I am, however, not *yet* convinced that ways of using it widely and effectively within the curriculum have been demonstrated. There is an air of 'it exists therefore we should use it'. Where there is a genuine reason for using it, the story may be different. Such genuine reasons could include the availability of large quantities of information appropriate to the curriculum, or the alleviation of the remoteness of some schools. Whatever the reason, so long as there are telephone charges, care will have to be taken to show effectiveness in terms of cost and effort.

LOGO OR NO-GO?

It is unusual to find programming being carried out in primary schools. Most teachers do not consider themselves qualified to teach it, although many felt obliged, in the early days, to attempt it using BASIC! LOGO has remained largely the province of the enthusiast, and very few schools use it in any systematic way. Where it is used, turtlegraphics rather than list processing (or its other facets) is dominant. Indeed, for many, LOGO and turtlegraphics are, erroneously, regarded as synonymous. Among the reasons behind its low uptake is the fact that this is one area which does not relate directly to a traditional area of the curriculum, although the problem-solving aspects are obvious. The commitment required, in terms of time alone, for teachers to feel comfortable with LOGO has largely precluded its use, despite the recognition by many of its desirability.

The most likely area in which programming is likely to develop in primary schools is through control technology. Many schools are beginning to look at an early introduction to design and technology through construction kits, and it is a logical extension of this that the computer should be used to control the workings of models. Children can program various devices by using a simple set of commands, either from LOGO or a derivative. As with turtlegraphics, the results can be assessed and the program amended or extended as necessary in order to solve the problem in hand.

PUBLISH AND BE DAMNED?

There have been numerous attempts to allow children access to desktop publishing techniques. To date, most have failed because teachers, quite simply, have found them too difficult to use in the classroom. What on a powerful machine is easy becomes tedious and involved on the machines found in the majority of schools – especially when the package tries too hard to ape its betters. Most teachers, very sensibly in my opinion, have stuck to cut-and-paste techniques, using their favourite word processor and, possibly, a graphics program. A less ambitious package with a well-thought-out user interface may change this, but it is unlikely that desktop publishing will become important in primary schools until they are given more powerful computers with libraries of pictures. Ways of importing children's drawings or photographs will also be essential. It will also be necessary to improve the standard of printout. When this does happen, we can look forward to the presentation of children's project work in a style which could rival or surpass their text books! Or will this lead to a bland output lacking in individuality and creativity? As ever, a balance will have to be struck.

SWEET DREAMS?

The foregoing may have painted in the reader's mind an idyllic scene: a classroom in which children are working at many different tasks, individually and in groups. Some groups are using computers. There is a purposeful atmosphere in the room punctuated at times by the whine of a printer and the stirring notes of the 'Granny's Garden' theme tune. Pupils go to and from the computers as the need arises. Everything is running smoothly . . . but then you wake up and find that it is all a dream.

The wide-awake reality of primary educational computing is that the teacher has perhaps one micro two days a week (last year it was only one day!), and has up to thirty-three children. This week those in the Kangaroo Group are using it for word processing their history of Foster's Lager; the Wallabies are building a database of Australian creatures; and five of the other children are being squeezed in to do some work on bearings because that is what they are doing in R2D2 Maths. The Kangaroos are not able to get a printout today because it is Mr Hacker's day for the printer, and he always locks his door at lunchtime, so they cannot get a printout even then. The teacher is thinking about how much better use could be made of the computer if it could stay in the room all the time. Then it really would be worth making up those overlays for the Concept Keyboard to help the children with their vocabulary for the Australian project. No chance – the television finally gave out yesterday and there is that new reading scheme. And the R2D2 Maths workbooks cost a fortune and the head is always rabbitting on about how £14 a year per child has to cover everything from books to glue. Perhaps the school fund could stand it? No, most of that is earmarked to help with educational visits and books. The school down the road could afford it: they are always having coffee mornings and jumble sales.

Sadly, this scene is neither imaginary nor exaggerated. While databases, word processors, and all the rest *are* being used, few teachers are in a position to use all of them naturally, with all children, as and when required. It will be no surprise that this is due, mainly, to a lack of funds. To put a figure on the number of machines required for thirty children is difficult, but I could, *as things are at the moment*, easily make good use of half a dozen. They would not be fully employed every moment of every day, but equally there would be times when there would be queues to use them. Some day it will be regarded as unremarkable that every child has constant access to a computer in much the same way as a pencil today. It is only the time scale of this which can be questioned, the fact is inevitable.

MONEY MAKES THE DISK GO AROUND?

Teachers have demonstrated their willingness to be involved with the new technologies. What they require is adequate training and the equipment to use, as and when required. This will involve the spending of a very large amount of money. Most of the computer equipment in schools has, to date, been financed by parents through fund-raising events, and it seems inevitable that children in less well-off areas will be increasingly disadvantaged if this continues to be the main source of funds. If the parents of the children are not, in effect, to pay directly for their children's education, this leaves two possible agencies: local and national government. It is, unfortunately, all too convenient for them to blame each other for not supplying the cash, but they must recognise their joint responsibility without turning the issue into the usual political football. Unfortunately, much the same arguments can be applied to all areas of public funding and the competition is enormous!

If, indeed, we are at the beginning of a new technological age, it is necessary that *all* children grow up with the opportunity to use the tools of that age in a free and natural way. They must not be denied this because of a lack of the essential equipment. One day, and it cannot be so far off, the micro will be used as naturally as a pencil – and whoever heard of a hundred children sharing one pencil! Solutions may be difficult, but let no one in years to come blame primary teachers for what will inevitably be regarded as a form of illiteracy!

THE WAY AHEAD?

Unfortunately, computers are necessary in order to run software. The ideal computer is one which does everything you want it to, never breaks down, and costs as little as possible. The reality is that such machines, if they truly exist, cost several arms and legs! Whilst it is tempting to have a range of machines, each one targeted at a particular application, the disadvantages in terms of support (leaving aside teachers' sanity) are overwhelming. The range should, therefore, be kept as small as realistically possible.

The idea of what constitutes a computer system in the primary school is changing. Today it may be an 8-bit computer, a monitor, a dot-matrix printer, and a floppy disk drive with access to a Concept Keyboard. In the near future we will require, for many tasks, a more powerful computer with a high-quality printer and a scanner. Networking of computers will be necessary to keep down the amount spent on peripherals, and as interactive video becomes genuinely usable it will have to be added to the system.

The trend in primary computing is towards using fewer packages. It is unrealistic to expect teachers to be using more than, perhaps at most, a dozen different applications. Although the use of any piece of software has to be justified in educational terms rather than in terms of computer use, it must be recognised that there has been a considerable extension to the set of basic skills required by past generations.

All children should be able to use a suitable word processor from an early age. As graphics tools improve, they should be able to process appropriate illustrations, such as drawings, diagrams, graphs, and photographs. The presentation of this information should, at a later stage, be enhanced by using desktop publishing systems. Before leaving the primary school, children should have experienced controlling external devices from a program they have constructed. At least some of these devices should be of their own making. As early as possible, children should be introduced to the concept of accessing a computer to store information. Even more importantly, they should be able to extract information from the system. These applications reflect the way in which computers are used in society today, and the skills they encompass will shortly be considered essential.

It is to be expected that teachers should use the computer wherever possible to enrich and enhance the learning process. Simulations and adventure programs may be used to develop problem-solving skills as well as to provide a vehicle for cross-curricular work. Simulations should be used only where direct experience is not possible, or where the direct experience may be enhanced. If educational justification can be made, other programs can be used as appropriate.

WHO CARRIES THE CAN?

On a school level, the computer must be taken seriously rather than as an adjunct to the 'normal work'. Its use can, and should, be integrated into the many and various areas of the curriculum as appropriate, and the progression of skills carefully structured. The initial responsibility for ensuring that this happens lies with the headteacher. The school cannot be held responsible for raising funds to purchase equipment where adequate provision is not made in the capitation allowance. Staff are entitled to expect sufficient training and resourcing to enable them to make proper use of the computer. They are not entitled to opt out.

At a regional level, training and resources must be provided. The money required to enable primary schools to use computers effectively must be made available. If it cannot be found from regional funds, representations must be made to higher authorities. Regions should supply schools with a common set of software and ensure the competence of all staff in its use. Software and files appropriate to the Region should be constructed and made available to schools to enhance environmental studies programmes. Failing agreement at a national level, a Region must decide what hardware it will support.

At the national level, the emphasis should be on supplying software appropriate to the educational needs of children in Scottish schools. The SCET, with 'Apprentice', has demonstrated that it is now capable of coming up with the goods. In order to facilitate this, it is highly desirable that there should be some agreement on the range of hardware to be used in Scottish schools, althought, at the time of writing, this would seem to be a vain hope. The ultimate responsibility for ensuring that primary schools in the country are adequately resourced lies with the government, and it may well be argued that the vast amount of cash required to get things going properly can come only from a centrally funded programme.

12

WHY COMPUTING STUDIES?

MELODY MCKAY

INTRODUCTION

During the past decade we have seen the mushrooming of microcomputers in our schools. According to a 1987 HMI report, the majority of Scottish secondary schools now have at least fifteen machines, and for those involved in educational computing the microcomputer has become as commonplace a piece of equipment as the textbook. Yet, despite this influx of computing power, education in general has not adopted information technology (IT) to the same degree as most of the rest of society. Teachers still have to do many record-keeping tasks which would have been automated long ago in any other large organisation, and the average teacher is unlikely to make much use of IT in his or her everyday teaching.

The major use of computers in secondary schools today is for teaching the new subject Computing Studies. Controversial from its inception, Computing Studies has come under fire for its syllabus, its choice of programming language, and for problems to do with hardware, software, and teacher training. Those who must cope with these difficulties on a day-to-day basis are in a better position to comment upon them than I am. My purpose in this chapter is not to discuss the content or implementation of any one computing course, but to look critically at the rationale behind the introduction of computing as a certificate subject at all.

To most people, the computer is just a tool which is used to increase productivity by doing things more quickly or more efficiently. In some cases it may even do things which were not possible before, but it is still just a tool. We do not have Calculator Studies, or Typewriter Studies, or even Telecommunications Studies; so why Computing Studies?

There has been a great deal of propaganda to persuade us that computers in schools are a 'good thing', but little discussion of *why* schools need computers, what teaching or learning objectives they may help to fulfil, and what alternatives to computers exist. Computer technology is expensive and, with limited funding for education, it is imperative to ensure that IT is introduced in ways which are of the most educational benefit. In this chapter I want to highlight some of the issues concerned with Computing Studies, such as the concept of 'computer literacy', and to challenge the main assertions and assumptions made in order to justify its adoption as a school subject.

MODELS OF COMPUTER USE

One of the main features of the microcomputer is its versatility. Even within a single domain, such as education, it can be used in a multitude of ways. For the purpose of this discussion, I should like to distinguish two basic types of computer use in education: I shall refer to these as the 'computer literacy' model and the 'computers across the curriculum' model.

The 'computer literacy' model

I have used the term 'computer literacy' to describe the use of micros to learn *about* computers and computing. This model usually comprises special computing classes which may vary from a few hours of hands-on experience to full-blown certificate courses such as Standard and Higher Grade Computing Studies.

There are two aspects to this type of model. First, there is what might be more accurately described as 'computer awareness'. This term implies an awareness of what computers can do and of how IT affects both individuals and society in general. Secondly, there is the teaching of specific skills. These may range from using a keyboard and other in-put/output devices, through handling various pieces of software, to computer programming. Different courses which I would include under the general heading of 'computer literacy' may emphasise one or other of these aspects, or encompass both. What all such courses have in common is an emphasis upon the technology and its effects as the main object of study.

The 'computers across the curriculum' model

In contrast, the 'computers across the curriculum' model involves the introduction of computers and associated technology into existing school subjects in order to provide additional and/or better teaching aids for that subject. This approach is characterised by the fact that computers are introduced to fulfil a teaching *need*; it is what is *done* with the machine which is important and there is no interest in the hardware and software for its own sake.

This model can be subdivided into the use of the computer as *teacher*, and the computer as *tool*. Computer Assisted Learning (CAL) packages fall into the first of these categories. The full potential of CAL has still to be discovered and it is at the centre of current research into 'intelligent tutoring systems'.

A more proven approach is the use of appropriate computer packages as tools for learning in different subject areas. Some examples of this sort of computer application are:

creative work using word processors or desktop publishing systems in English

using LOGO to explore the world of Mathematics

controlling robots or using Computer Aided Design/Computer Aided Manufacture (CAD/CAM) in the technology lab

working with interactive video systems to help in learning foreign languages

using micros and synthesisers to create original music

electronic information processing in Business Studies

It is possible to find computers being used in ways which encompass both approaches and, in practice, the two models are not necessarily mutually exclusive. However, one can normally place a particular application under one heading or the other on the basis of the major learning objectives being pursued.

Although both approaches may exist within a school, 'computer literacy' in various forms is currently the dominant model. This can be seen when there is competition for limited resources. The Scottish Education Department (SED) report, *Learning and Teaching in Scottish Schools: The Use of Microcomputers* (1987), differentiates between 'the use of microcomputers in learning and teaching across the curriculum', 'computing courses leading to certification', and 'computer awareness courses'. The report notes that 'the main thrust of hardware provision is directed towards supporting computing courses; and:

> In several of the schools visited, the need to meet demands for access to facilities to support computing courses had led to limitations on the use of microcomputers more generally in learning and teaching. The increasing use of computer rooms for computing courses was progressively inhibiting access by larger groups from other departments. [SED 1987]

THE INTRODUCTION OF COMPUTERS INTO SCHOOLS

An examination of how computers were introduced into schools sheds light upon how this prominence of 'computer literacy' -type courses and their monopoly of computing resources came about.

The first report on computers in education, the 'Bellis Report' of 1969, recommended the use of computers across the curriculum rather than the introduction of certificated computing courses. However, the practical circumstances under which microcomputers were introduced into schools favoured the adoption of the 'Computer literacy' model over the 'Computers across the curriculum' model.

The UK pioneered the introduction of IT into education with its government initiatives of the early 1980s. The Department of Industry's (DOI) 'Micros in Schools' project offered reductions on selected hardware. Its stated aim was to ensure that every school had at least one microcomputer.

The Microelectronics in Education Programme (MEP) aimed 'to promote within the school curriculum, the study of microelectronics and its effect' (the 'computer literacy' model) and 'to encourage the use of technology as an aid to teaching and learning' (the 'computers across the curriculum' model). In Scotland, the Scottish Microlectronics Development Programme (SMDP) was established in 1980 to support and develop the use of micros in Scottish education.

The DOI initiative brought substantial benefits for the British computer manufacturers whose products were supported. The government also gained useful publicity. It could claim that the UK was the most advanced country in the world in terms of the percentage of schools possessing at least one computer.

The immediate benefits for schools were more arguable. The initiatives have been widely criticised for inadequate funding, especially for software development and training. The major weakness, however, was the lack of an integrated policy on IT in education, based upon agreed pedagogical objectives, and encompassing regular funding, software design, machine purchase and replacement, and teacher training.

To a computer professional, the fundamental mistake was to place computers in schools *before* identifying the purposes for which they would be used. The generally accepted sequence for introduction of IT into an organisation is:

(*i*) analysis of *needs*

(*ii*) specification of *software*

(*iii*) identification of *hardware*

The 'needs' of education are probably more varied and less easy to define than those of a commercial organisation. This makes it even more important to investigate thoroughly and analyse requirements before making decisions about equipment. However, in Scottish education (as in England and Wales): 'the early approach was to supply hardware to enthusiasts to stimulate the production of ideas for software' (SED 1987). This topsy-turvy policy, in which the choice of hardware came first, severely limited what could be done with the machines. It completely ignored the question of *why* computers were needed, and, hence, prevented the exploration of alternatives. This was of particular significance as the DOI-supported micros were incompatible with existing educational software, which was largely for American machines. Since the policy did not standardise on *one* machine or *one* operating system, it made it difficult for any widespread software support to become established.

THE EFFECTS UPON COMPUTER USE IN SCHOOLS

Many schools enthusiastically purchased computers under the DOI scheme and were then left puzzling over what to do with them. This dilemma was exacerbated by the shortage of teachers who felt competent to use a computer. Every school which acquired a micro under the government initiative supposedly had two teachers who had participated in 'a period of suitable in-service training in the use of microcomputers in education'. This vague definition was open to a liberal interpretation.

In industry, departments which acquire computing resources due to directives from outside rather than to satisfy their internal needs rarely use such systems effectively, especially if no suitable training is provided. The same axiom applied in education. In many schools the new machine was soon left unused in a corner or a cupboard. Elsewhere, the computer was placed in the hands of a member of staff with a personal interest in computing. The stereotype of this teacher – a male Maths teacher with a penchant for writing programs in BASIC – is familiar to most.

Thus, the first micros were machines searching for a purpose. They were used exclusively by computer 'enthusiasts', people who were fascinated by the machines themselves. In most schools no one else was interested in the strange new machine as they had no idea of what they could do with it! This context, plus the propaganda about 'computer literacy', set the scene for computers in schools to become objects of study in their own right rather than tools for all.

THE SCHOOL 'SUBJECT'

Another strong influence upon the development of computing courses was the structure of secondary school education. In this country knowledge is perceived as being divided into relatively tightly defined subject areas. We have separate departments for each subject, which are responsible for a particular part of the curriculum. Each subject has specialist staff, some of whom are in promoted posts. Attempts to introduce cross-curricular courses have met with little success.

An additional feature of these departments is that they form a 'hidden' but nevertheless strong hierarchy. The English and Maths departments are seen by many as being at the top of this hierarchy; technical and craft subjects fall at the opposite extreme. the 'ranking' of a subject depends upon its perceived academic merit. This may be judged by various criteria, but of particular significance is the number of pupils who take certificate courses, especially Highers, in the subject.

The early computer enthusiasts were mostly Maths or Physics teachers, both 'high status' subjects. They used micros within their own department and tended to concentrate upon calculation rather than data processing. In a worthy attempt to broaden the application of computers, many schools appointed specialist 'Computing' teachers. The only way to attract or keep suitable teachers, within the traditional system, was to establish Computing as a separate academic subject in its own right, with certificate courses at Standard and Higher Grade. Eventually promoted posts in Computing were created. Once this situation was established, there was a strong disincentive to promote a 'computers across the curriculum' approach in favour of certificate computing courses.

THE RISE OF COMPUTING STUDIES

The original recommendation for computers to be used across the curriculum was, thus, gradually engulfed by moves to introduce a range of courses in computing, such as 'computer awareness' courses, Standard and Higher Grade Computing Studies, and various scotvec (Scottish Vocational Education Council) computing modules.

The rationale for this complete swing away from a 'computers across the curriculum' model to a 'computer literacy' model has, to the best of my knowledge, never been widely debated. The 1987 HMI Report tells us that it took place 'in response to pressures within the system and developments elsewhere' (SED 1987), although these pressures and developments are not made explicit. And where is 'elsewhere'? I hesitate to think that the SED might be responding to initiatives south of the border!

I have indicated that the major pressures which existed were not pedagogic but social and economic. They included the interest and ambitions of the early enthusiasts in schools, the division of education into 'subjects', and the lack of adequate funding for software and training. More covert political motives may also be discerned.

I have already mentioned one important concept which fuelled the introduction of computing courses. Schools were encouraged to ensure that their pupils were 'computer literate'. It is curious that this term is applied only to computers. I have yet to hear concern being voiced over whether pupils were 'telephone literate', or 'calculator literate', or even 'electricity literate'. I believe that a closer examination of the concept of 'computer literacy' reveals that is it misleading; what such courses actually teach would be more accurately described as computer *acceptance*.

WHAT IS 'COMPUTER LITERACY'?

The term 'computer literacy' is intended to imply an analogy between the acquisition of computing skills and the more traditional skills of reading and writing. It is a powerful image, carrying with its antithesis the stigma of illiteracy.

However, whereas many people might agree upon what is meant by literacy, there is not the same consensus about what it means to be 'computer literate'. Does it imply merely basic keyboard skills? Does it require an understanding of the workings of a computer, or the ability to write computer programs? Or might it be experience with a number of packages? I shall not attempt a definition of the term, as I believe it to be a spurious concept based upon mistaken beliefs about the human–computer interface.

Nevertheless it is interesting to consider the analogy in the context of current debate on literacy in general. Many writers in the field now favour an 'ideological' model of literacy, believing that it encompasses a set of conceptualisations and beliefs about the world rather than simply a neutral technical skill. They see literacy as having a social context and talk in terms of 'literacies' rather than a single 'literacy'. With this interpretation, literacy programmes, such as are promoted in the Third World, can be seen as based upon 'culture transfer' rather than merely 'technology transfer'.

It is thought-provoking to relate this to computing. One of the main criticisms of computer literacy courses is that they often carry with them very definite, but often non-explicit, views about computers and the world, which influence their content.

A common example is the belief that IT is a 'neutral' technology, the developments of which are *technologically* determined rather than deriving from *socio-economic* considerations. This implies a lack of individual choice, and acceptance rather than control of change. I suspect that such an outlook may lie behind the statements:

> It is important . . . to understand and be able to adapt to continuing technological development. Equally it is essential to learn to cope with its effects on everyday life . . .

> Such a grounding is important . . . in helping the pupil to react positively to technological change [SEB 1987]

I am uneasy about any literacy which places such importance upon 'accepting' and 'coping' with development, and 'reacting positively' to technological change. This emphasis clearly favours the adoption of a passive attitude towards change, rather than fostering the critical analysis of *why* particular changes take place; *what* decisions are taken in implementing these changes; and *how* developments are selected and used to meet specific needs. If these aspects are ignored, IT courses become 'propaganda which parades as public enlightenment' (Noble 1984).

It is interesting to note what is *not* included in most computer literacy courses. Many purport to foster a general 'awareness' of IT, and they may look superficially at the effects of IT upon society. However, they usually ignore the economic and political influences which *shape* the technology. Pupils do not examine the role played by defence budgets in determining the direction of IT research, or consider the powerful influence of large financial organisations and multinational companies (who can act without recourse to national government) in determining how developments are implemented.

A major feature of the world today is the convergence of computer and telecommunications technologies, faciliating international data exchange. Yet IT courses often concentrate purely upon computers, ignoring the implications of more recent developments. Pupils will not hear much about how these can increase inequalities, both in our own society and between the Western world and underprivileged nations. They will learn little of the growth of credit information and customer profile agencies; of how police and government departments are adopting increasingly integrated systems which can exchange data rapidly within and across national boundaries. On most courses they will look almost exclusively at small packages running on microcomputers, even though the main impact of IT upon society is through large networked systems which may be inaccessible to public scrutiny.

I leave it to the reader to decide to what extent the following comment on literacy programmes in developing countries might also apply to *computer literacy* courses:

> Through their literacy programmes governments can give an appearance of appropriate action and good intention that would be difficult to challenge, while at the same time maintaining and disguising the real power relations and forms of exploitation that create the problems they claim literacy can solve. [Street 1987]

THE RATIONALE AND AIMS OF COMPUTING STUDIES

Let us now turn from the hazy notion of computer literacy to the explicit claims made to justify the introduction of Computing Studies as an examinable subject. An examination of the rationales for Standard and Higher Grade Computing Studies reveals that they contain three main assertions about pupils' needs and the extent to which these can be met by Computing Studies.

First, we find the suggestion that an understanding of computers is necessary for *everyday life*. The second claim is that Computing Studies can provide pupils with qualifications and skills which are relevant to their *future employment*. Finally, it is implied that Computing Studies is a valuable prerequisite for *Higher Education* in IT. I challenge all three of these contentions.

Understanding computers for everyday life

Many people were afraid and worried about computers when they first became widespread. It was felt that only the provision of courses about computers, which would lead to an understanding of how they worked, would dispel this fear. I believe that these ideas stem from misconceptions about the nature both of computers and humans such as:

– there is something intrinsically frightening about computers
– there is something inherently difficult about using a computer
– the only way to overcome fear of computers is by understanding how they work.

Fear of new technology has always been with us. It is not so long ago that people were afraid of getting radiation sickness from the new-fangled television sets. Adults to whom computing technology is new may retain their fear for some time, but children who have grown up with computers find them no more frightening than telephones, televisions, videos, or any other piece of household technology.

Many adults also find computers difficult to operate. Again, this has often been the case with new technology, but, once the technology proves its worth, public demand leads to it being made simpler to use. The proponents of many computing courses seem to think that humans will have to learn to adapt to the machine. I believe the reverse to be true: the machines will be adapted for easier human use. We have already witnessed this type of development. Software is now designed to be 'user friendly', carefully guiding and prompting the user through each step of the program, and dealing effectively with mistakes. Operating systems with WIMP (Window Icon Menu Pointer) interfaces allow the user to carry out commands simply by pointing at icons. Eventually, it is possible that computer–human interchange will be largely through speech. Without doubt, tomorrow's software will become, to borrow a phrase from a current television advertisement 'so simple that even grown-ups can use it'.

The delusion that humans need to understand how computers work in order to use them also has historic parallels. The first automobiles, for example, were driven by chauffeurs who were familiar with the internal combustion engine. Driving was considered difficult and dangerous, and knowledge of how the engine worked was thought to be essential. Yet today millions of people drive cars without the slightest understanding of what goes on under the bonnet. Automatic starting, power-assisted steering, automatic gear-changing, and countless other innovations have made driving possible for even a novice. *Design improvements*, coupled with *familiarity*, rather than *understanding*, seem to have been the key factors in the change of attitude. I believe the same will happen (indeed is happening) with computers.

The increased mobility brought about by car ownership has led to fundamental changes in society, and driving a car is an important accomplishment for modern life. It is potentially more dangerous and certainly requires far more skill than using modern software. And yet I know of no great movement to introduce Driving Studies into the curriculum.

I have often witnessed pre-school-age children using computer technology with a grace and ease which would be the envy of most adults.

These children have no fears and difficulties. Neither do they have the slightest understanding of how the equipment worked! I wonder if the demand for computer literacy courses is not merely a hysterical reaction of the middle-aged?

Knowledge and skills for future work

If Computing Studies is not needed to prepare pupils for everyday life, can it be argued that it is essential for imparting specific knowledge and skills needed for future employment? The *Arrangements in Computing Studies at Higher Grade* cites figures from the European Commission which indicate that 60 per cent of all jobs in Europe are significantly affected by IT. They argue that 'education systems must produce young people who enter the labour market with qualifications and skills relevant to their employment' (SEB 1988).

British education has often been criticised for emphasising academic subjects over practical and vocational subjects. Whilst I do not want to enter into this debate here, I have some sympathy with the view that secondary schools should provide *both* a *general* education *and* some vocational courses for older pupils. However, I see no evidence that Computing Studies is the best way to provide pupils with vocational skills and knowledge.

For example, the majority of jobs will require the use of some form of keyboard, since most data will continue to be entered in this way for many years to come. Surely in the 1990s we could expect *all* school-leavers to have basic keyboard skills? However, Computing Studies is not taken by all pupils, and does not focus to any large extent upon the acquisition of keyboard skills. I would argue that a short compulsory typing course would be a better way of meeting this objective than an optional two-year computing course. Perhaps some of the S1/S2 'computer awareness' courses might be profitably replaced by such courses?:

Apart from being able to use a keyboard, the specific IT skills required in most work situations normally fall into a narrow spectrum and will almost certainly be taught on the job.

If it is considered desirable for schools to teach more general IT skills for work, then research should be carried out to ascertain from employers exactly what should be taught. Only then will it be possible to determine whether Computing Studies is the most effective way to meet this need. It may be that short training courses in specific systems would be more appropriate. In order that the skills taught are not obsolete before the pupils enter the job market, the courses should be as up to date as possible, using the sort of systems to be found in business and industry.

I doubt whether schools themselves will have the resources required to provide such courses. Other alternatives may need to be explored, such as regional training centres run by Education Authorities *in conjunction with* business and industry.

We currently have both high unemployment and 'skills shortages' in certain areas, including computing. Slogans such as IBM's 'training the workers without jobs for the jobs without workers' intimate that IT training can cut down unemployment. Claims such as these should be seen in perspective. It is estimated that by 1990 there will be a shortage of approximately 10 000 IT professionals. Comparing this against current unemployment statistics of over 2 million, it is easy to see that IT training alone cannot reduce the jobless total to any significant extent.

I contend that the assertion that Computing Studies can provide pupils with skills needed for their future employment is similarly exaggerated, and is unsupported by any real evidence.

Higher education

Much of the school curriculum is geared towards entrance to tertiary education. Whilst it is quite valid to question to what extent this should be the case, my concern here is not with that issue. I wish to deal merely with the questions of whether there is a demand from institutes of Higher Education for potential students in IT to have computing qualifications, and whether Computing Studies is a good prerequisite for pupils who wish to pursue careers in Computing Science.

What sort of qualifications do universities and Colleges of Further Education look for in their computing students? I found universal agreement amongst colleagues to whom I posed this question. They want school-leavers who have the ability to *think logically* and to *communicate clearly*; in other words those skills which have always been seen as important in Scottish education.

The preferred qualifications for entry to computing and related studies were Highers in Mathematics (which gives pupils experience in manipulating symbols and in the abstract representation of problems) and English (good communication skills are essential for understanding and interpreting user requirements, and for designing and documenting systems). Attitudes towards Computing Studies ranged from indifference to antipathy. Computing lecturers generally did not see any advantage in schools teaching pupils about computers and computing. Some even expressed concern that problems might arise if pupils were taught by teachers who were inadequately qualified or who had an insubstantial background in computing. I cannot claim to have carried out any formal research on this point, but, during numerous discussions with lecturers in several colleges and universities, I have found no evidence of any real demand from the tertiary sector for Computing Studies to be taught in schools.

None the less, schools may wish to help pupils who are considering a career in IT. I welcome the current trend towards short courses for sixteen-plus pupils. These modules could be used as 'taster' courses by those seeking entrance to Higher Education. In addition to conventional programming modules, introductory units in logic and linguistics, if available, could benefit future programmers. A major disadvantage faced by most students who come into computing straight from school is a total lack of knowledge about, or experience of, how the commercial world functions. Rather than introducing a new school subject, potential systems analysts and programmers might be encouraged to take modules in Business Studies or Modern Studies.

The increasing emphasis upon the human–computer interface will require students to have a mature appreciation of user requirements. Throughout their school career, it would be beneficial for computing students to have had a broad experience of using various programs as 'consumers'. As far as possible these should be used to carry out *real* tasks, rather than simply being looked at in a superficial way. It is only by using a piece of software for the purpose for which it was intended that its merits and weaknesses can be identified. For example, in writing this chapter I have discovered a lack of certain features of my word processing program that I would not have noticed in a general evaluation. I would, therefore, argue that 'computers across the curriculum' can provide as good a background for potential Computing Scientists as Computing Studies.

THE WAY AHEAD

One disadvantage the UK had, as a pioneer of computers in schools, was that we were not able to learn from the experiences and mistakes of other countries in implementing an IT policy in education. This was compounded by a failure to learn from the experience of other sectors of society.

In order to identify aims and objectives for the future, it is crucial to begin with a thorough analysis of the needs both of teachers and pupils which might be met by IT. The teachers' needs might include access to ideas, teaching resources, and materials, help with assessment and recording, and in-service training. Pupils' needs might include individual attention, extra help with particular problems, access to resources, and information relating to their studies and future careers. The genuine needs of pupils for future work and/or study should also be ascertained in consultation with employers and Further Education.

Only after this analysis has been done can the potential of different approaches be evaluated. The relative merits of computing courses as opposed to using 'computers across the curriculum' can be considered, bearing in mind the resource implications of each, and total IT budget restrictions. This approach should lead to a proper IT policy, based upon sound pedagogic principles.

I welcome the advice that Education Authorities should issue a written policy statement to all schools:

> The statement should provide guidance on matters such as the expected nature and extent of pupils' experience of microcomputers, in particular the balance to be achieved between the subject of computing studies and the learning and teaching applications of microcomputers across the curriculum, coherence and progression in that experience from primary through secondary school, management and communication, funding, staffing, staff development, accommodation, provision of hardware and software, support services, links with national agencies, monitoring and evaluation. [SED 1987]

In order to avoid the mistakes of the past, this policy should be drawn up only after a thorough analysis of the needs of teachers and pupils.

Most businesses now recognise the importance of IT, and this has resulted in a change of attitude towards the management of data processing. Rather than being seen as a subsidiary of some other department (e.g. finance) it is increasingly being recognised as a service function to every part of the organisation. This change is reflected in current debate as to whether the data processing manager should have a place on the Board.

An important parallel step in education would be the recognition of the importance of IT throughout the school by the appointment of a specialist senior manager. This person would be responsible for encouraging and training teachers to use existing equipment, for evaluating innovations, supervising implementation, and acting as a consultant to the staff. He/she would require an understanding of technological, pedagogical, and managerial issues.

The 'HMI Report' recommends that each school should have a written policy statement on the use of microcomputers. I concur with this, but would add that IT should be seen as part of a *total* system, which includes teachers and pupils.

In conclusion, I would urge that, within this system, the introduction of IT should be purely 'needs-driven'. Computers should not be put into schools to help industry, to promote competitiveness with other nations, to encourage the unquestioning acceptance of new technology, or even to placate parents who feel that their children might be disadvantaged. If computers are introduced for any reason other than to solve a particular problem, they are there not as pedagogical tools but as political ones.

REFERENCES

House of Lords Select Committee on Science and Technology (1985). *Education and Training for New Technologies*, London: HMSO.
Noble, D. (1984). 'The underside of computer literacy', *Raritan Review*, 3, Spring.

Robins, K. and Webster, F. (1987). 'Dangers of Information Technology and Responsibilities of Education', in *Information Technology: Social Issues*, Sevenoaks: Hodder and Stoughton Educational.

Scottish Education Department, SED (1987). *Learning and Teaching in Scottish Secondary Schools: The Use of Microcomputers*, a report by HM Inspectors of Schools, Edinburgh: HMSO.

Scottish Examination Board, SEB (1987). *Revised Arrangements in Computing Studies at Foundation, General and Credit Levels.*

——(1988). *Arrangements in Computing Studies at Higher Grade.*

Street, B. V. (1987). 'Models of "Computer Literacy"', in *Information Technology: Social Issues*, Sevenoaks: Hodder and Stoughton Educational.

13
COMPUTING STUDIES HAS A FUTURE

PETER COPE

The title of this chapter reflects a belief in the potential of courses which are made possible by computers; courses which do not have a place elsewhere in the curriculum and which have worthwhile educational goals. We do not have such courses at present. In fact, Scotland's implementation of the subject of Computing Studies illustrates perfectly how the education system often seems doomed to administer the kiss of death to anything new and exciting. Scrutiny of our Computing Studies courses as they now stand reveals products which exemplify the immaturity and inflexibility of educational computing Scotland.

With a little imagination and the removal of the constraining effects of SEB[1] syllabuses, there is room for a variety of new courses based on the availability of powerful microcomputers. It would be strange indeed if no such new areas did, in fact, exist, and it would be negligent of those charged with curriculum design if they were not exploited. But such exploitation depends on a new approach to the development of computing courses, an approach which depends on a willingness to experiment and to discard efforts which fail.

CURRENT COMPUTING STUDIES COURSES

It is unfortunate that there are no published articles which describe and defend existing SEB Computing Studies courses. Interested readers are referred to the appropriate course descriptions of S-Grade and H-Grade Computing Studies (SEB 1987, 1988). Briefly, both courses are based on an 'applications' approach to the subject, where a large part of the course consists of case studies of particular uses of computers. The flavour of the courses can be obtained by looking at the compulsory S-grade case-study topics. These are word processing, databases, robotics, and mail-order processing. Optional topics include stock control, aeroplane seat-booking, and banking. S-Grade Computing Studies has been a major focus of Scottish educational computing in the decade between 1980 and 1990, but a close examination of the course reveals some lamentable deficiencies.

S-GRADE COMPUTING STUDIES

The rationale

One might reasonably look in the SEB publications mentioned above for justification of the dreary content of the Computing Studies curriculum. It is a disturbing feature of such documents that the rationale and aims sections are bland, uninformative, and provide little in the way of analytical argument. In keeping with the poor quality of educational analysis, there is no reference made to any other educational literature. If there is any coherence to be found in the rationale, it seems to be based on an appeal to naive vocationalism. The opening sentence refers, albeit somewhat vaguely, to Circular 1093, which echoes current government ideology concerning the importance of technical and vocational education.

The aims and objectives

There is an alarming mismatch between the course structure of S-Grade Computing Studies and its aims and objectives. In the latter, we find that pupils are required to develop both knowledge and problem-solving skills. Lip-service is paid to the problem-solving component by making this one of the assessable elements. But the course content is totally inappropriate for the pursuit of this aim. In fact, the content of the course is so incompatible with its aims and objectives that one cannot but suspect that the latter were tacked on as an afterthought. Certainly, no attempt has been made to select the content from those areas of computing which might provide rich sources of suitable problems. It is far from clear how forcing pupils to study mail-order or word processing will foster the development of problem-solving skills. Yet computing is not short of challenging areas to study, and it is incomprehensible that anyone with a real concern for problem-solving interpretations of the subject could have created such a syllabus.

The approach

The 'applications approach' is the linchpin of the S-Grade syllabus, and yet there is no attempt to justify its selection or to discuss alternatives. Instead, the approach upon which the whole syllabus is based is dealt with in one sentence contained in the course rationale:

> It is considered important that the theoretical aspects of the subject should be approached through experience of a variety of applications and case studies in industry, commerce and education. [SEB 1987 p. 4]

This sentence leaves a number of crucial questions unanswered. Why, and by whom, is it 'considered important'? How does this terse statement lead to the prescription of particular case studies? If, for example, the case studies are to be used to illustrate theoretical aspects, why must the case-study topics rather than the theory be prescribed? Examination of the syllabus shows that the theoretical areas are, in fact, grouped around the case-study topics. Thus, although it is implied that theoretical considerations determine the course structure, with applications being used to illustrate them, in reality, the opposite is the case. It is difficult to avoid the conclusion that the content was chosen first and the theory was tacked on afterwards.

The obsolescence

There seems to be little doubt that SEB Computing Studies courses are in trouble. Readers are invited to compare Ian Singer's description of computing in the primary school (elsewhere in this volume) with the S-Grade syllabus. Primary school children use databases and word processors, and are beginning to use a variety of buggies and robots. Although there have been problems of resourcing and training, the lack (hitherto) of centralised control of the primary curriculum has meant that primary computing has developed in a far more natural way. Primary teachers have been able to experiment and discard software which does not seem useful. What are children who have benefited from such classroom experiences likely to make of courses which appear to cobble together a subject from applications they have been using in more appropriate contexts since they were six or seven years old? Is the study of stock control and the computerised booking of aeroplane seats going to be enough to convince them that computers have something else of significance to offer them in the secondary school?

Conscious of the irrelevance of the S-Grade course, some members of the Computing Studies Examinations Panel are now pressing for a review of the syllabus. But the last revision of S-Grade Computing Studies was completed only in 1987. The revision was made necessary by the unrealistic assessment arrangements of the first syllabus, and did nothing to update the content in any way. Nevertheless, the SEB is unlikely to welcome the idea of changing the course again so soon. Should the pressure prove sufficient to impress the SEB, a new Working Party would be necessary to carry out the review. Schools would then require two years' notice before the revisions could be brought into operation. By that time another review will be long overdue.

H-GRADE COMPUTING STUDIES

Many of the criticisms made above of S-Grade Computing Studies also apply to the Higher Grade course. The H-Grade rationale is based on vocationalism, and the course maintains an 'applications approach' to the subject. Much of its content is prescriptive, and no mechanism is provided to permit the constant updating which will be required if it is not to become out of date. There is little opportunity for any innovative computing, and this weakness will be exacerbated by the exam-driven two-term rush which is so characteristic of H-Grade in other subjects.

In addition, the course content is regarded by some as so challenging that, although INSET[2] is normally provided by Colleges of Education, the SED[3] has attempted to enrol university Computing Science departments to provide training for the Higher Grade. This probably reflects on the poor standards of teacher education and training in computing rather than on the course itself. The specimen question paper circulated with the H-Grade syllabus is trivial. For example, the question on knowledge-based programming could be answered by any intelligent lay person, irrespective of any prior knowledge of the subject. Nor is the H-Grade course considered to be difficult by the SUCE[4], whose judgement was that the course is too broad and too shallow.

The declining fortunes of computing courses

The implementation of the S-Grade Computing Studies course, with all its specific limitations and drawbacks, has occured at a time when other countries are re-examining the role of computing courses generally. In England, there has been a decline in uptake in sixteen-plus Computer Studies exam entries since 1985. The decrease between 1985 and 1988 was around 31 per cent. Until that time, the uptake had been growing at a rate of around 25 per cent each year (Leaton 1989). The reasons appear to be associated with the decision to transfer support from the subject to a more general usage of IT[5] across the curriculum.

There are clearly doubts in England about the appropriateness of studying computers rather than using them in context. These are articulated, for example, by Cotterell, Ennals and Briggs (1988), who see studies of the computer itself as becoming increasingly irrelevant as computers become integrated as part of normal teaching and learning. Evans (1989) charts the attempt to keep Computing Studies courses educationally relevant by moving towards an 'applications-based' curriculum. But he points out that one of the weaknesses of this approach is that studying applications out of context makes little sense:

> a computer studies class is not necessarily the right forum for development of skills in computer applications when it is in fact devoid of any context for the use of those applications.

Thus, while a database management package is of great potential in History or Geography, there is no merit in studying it for its own sake. Word processing could be of enormous benefit in the teaching of creative writing, for example, but to study the process itself seems perverse. The absurd nature of this approach is more evident when it is taken to extremes. In Higher Grade Computing Studies, which tries to make a theme of 'objects' and 'operations', pupils are to learn that the 'objects' of word processors are letters, words, and paragraphs and that the 'operations' which can be performed are creating, inserting, deleting, etc. How committing such knowledge to memory will benefit the unfortunate pupil is not obvious.

The temptation to drop Computing Studies altogether will be a strong one. But it would surely be unreasonable to do so simply because the current architects of the subject have failed. In another chapter of this book, Bob Munro suggests that the past failures of the use of IT in the social subjects should be looked upon as a necessary period of experimentation which may now lead to a more realistic phase of development. Such an eminently sensible approach should be extended to Computing Studies courses. What prevents us from doing so is the interpretation of the subject through SEB courses which are not amenable to even minor adjustment without enormous bureaucratic obstacles. Yet the notion that the S-Grade computing course designed in 1983–4 will serve us into the 1990s is absurd.

DESIGNING FUTURE COURSES

One lesson to be learnt from the experiences of the 1980s is that prescriptive courses are not the best way to make progress in the educational computing area. First, we simply do not know enough about the potential of computing in schools to prescribe course content on any rational, principled basis. Secondly, prescriptive courses largely prevent teachers and learners from trying anything new, and experimentation is crucial to the successful exploitation of computing in schools. Computing is a dynamic area, and attempting to confine it within limits can only mean that we lose out on any new areas which may seem potentially worthwhile. Thirdly, SEB courses are too long. It is debatable whether we are in a position to put together quality computing courses of 120 or 160 hours' duration as the H-Grade and S-Grade demand. A more reasonable type of course structure could be arranged around shorter modules which would provide the basis for the flexibility and experimentation necessary for the healthy development of computing.

We should learn also from the attempts to base school computing courses on a vocational rationale. Computers are, without doubt, of great importance in the 'world of work', a world which has now become the focus of much educational discussion. But the view that school Computing Studies can enhance the employment prospects of pupils is unsupported by any evidence. Unfortunately, such a view is implicit in much of the discussion about the role of Computing Studies courses. For example, in a recent book about computing in schools jointly authored by the Chairman of the S-Grade JWP[6] for Computing Studies and an HMI in Computing, an instance is given of a school where it is claimed that the provision of word processing courses subsequently helped pupils to get jobs (Williams and McLean 1985, p. 117). There was no evidence offered to support this claim.

Of course, there has never been any evidence to suggest that learning to word process on a BBC microcomputer is likely to impress prospective employers. Industry and commerce are not short of skills at this level, because such skills can be attained during a short period of on-the-job training. After all, word processing occupies seven hours of the S-Grade course at the most, and this level of training is hardly significant. There is a profusion of literature which clearly demonstrates that the serious projected skills shortages are at graduate level (see Wellington 1988 for a bibliography). The way to tackle such shortages is to make school computing interesting enough to attract pupils to further study. Basing the course on cut-down versions of commercial software is hardly likely to achieve such an aim.

The inappropriate nature of the vocational rationale is compounded by our ignorance of the types of skills which will be required of the workforce in the future. The sort of primitive applications so central to S-Grade Computing Studies will have evolved into forms which will be unrecognisable to our current pupils by the time they start work. Careful consideration of exactly what will be required of the workforce in the future of rapidly changing technology seems to have got lost in the rhetoric of the vocationalists. Almost certainly we will need flexible and creative individuals who are able to apply skills of general problem-solving and scientific investigation to a variety of areas as they move through their working lives. It is somewhat ironic that such goals would, perhaps, be more compatible with the traditions of a liberal education than with the vocationalism of current courses.

Further lessons may be drawn by considering the hidden curriculum encompassed by current computing courses. In many of the applications, pupils play the roles of the personnel involved in the various parts of the process being studied. Thus, in the study of aeroplane seat-booking, a pupil will play the part of the travel agent and of the terminal staff. In the mail-order processing case study, pupils pretend to be the keyboard operators, the stock managers, and the invoice clerks. Computers are presented as artefacts of office technology. While business computing is undoubtedly an important application area for IT, it underrates the likely significance of computing, reinforces the social status quo, and provides a poor opportunity for problem-solving experiences. As such, it is difficult to see why it should be part of a school computing course.

The design of educational computing courses requires careful analysis of what we consider to be educationally worth while. We could, for example, use these powerful educational tools to create an atmosphere of investigation and of scientific endeavour in which more thought-provoking issues were raised. Undoubtedly, most of the computing knowledge required by most pupils can be achieved by using computers across the curriculum. But we should not ignore the educational potential of courses which are made possible by computers but which are not 'about computers' and which do not fit readily into other areas of the curriculum. These new courses emphatically do not include studies of applications software. If such software is worth using in schools, it is because it can be applied in the appropriate area of the curriculum, not studied out of context. In order to justify its study, software must contain the potential for developing problem-solving, for encouraging investigation, or for raising important human and social issues.

DEVELOPMENT OF PROBLEM-SOLVING SKILLS

That problem-solving is a crucial part of the rationale for large sections of the curriculum would not be disputed. In fact, the phrase has become ubiquitous in educational literature in recent years. The 'Cockcroft Report' (Cockcroft 1982) stated the importance of problem-solving as a curricular goal, but warned that we need to know more about the way in which it develops and how it can be taught. Mathematics has been the traditional home of problem-solving in the curriculum, but clearly a large number of its clientele have not been convinced of its benefits. There is now an unprecedented opportunity for experimental courses devised to teach problem-solving techniques. One way of attempting this would be through the medium of computer programming.

Programming has had a sad history in schools. The 'Alvey Report', for example (Alvey Committee 1982), speaks of the existence of remedial programming courses given by universities to entrants with A-Level Computing Science such was the poor quality of the instruction they had received. But there are discernible causes for its unfortunate reputation.

First, the reasons for including it in the curriculum in the first place have been badly thought out. There is no place in schools for programming as a preparation for a career in that area. If we wished to do this, perhaps we should teach COBOL since it is the major language of commerce and industry.

Secondly, the choice of language has been determined by the firmware of the microcomputer rather than by considerations of the aims of the course. Most courses have been taught in minimal BASIC, which is now infamous for being inappropriate to learners. The use of BASIC used to be forced upon the teacher by the limited facilities of the early microcomputers, but such is not now the case.

Thirdly, most teachers involved in teaching programming have been unqualified to teach it. In England, 76 per cent of staff teaching Computer Studies in 1984 had no qualifications (Leaton 1989). In the USA, the vast majority of pre-college computing courses in the 1980s were BASIC programming courses taught by teachers with no qualifications in the subject (Lockheed and Mandinach 1986). In Scotland, the S-Grade Computing Studies course prohibits any serious treatment of programming. It allows only thirty hours for the topic, the language is prescribed, and the impression has been given that the methodology for teaching programming has been satisfactorily researched. A single model of problem-solving has been adopted, and no efforts have been made to explore alternative paradigms.

There is now an abundant literature on the difficulties of teaching programming and problem-solving (see Goodyear 1987 for a review). The one thing that all contributors agree on is that teaching programming is not easy. Hence, to judge the appropriateness of programming on the basis of what has been achieved by unqualified teachers, however well-motivated they may have been, is unreasonable. It has been argued that pupils cannot learn anything about problem-solving unless problem-solving is an explicit curricular aim of the programming course (Johanson 1988). Hence, it is crucial that any programming course has problem-solving as its overall and predominant goal. We are not certain how to construct such a course at present, and the kindest thing that could be said about the current restrictions on programming language and methodology in Scottish schools is that they make it difficult to explore the area.

However, most teachers of computing will have experienced pupils who are highly motivated by programming. The high level of interest often induces behaviour of the type sought in other areas of the curriculum. This typically includes working out of lesson time, being able to focus on a problem and pursue it without constant supervision, and having a positive attitude to the subject. Surely this sort of behaviour is worth pursuing, even if we do not yet know how to trigger it in the majority of our pupils?

On the optimistic side, we now have much better tools at our disposal than the minimal BASIC which was so typical of the early attempts. Microcomputers are now powerful enough to run high-level languages with a greater potential for problem-solving. Prolog and LOGO are two obvious candidates. Both have been available for only a few years and both require a powerful computer to make them accessible to the learner, but such computers are now not uncommon in schools. The advantage of both of these languages is that they are languages of AI[7] and, as such, they support a rich variety of problem-solving techniques. The single technique stressed by conventional programming courses is that of top-down analysis. But even this technique is rarely successfully applied by pupils in schools. Recent research suggests that pupils get bogged down in the syntactic complexities of BASIC COMAL-type languages (Perkins, Martin and Farady 1986). AI languages, on the other hand, display a number of significant advantages, such as the explicit representation of knowledge and the direct use of logical inference. A wide variety of problem-solving techniques is accessible, including, for example, searching through the space of possible solutions and the use of heuristics. These languages seem to be promising candidates for problem-solving courses in schools, but there are other programming languages which also show potential for education. Examples include functional languages, object-oriented languages, and parallel languages.

DEVELOPMENT OF ANALYTICAL THINKING SKILLS

The attempts of the S-Grade course to study software have not been successful partly because it is the software itself, rather than any fundamental idea behind it, that is the focus of attention. A further limitation is that the software selected is concerned with making computers behave as rather sophisticated typewriters or filing cabinets. A source of more challenging ideas with worthwhile underlying theories and principles comes from AI. Here, software reflects attempts to do more than merely make office practice more efficient or carry out the role of warehouse personnel. AI is concerned with such fundamental human activities as learning, acquiring knowledge, planning tasks, understanding language, and interpreting visual information.

Definitions of AI vary. Some reflect its concern with modelling the human mind in order to increase our understanding of ourselves. Others emphasise the goal of creating machines which act intelligently, irrespective of their similarity to humans. The richness of this area of human endeavour as a source of powerful and stimulating ideas is apparent from these two viewpoints of its aims.

A topic such as machine learning raises important issues about the nature of learning itself. The questions addressed by a course in the area of AI are not trivial, and they do not necessarily come equipped with easy answers. Studying machine learning involves an examination of human learning and an attempt to classify the different types of learning which humans seem to display. Questions arise as to how learning differs from problem-solving behaviour; whether the storage of large amounts of data is equivalent to 'rote learning' in humans; why, if this is so, machines are so much better at it than humans; and what are the limiting factors. In a sense, to study AI is to study ourselves. The benefits of metacognition, with its insight into the pupil's own thought processes, have been discussed by such authors as Papert (1980) and Jensen (1987).

Investigations of examples of machine learning software would provide pupils with the opportunity to explore these ideas for themselves. Pupils might examine Winston's classic concept learning program, expert systems which appear to 'learn' by induction, programs which are able to learn by analogy. The emphasis would not be on the skill of handling a particular piece of software but on the investigation and understanding of the principles behind it, principles which can give insight into large areas of human behaviour.

Equally important would be the study of the implications of the development of such human-like activities in a machine. The social effects of the implementation of AI are likely to touch our lives fundamentally in the near future. It is important, for example, that people are able to make informed judgements about the problems that might be involved with using AI techniques to control 'star wars'-type weapon systems. Instead of preparing pupils to adapt themselves to the technology, as the S-Grade Computing Studies syllabus suggests, we should be preparing them to adapt technology to the needs of society.

Some moves have been made towards introducing AI modules into the school curriculum. The AIMS[8] group, a group of interested teachers, academics, and computing professionals, has produced a small number of SCOTVEC[9] modules in the area. So far, these have covered Prolog programming, machine learning, and natural language interpretation. The philosophy has differed from that of SEB courses in several important respects. The goal of the group has been the inculcation of an investigative spirit rather than production of a 'passively trained consumer'. The courses have been designed with flexibility rather than prescriptiveness in mind.

This approach is based on the belief that nobody knows enough about school computing courses to specify content and methodology in a rigid manner. It is hoped that the modules will evolve rather than remain static, and that this evolution will emanate from close consultations with those in the best position to make the necessary judgements, i.e. teachers. The decision to have modules in specific areas of AI rather than a single general module results from the belief that it is depth rather than breadth which is important in such a wide and diverse field. H-Grade Computing Studies, which has been described variously as too difficult and too easy, acts as a warning about the consequences of trying to cover wide areas of computing with a single course.

There will be problems with the implementation of these new AI courses. Resources have been inadequate, software has been difficult to tailor to the requirements of schools, and most of the work has been carried out in the spare time of a small number of committed individuals. They represent one avenue of potential for school computing courses – there may well be others. Indeed, although it has been suggested here that AI provides a source of educationally worthwhile ideas in the area of computing, the intention is not to replace the old orthodoxy with a new one. New areas may develop and different people may come up with new and better ideas.

Many teachers might feel uneasy about the idea of branching out from the prosaic contents of current computing courses to experiment with those dealing with bigger questions. Such feelings are entirely understandable, especially given the inadequacy of much of the INSET in the area of computing. If new courses are, in fact, worth developing and teaching, it would be necessary to invest in teacher education rather than in narrow skills-based training. But if we cease the sterile attempts to run 160-hour applications-based computing courses, there would then be more time available to the computer specialist. Some of that time should be used to allow the computing teacher to fulfil a consultancy role to the rest of the school. But it should also be recognised that, in an area as dynamic as computing, the teacher should have time allotted solely for the purpose of the development of his or her knowledge and of the area itself.

CONCLUSION

The birth of Computing Studies in Scotland was announced in 1982. After eight years, the subject has not fulfilled the promise of the early days of Scottish educational computing. What we have lost in those eight years is the excitement of discovery – an excitement which was shared between pupil and teacher and which made computing unique in its capacity to motivate. A flavour of this motivation is given by Smith (1986) when he talks of a 'practitioner led revolution' and of 'a community of "barefoot curriculum developers"' in the context of classroom trials with Prolog. This colourful terminology sums up perfectly what has been sacrificed in the process of institutionalising Scottish computing.

The main effect of the 1980s computing course has been to show that, in spite of its inherent interest, computing can be made to outdo other subjects when it comes to tedium and drudgery. Our goal for the 1990s should be to recapture the vitality of the subject. This will require a return to bottom-up curriculum development, with the curriculum being rooted in the study of theories and principles rather than of the latest technological gimmickry. If Computing Studies withers and dies, as it shows every sign of doing, it will be because it has been constrained to the point of suffocation. Surely it is now time to break free of the stranglehold and allow Computing Studies to approach its real potential.

NOTES

1. Scottish Examination Board.
2. In-service training for teachers.
3. Scottish Education Department.
4. Scottish Universities Committe on Entrance.
5. Information technology.
6. Joint Working Party.
7. Artificial Intelligence.
8. Artificial Intelligence Modules for Schools.
9. Scottish Vocational Education Council.

REFERENCES

Alvey Committee (1982). *A Programme for Advanced Information Technology: The Report of the Alvey Committee*, London: HMSO.
Cockcroft, W. H. (1982). *Mathematics Counts*, London: HMSO.

Cotterell A., Ennals, R. and Briggs, J. H. (1988). *Advanced Information Technology in Education and Training*, London: Edward Arnold.

Evans, N. (1989). 'Cross examination', *TES*, 17 March, p. 88.

Goodyear, P. (1987). 'Sources of difficulty in assessing the cognitive effects of learning to program', Journal of Computer Assisted Learning, 3, 214–23.

Jensen, A. R. (1987). 'The Plasticity of "Intelligence" at Different Levels of Analysis', in D. N. Perkins, J. Lockhead and J. C. Bishop (eds) *Thinking: The Second International Conference*, New Jersey: Lawrence Erlbaum Associates Inc.

Johanson, R. P. (1988). 'Computers, cognition and curriculum', *Journal of Educational Computing Research*, 4 (1), 30.

Leaton, E. (1989). 'The great computer crash', *TES*, 6 January, p. 22.

Lockheed, M. E. and Mandinach, E. B. (1986). 'Trends in educational computing', *Educational Researcher*, 15(5), 21–6.

Papert, S. (1980). *Mindstorms*, London: Harvester Press.

Perkins, D. N., Martin, F. and Farady, M. (1986). *Loci of Difficulty in Learning to Program*, School of Education, Harvard University.

SEB (1987). *S-Grade Revised Arrangements in Computing Studies*.

——(1988). *H-Grade Arrangements in Computing Studies*.

Smith, D. (1986). 'How long is a piece of string? Issues in the classroom evaluation of Micro-Prolog', PEGBOARD, 2, 108–23.

Williams, R. and McLean, C. (1985). *Computing in Schools*, Edinburgh: Holmes McDougall Ltd.

Wellington, J. (1988). *Policies and Trends in IT and Education*, ESRC Occasional Paper ITE/28e/88.

14

COMPUTING STUDIES: HOPES AND ILLUSIONS

NEIL KENNEDY

INTRODUCTION

In this chapter I set out to pose many questions about the present state of Computing Studies courses in Scotland. Unfortunately, I provide few answers to these. I am certain you can provide your own, so I would not dream of imposing upon you my vision of what educational computing ought to be about. After all, I am a practising teacher of the subject and, as such, like many of my fellow teachers, have no real 'outside' experience of computing, either in the big bad world of business and commerce, or the challenging atmosphere of the research lab. My experiences are mainly classroom ones – many of which I would like to forget! I have read the odd book or two, and occasionally talked to 'real' computing people. This lack of involvement, other than in educational computing, sometimes makes me, and perhaps other teachers in this area, feel vulnerable. Does our not being 'real' computing people put a question mark over our competence? Perhaps this is just paranoia, or an awareness of the 'those who can, do; those who can't, teach' charge which is often levelled at other subject areas. I feel that in relation to computing this is not necessarily the case. Because of the relative newness of the subject, teaching is perhaps as valid and valuable a skill as any other in the computing area.

What about Computing Studies as a subject? Does it match up to much of the hype which surrounds it? I feel that there are many problems in our subject area, due mainly to the lack of meaningful discussion and consultation about the way the subject has developed. If more individuals and groups shared the desire to produce a creative and innovative course, Computing Studies would be in a much healthier state than it is at present.

A BIT OF HISTORY – EARLY EXPERIENCES AND HOPES

Let me start with a short flashback to the heady days of 1983. As I sat in front of my ZX81 wondering how on earth I was going to fill a whole 16K with my latest BASIC program (even with the help of the useful GOTO statement – a useful pointer to my lack of experience in these early days!) I mused on the possibility of teaching children about computing. As a beginner, the subject fascinated me. I enjoyed the challenge of 'finding out' about languages and operating systems, and tackling problems in a creative way. It seemed to me that I could easily capture the interest and enthusiasm of pupils in my school if I had the opportunity to teach them computing skills. All the fun of challenging problem-solving and the selection and implementation of strategies in a new and practical fashion – all the things that real education should be, but, because of the various strait-jackets often imposed upon it, so often it is not. The subject could be creative, exciting, and reformative. There would also be the benefit of real interaction; the opportunity, as stated by Bork (1988), to 'make education an active learning experience for students, replacing the passive experience of the typical class'.

Although at that time, I had some idea of what would constitute a Computer Studies course, my ideas had not had time to develop fully. I was involved in extra-curricular computing – the early computer clubs for which there was so much enthusiasm. My 'computing classes' consisted of groups of enthusiasts who gathered in the computing room during lunch hour or after classes. When I say 'computing room' I am being a little fanciful as, at that time, there was a lack of accommodation and equipment. Not much has changed I hear some of you say! Members of the group used ZX81s or Research Machines 380Z micros – mainly for programming; although some 'word processed' with TXED, the CP/M text editor, as well as investigating ASM and other 'mysteries'. People involved with this group often waited at the computer room door before school started in the morning, or requested permission to come back after lessons, and these sometimes included interested members of staff, not just pupils. There was a real desire to learn about the subject. I felt that if only I could generate such enthusiasm for my day-to-day teaching, there might be fewer times when I scanned the situations vacant column in the newspapers.

S-GRADE COMPUTING STUDIES

I had to wait until September 1984 until my dream was realised – Standard Grade Computing Studies, or at any rate the Foundation Course pilot! At last, I thought, a course which will be fun to teach and fun to participate in; as well as the future potential of General/Credit Computing Studies, which would have the necessary rigour to challenge the more-able pupil. It is interesting to note that, at this point, there was no debate about whether computing should be experienced as a distinct subject in its own right, or whether it ought to be absorbed as a 'transferable skill' as part of the learning process across the curriculum. At that time the chance of seeing a micro in a subject classroom was pretty slim. I often feel many people would like to return to that state of affairs, some teachers of Computing Studies amongst them.

My school did not participate in the O-Grade pilot of 1982, but I was convinced that the wait for S-Grade was worth while – after all, the philosophy of Standard Grade was sound ... wasn't it? The view adopted by Sperry (1982) that

> The more we learn, the more we recognise the unique complexity of any one individual intellect ... The need for educational ... policy measures to identify, accommodate and serve differentially special-ised forms of individual intellectual potential becomes increasingly evident.

was catered for by the 'Munn Curriculum' which, if properly imple-mented, seemed to fit the bill. Does the S-Grade Computing course measure up to this? I think not. I (as did many others at that time) rushed headlong into the course, fired with enthusiasm and with the recog-nition that money had been spent and perhaps, more importantly, that more was to be spent. This disposed of the major problem of having a syllabus without proper resources: BBC Micros appeared as if by magic. As a Joint Working Party (JWP) had been set up and a lengthy document produced, support for the pilot was going to be substantial. Advice was at hand and comments would be noted for future development. In fact, everything in the garden was rosy.

Sadly, this was not to be the case. Once I had read the proposals document a couple of times, I began to compare it with my ideas of the creative, exciting, and innovative course that Computing Studies ought to have been. This was when I experienced my first stirrings of disquiet. What did I find in the document?

(*i*) content, some of which I could endorse but which seemed a little prescriptive.

(*ii*) a choice of programming language (but LOGO, the natural selection for many, was soon removed).

(*iii*) assessment arrangements which could at best be described as complex, or at worst as unbelievably stupid and completely unworkable.

(*iv*) in addition, there was project work to cater for, so I thought, the creative side of things – more of which later.

The proposals then were too prescriptive, even to my inexperienced eyes, but I felt that as this was a pilot course, there would be ample opportunities to put things right!

As far as detailed content went, the 'applications approach', which had its origins in the development of the O-Grade, continued. Appli-cation areas with compulsory and optional case studies based on busi-ness and industrial computing were the order of the day. The compulsory case studies included use of a database and a word pro-cessor: empty vessels, to be filled with what? This vocational approach appeared to be based on the maxim that knowledge of data processing and the electronic office was 'a passport to a job, if not to wealth and happiness ever after'. Did we sell this idea to the pupils, even indirectly; and did they buy it? 'The answer to both of these questions is 'yes', on both counts. A capacity for recognising fools and fools' gold might have been more appropriate. Computer systems and common themes teaching ran throughout the course, which seemed a sensible decision. Comal, an emasculated Pascal, was to be used for programming. As mentioned previously, there was the option, in the initial stages, of using LOGO. However, since little mention was made of it and no support offered, I (in line with the majority) opted for Comal. Besides, I was promised some 'Demons' to solve all my problems, as well as bi-directional parameter passing – every programmer's dream, I was informed.

EXPERIENCES DURING THE PILOT

So I got down to teaching, and learning, the course. In the early days of the pilot there were regular meetings at the Northern College of Education (Dundee Campus) for those involved in the development of the course. As well as disseminating information, I hoped that these would be a real forum for discussion of the course and how it was to develop. The mix at these meetings was ideal for proper consultation: teachers, college lecturers, members of the Inspectorate, and so on. The majority of the teachers involved with the pilot were enthusiastic amateurs. All had much the same level of computing expertise, albeit some had more confidence or arrogance than others. (There was always someone trying to sell his or her latest program, or hiding his/her worksheets, usually autographed, from those with access to a photocopier. What happened to the free exchange of ideas, materials, and teaching strategies? Thankfully, these people were in the minority – at least in the initial stages.) With this basis the course should have developed apace, but the pilot went sour: why?

I believe this happened for two reasons: first, the industrial action taken by teachers, which, by all accounts, should have stopped the pilot in its tracks. This resulted in many enthusiastic and innovative people, for reasons of conscience, being unable to continue with the necessary development work. This left one or two truly dedicated individuals to carry on, but many with more questionable motives. Secondly, it became obvious that many involved with the administration of the pilot scheme were not interested in listening to criticism, however valid, of 'their' course. Many constructive comments were disputed and certainly not 'taken on board'. Nowhere was this more obvious than during the discussion of the cumbersome assessment scheme proposed for the course. This, above all, sapped the energies of those of us involved in the teaching of the subject. Did we spend most of our time developing interesting materials and alternative strategies for teaching and learning? No, we spent our time thinking about process skills, Grade Related Criteria (GRC) and whether we would be able to assess all we were meant to assess in the time available. Obviously, these things are important, but to spend a disproportionate amount of time on them did little for many teachers' motivation.

ASSESSING THE ASSESSMENT

There were many questionable assumptions about learning and knowledge in the arrangements:

could we neatly divide knowledge into the areas presented in the document?

could we develop real problem-solving on word processing or mail order?

did the assessment match the content?

when we had content-free GRC which were difficult to put flesh on, was the resultant assessment reliable and valid?

and, of course, what did the pupils need from the course?

I am certain all these questions and more were asked, but few were answered satisfactorily. I recall discussions on formal tests when groups attempted to devise marking schemes for pre-written questions. There was much agonising over the GRC: is this PS3 or PS4?; how can you have PS without KU?; what is the difference between PS and KU?; how can we assess communication? – each group came to different conclusions, no one really agreed. At first, this was not taken as an indication of the vagueness and inadequacy of the GRC approach. My questions about the validity of wandering round the classroom with a checklist playing the game of 'I spy a grading opportunity' were met with raised eyebrows and a mention of 'correct classroom management techniques'. Later on in the life of S-Grade, the Short Life Working Group (SLWG) and the resultant revised arrangements made the in-class assessment more manageable for the classroom practitioner by lightening the assessment workload. However, the questions of validity and reliability were not tackled. Even with the new arrangements, I feel we can put little faith in the assessment arrangements giving us a meaningful outcome about a child's grasp of problem-solving, or his knowledge and understanding of the subject. Despite the changes by the SLWG, the opinion expressed by Brown (1987) holds true:

> In the case of the Standard Grade, the developments have attempted the ambitious task of constructing a system which by the introduction of Grade Related Criteria attempts to retain the apparent simplicity of the single grades awarded in the past, and at the same time to provide detailed descriptions of achievements to inform teaching and learning. It is clear that the price to be paid for trying to be all things to all people, whether of a norm- or criterion-referenced turn of mind, is a very complex system which has to

make major, and questionable, assumptions about the structure of
knowledge and pupils learning.

So the pilot foundered because of the withdrawal of many schools from
the initial trial during industrial action, and because of the perception
among many of the lack of real consultation by the JWP. Some might say
that the meetings at Dundee College provided ample opportunity for
consultation of this type. I would beg to differ; how can a classroom
teacher, perhaps a little insecure in his knowledge of the subject (and, on
occasions, with an eye to future promotion) voice criticism of a course to
lecturers, Inspectorate members, and the JWP which proposed them in
the formal surroundings of a boardroom? A tremendous pressure to
conform exists under these circumstances. From the earliest point,
teachers at the chalk-face should have been consulted officially. Course
development should not have been left to communication through an
'interested body' such as a professional organisation or the Advisory
service, with the unavoidable dilution of individual opinion and expertise which occurs under these circumstances. Furthermore, I did not,
and, nor to my knowledge, did any other teacher involved in the pilot,
complete a formal report on our experiences or see conclusions from any
such survey.

Proof of the ineffectiveness of consultations came when the final
arrangements document was published. It varied little from the pilot
proposals: the tidying-up of the assessment arrangements with the
effective removal of the communications element; the aforementioned
removal of LOGO as an alternative to Comal; and the loss of the compulsory 'training simulation' case study being the major changes. This
suggests either that the JWP got it right first time or that the pilot was a
sham.

THE LATER STAGES

When S-Grade Computing Studies got under way, following its rapid
promotion from phase 3 to phase 2 (effectively phase 1) of the S-Grade
development program, I feel that pupils' and parents' perceptions of the
course content began to cause trouble. Many children (as well as parents,
guidance teachers, headteachers) had misconceptions of what computing was all about. In spite of the fatal 'arcade game' mentality which still
affects the subject to some extent, many children are interested in programming, not applications. Even the less academically gifted pupils like
to get the computer to do what they tell it, even if this is just writing their
name in colour all over the VDU. Unfortunately, traditional imperative
programming (as prescribed by the present syllabus) is often demotivat-
ing, except with academically able children. Syntax of languages causes
untold problems for those with learning difficulties: if you do not get it
absolutely right the program does not work. When using the Comal
'Demons' a simple mistake can cause exit from within the pre-written

procedure which has been called, with the resultant error message causing confusion. Could these difficulties be a problem of the prescription of language and technique? Would it be possible to find the 'motivating spark' for these pupils if alternatives were made available? I would like to think that graphics programming using LOGO turtlegraphics and some declarative programming, using the SIMPLE or preferably MITSI front end to micro-prolog would provide this. (For the cost-conscious among us, a 'stand alone' – compiled – version of MITSI is now available for PCs/Nimbus from its author Jonathan Briggs.)

With many of our pupils turned off programming, what will make them come back for more? With the possible exception of the more practical aspects of the automated systems section, not a lot in the current syllabus! In extra-curricular computing, pupils often come back to the department for programming practice or occasionally for use of a word processor or database in a cross-curricular capacity. I have yet to hear a pupil banging on my door demanding another run of the mail-order package.

So, with S-Grade, a potentially creative, innovative, and exciting subject has, to some eyes, been institutionalised to form another 'ordinary' course. The creative aspects of the subject have been curtailed by a tight syllabus and examination constraints. Projects, the main creative outlet for pupil potential in S-Grade, are supplied with prescriptive grading schemes, thus limiting the creativity which they ought to engender. This sort of prescription, also exemplified by the 'Demons' approach to programming, underplays the creative side of our subject which would have attracted many to Computing Studies and made it accessible to those who need the life skills of information processing.

HIGHER THINGS

So much for S-Grade. What about Higher Computing Studies? Here the picture is a little brighter. Although Higher 'articulates' (please pardon the use of SEB[1] terminology here!) with Standard Grade and so provides to some extent an extension of S-Grade content, there was, at the design stage of the course, the opportunity for stimulating new areas of computing to be explored. Was this opportunity taken up by the JWP (which, it is worth noting, contained a significant proportion of those associated with the Standard Grade developments)? As with the S-Grade, there appears to have been little consultation with practising Principal Teachers or other individuals outwith the circle of the JWP. There are two dimensions to the course: the 'unifying themes', and the topics themselves. The unifying themes (stimulus to development, objects/operations, software levels, hardware levels, the human computer interface, integration, applications, and implications) seem to be pretty sound – with the exception of the pseudo-scientific 'objects and operations'. The topics (general purpose packages [GPAPS], knowledge-based systems [KBS][2], programming, communication systems and networks[2], interfacing and control[2]) showed that the Higher had the potential to be an excellent course. The exception was, of course, GPAPS. Although I appreciate that a look at integrated software is essential, this, in my view, provided an unnecessary distortion of content (were our most-able pupils to be thrilled by word processing and databases, yet again?) Why was this topic included as a compulsory area of study? I do not think we are short of interesting things to investigate. GPAPS should have been offered as an optional topic so that those who were happy with this sort of computing could have selected it. Obviously, the compulsory topic to replace it should have been KBS.

The assessment arrangements for Higher are more sensible than those proposed for S-Grade, but are not as fully criterion referenced as they ought to be. The objectives of the course are not deep enough for detailed exploration of the subject. A real chance for creativity comes with the investigation – an approach prevalent across the curriculum. It is a pity that the time allocated to this is so short. In fact, the whole course is rushed in the time available. This criticism can, of course, be levelled at the majority of the present Higher Grade courses, and the argument for a two-year Higher course on the grounds of allowing adequate time for depth of study must surely be a strong one. The optional topics provide the chance to study knowledge-based systems, surely the most exciting area of computing at the present time. This gives the course a major plus point.

As with any new course the Higher will be a success only if it is adequately resourced in terms of hardware, software, and in-service training. Early indications as to whether this will happen vary from Region to Region, but only time will tell if adequate funding will be forthcoming or if, once again, the course will be carried by committed innovators willing to spend a disproportionate amount of their own time developing materials and running the course by sheer force of personality and enthusiasm.

CONCLUSIONS

The state of Computing Studies in the late 1980s is mixed. On the one hand, we have a Standard Grade course producing software users as opposed to enthusiasts or innovators, a role better suited to other departments in the school. Indeed, with the introduction of S-Grade Office and Information Studies as well as Technological Studies and the plethora of short courses (SEB short courses as well as SCOTVEC[3] modules), it seems that other subject areas already have a justifiable claim to large chunks of 'our' course content. It is certain that the Standard Grade has a limited shelf-life in its present form, because of outdated content and the method of its implementation. In fact, it may already be past its 'sell-by' date! It remains to be seen if the review of the course due to take place has the courage to make the necessary changes to ensure survival of the subject. These would include: the 'deregulation' and extension of the time allocation for programming, the removal of the compulsory case study on mail-order; and the introduction of a new application area, Artificial Intelligence, with its accompanying expert systems case study. Projects could be 'multi-level' and more open-ended. In addition to this, the 'common themes' section and the assessment arrangements ought to receive a thorough 'seeing to'! How this review is organised is a cause for concern. Are we to have a new JWP, or are the 'examining team' and Computing Panel to provide us with another snapshot of computing – this time of how a group of individuals see the subject in the late 1980s and early 1990s as opposed to the present mid-1980s scenario? In view of the opinions expressed earlier, I wonder if we need another prescription. Would it not be better if practising teachers were given the time and help to develop Computing Studies? As far as the SEB is concerned, any changes suggested now and implemented as soon as possible will not be the subject of an arrangements document until 1993 at the earliest. Will this be too late?

On the other hand, we can be optimistic about the Higher Grade and other developments such as those produced by the Artificial Intelligence Modules in Schools (AIMS) group. All in all I look optimistically to the future of Computing Studies, if it can escape further top-down developments and concentrate on skills which can be transferred to the learning process in other subjects in conjunction with exploring the unfolding science of computing. I leave the last word to Sloman (1982), who predicted:

> Unless there is a coordinated effort at national or even international levels to look ahead to the needs of the future, there is a real risk that many schools will be stuck with an out of date approach to computer education . . . this can do permanent damage. I've seen evidence that some children are being turned right off computing by what they currently experience in school.

NOTES

1. Scottish Examination Board.
2. Optional topics, one from the three being chosen.
3. Scottish Vocational Education Council.

REFERENCES

Bork, A. (1988). Professor of Education at University of California (Irvine) speaking at the Fifth International Conference on Technology and Education in Edinburgh.

Brown, S. (1987). in *Assessment – a Changing Practice*, Edinburgh: Scottish Academic Press.

Sloman, A. (1982). 'Beginners Need Powerful Systems', in M. Yazdani (ed.) *New Horizons in Educational Computing* Chichester: Ellis Horwood Ltd.

Sperry, R. (1982). 'Nobel prize speech (8 December 1981), *Science*, 23 September, 1223.

15
PRIORITY NO. 1

TOM CONLON

I

Chris smiled and put down the book, '*Computing in Scottish Education: The First Decade and Beyond*'. What a dusty old tome! For some reason it had caught her eye that afternoon as she had been browsing idly through the library's archives. She certainly hadn't intended to spend so much time with the thing, but there had been something irresistible about those stories of EdfoTech back in the 1980s. What a mess they had made of those early efforts! And how much had changed in the last ten years! But now she really must get on with the preparations. The kids would be here in an hour or so, and, of course, they would be expecting something special. Chris powered up the Nutrimatic. She would let them have ice cream and Zuper squash – why not? 31 December 1999 was no ordinary old date, after all . . .

II

The Nutrimatic whirred gently in response to her commands: 'Ice cream, fourteen portions, half strawberry, half vanilla'. 'OK', the machine replied. She hardly knew what she was saying: her mind had gone back to that old book. 'Zuper squash, fourteen glasses with ice'. 'OK', the machine replied again. Education was so much healthier now – everybody said so. As the Nutrimatic's food sourcer began to run through its program, Chris let her mind wander back over the decade. Of course, the Act of 1992 had been the main turning point. What had that Act been called again? Moving over to the console she tapped in a few brief queries. The screen blanked out for a moment and then came up with the information:

Education (Priority No. 1) Act, 1992
Principles:
(1) *Young people to be recognised as the country's most important resource: education to be recognised as the national Priority No. 1.*

(2) *The education system to be reorganised along non-hierarchical lines. Decision-making shall be shared and each shall be accountable to all.*

(3) *Schools to be based on community comprehensives, irrespective of race, class or religion, with democratic local control over the curriculum.*

(4) *Young people up to age 18 to be guaranteed equality of access to knowledge and culture, freedom from vocational pressures, and freedom from all forms of harmful competitive testing.*

As Chris read the text the Nutrimatic let out a beep: 'Out of protein powder. Please attend.' Distractedly, she fished out a dispenser and poured some into the machine, then hurried back to the console. The history was getting interesting.

III

So much had happened since the Settlement had transferred power to the National Convention that it was hard to keep track of it all. But Chris really owed her job as an LTS'er – Learning Tools Supporter – to that Act, and the whole educational scene, not just EdfoTech, had been transformed by it. She tried to remember what things had been like before. Tapping the keys again she retrieved a news shot. It was from the *Scottish Herald*, dated 12 July 1991:

> There was uproar in the National Convention yesterday when members heard the report of the Inquiry into Education. The report revealed that in the 1980s under the pre-Settlement regime, spending on education had dropped below that on weapons of war; the country's school buildings had fallen into a disgraceful state of disrepair; the management of education had been bureaucratic, hierarchical, and nepotistic; the curriculum had been dictatorially controlled by the state; teachers had been oppressed and demoralised and many had ceased to work in a creative fashion; tests and examinations had been used as instruments of social control; education had degenerated into job-related training.

There was much more in the same vein. Chris remembered that some people had called the 1980s decade 'The Era of Greed': it had been a time when practically nothing was done unless it was to make the rich richer. And to sell their wretched ideology, the old rulers had tried to persuade everyone to adopt the mentality of a small shopkeeper. Even education had been forced to behave as if it was a grocer's shop or some kind of profit-seeking business. To think of some of the things they had tried to do made Chris shudder: the payment-by-lesson proposals; the forced testing and streaming of seven-year-olds; school boards dominated by the Chambers of Commerce; Standard Grade Enterprise made compulsory . .

Of course, none of that had been wanted by the Scottish people. It had all been imposed by the civil servants at St Andrew's House, who were acting on orders from the South. After the Inquiry, the Convention had sent them packing: the new non-hierarchical decision-making arrangements meant that they weren't needed, and anyway how could they be trusted again after doing those things to children?

IV

The Nutrimatic was still humming busily, but Chris hardly noticed it now. Hadn't the Inquiry had quite a lot to say about EdfoTech, or Educational IT as it had been known then? Chris felt curious: this was her area. She typed another command into the console and skipped through the screen pages until she found what she was after:

IT: *the Resource Problem*

The educational potential of IT has not been fulfilled. Partly this is due to a lack of resources. Schools between them have around 10 000 microcomputers, but almost all are primitive 1970s models which everybody else threw out a long time ago. There are no technicians to help and teachers have not been allowed time to learn how to use the equipment. Schools have been forced to steal software by copying it because there has been virtually no money to buy, and the educational software publishing industry has collapsed. Research and development in educational computing is almost non-existent.

Chris remembered how she had been struck by the clear, direct language of this report when she had read it at the time. The style of the official reports which had come before the Settlement had nearly always been devious, bland, and bureaucratic. Had that been to protect the rulers, she wondered, or was it because the authors were really like that themselves? Chris clicked to the next page:

Recommendations

(1) *Immediately replace all school microcomputers with up-to-date models. The cost will be £10 million, which is trivial. A single Tornado jet aircraft costs £26 million and the former UK Government bought 394 of these in 1989 alone.*

(2) *Set up an educational IT systems manufacturing base in Scotland. One possibility is to acquire and relocate Acorn – the company's 1989 USM value is £19.3 million, which is only a little more than twice the £9 million paid in that year by the UK Ministry of Defence for a single Cray machine alone.*

(3) *Increase the annual R&D budget for educational IT to £3 million. This is a 1000 per cent increase over the 1989 figure but equates only to the amount spent by one Scottish bank (the TSB) just on the annual maintenance of its computers.*

(4) *Budget for £5000 million to be spent on educational software production and staff development through the decade. This is about the same as the sum which UK companies will spend on automating their marketing departments in the 1990s, or, alternatively, it represents a few months' profit for IBM.*

As far as Chris could remember, all of these recommendations had been implemented. Well, who could have argued against investment in Priority No. 1? The marvellous thing was that as well as transforming schools, the spin-off for the Scottish economy had been terrific: world leaders in EdfoTech, a huge export growth area! Who would have guessed as much back in the late 1980s, when the UK actually had a large net deficit on trade in IT?

v

There was a whole lot more stuff like this, but really it all boiled down to the same thing. The resource problem was just a matter of priorities. The old rulers had put education near the bottom, and short-term private profit had been placed before almost everything else. They had tried to build a whole society on one single, immoral, deceitful idea: 'self first'. Chris skipped to the section on secondary schools:

IT: the Secondary Curriculum

As with Primary, the Secondary schools have been grossly under-resourced for IT but they also have special problems. Their curriculum has been tightly controlled by the state and it is extremely inflexible, being rigidly divided into subject empires and dominated by unnecessary examinations. Management is so hierarchical that nobody does anything unless they are told, and teachers have become so alienated and defensive that they automatically resist anything new. In these conditions it is hardly surprising that IT has made very little general impact. Most of the IT resources that do exist are locked into Computing Studies. This subject has been disgracefully mismanaged: its syllabuses are prescriptive, dull, and out of date, being either redundant 'computer literacy' courses or else misguided attempts at vocational training. Its teachers have been forced to waste thousands of hours in making pointless 'assessments' of the miserable bodies of knowledge which are the compulsory content

At this point a button labelled 'Evidence' flashed up. Chris clicked on it and a document marked SEB *Computing Studies, Examination 1990* appeared on the screen. She flipped through it: this must have been one which some of her own pupils had taken at the time. Poor creatures! There were questions about computerised stock control, automated factory pallet-stacking, and airline ticket-booking – what on earth for? Others asked about computer systems design, but evidently these

questions referred to machines which were built on the old von Neu-
mann scheme. Surely that had been well on the way out, even in 1990?
Still more bizarre were the factual recall questions about long-forgotten
peripherals and ancient communications protocols. There were also
some fragments of program code. Chris tried to identify the language: it
was some primitive sequential, imperative thing, one of a kind which
had long since disappeared. Did its name begin with a 'C'?

She skipped back to the 'Evidence' button. There was much more:
graphs showing how the SEB's courses had been skewed against female
pupils; transcripts of interviews showing that the claims that the courses
would enhance job prospects had been false; statistics from colleges,
universities, and industry suggesting that the courses had actually had a
negative effect on advanced level IT; curriculum analyses showing how
much of what was done merely duplicated ground which was covered
elsewhere – in primary, at home, and in other school subjects. What
Chris found most depressing was the evidence from teachers explaining
how it had all been allowed to happen. She had almost forgotten the
insidious effect of the old hierarchical system, and how it had engen-
dered a degrading foot-soldier mentality among teachers: 'they know
best; ours not to reason why.'

Chris returned to the main text:

Recommendations

(1) *The most important use for computers in school is to provide tools for
learning across the curriculum. All schools should appoint at least one
teacher as full-time Learning Tools Supporter to promote this role.*

(2) *'Vocational' computing courses should be banned. 'Computer literacy'
courses should be discouraged: basic IT knowledge and skills should be
acquired in meaningful curricular contexts.*

(3) *SEB Computing Studies courses should be abolished. All computing
teachers should be given a year's sabbatical leave to recover from their
maltreatment, followed by another year in which to investigate how the
school subject of computing might be reconstructed in educationally
justifiable ways.*

VI

The Nutrimatic was silent now. Chris looked up and noticed that the ice
cream and the Zuper squash had been set out neatly around the kitchen
table. Outside it was growing dark; the last evening of a dying millen-
nium. The children would arrive at any minute.

Her job had changed beyond recognition since Chris had become an
LTS'er. In the first couple of years she had had her work cut out just
supervising the introduction of the new equipment and helping to
introduce its use across the school. But gradually things settled. The

STSU (School Technical Support Unit) had helped a lot, and so had the new non-hierarchical policies, which meant that everybody shared in the decision-making and in taking responsibility for doing things.

Nowadays she worked mainly on project collectives. Chris was very active in the Learning Web, an informal grouping of teachers who were committed to widening access to learning to all groups in the community: she convened the Web's HyperMedia team. But all LTS'ers were up to different things. Just now a lot of them were into Satellite Learn-Links, for example. Others were building a variety of tools: mostly expert systems, tutoring systems, simulators, and auto-counsellors. When they weren't doing those things, they were studying (there were two days per week for that, guaranteed) or writing articles for one of the many journals in the EdfoTech field, or just meeting together to drink coffee and talk.

There was plenty of time and resources to do it all. The Convention's policies had been to put science and technology to good use: there were higher living standards for all, and much better opportunities for leisure, culture, and education. Almost all of the routine jobs had been automated, and education was the main growth industry. Priority No. 1 had been the right idea, sure enough.

Chris wasn't involved in Computing Studies any more. But she knew people who were: they had come back from their two-year leave frothing over with ideas, and experimental short courses had soon sprung up everywhere. Like the LTS'ers, the computing teachers spent a lot of the time studying, writing, and debating – especially debating. Chris had been surprised at this group's enthusiasm for that; they would argue for hours about their educational philosophy, or about why this or that topic was significant, or about the relationship between what they were doing and what was happening elsewhere.

Nowadays the computing courses concentrated on principles rather than on technology. Of course, nobody studied routine IT any more – computers were everywhere, after all, and you learnt about them casually, just like you learnt about cars and televisions – but lots of the kids took one or two modules just for interest, and they were especially popular with the adult students. The variety was stunning: there were modules on machine learning, logic, parallel problem-solving, ethics of AI, algorithmics, judgement versus calculation, computers and emotion, natural language processing, knowledge form and meaning, and many more. And for some reason, the applications for post-school computing courses had gone through the roof. It couldn't be to do with money, because IT workers were paid slightly less than most people, on account of having such enjoyable jobs.

VII

Yes, thought Chris, things had certainly changed since that book was written. She switched off the Nutrimatic and picked up the book again:

Computing in Scottish Education: the First Decade and Beyond. There was just one chapter still to read.

From outside the room came a crash. Chris turned and saw the door fly open. Simultaneously, fourteen children rushed through, jostling and shouting and waving bags. Some things would never change. 'All right, you lot! Calm DOWN! ALL RIGHT!'

VIII

The book hit the classroom floor with a thud, and Chris suddenly realised that she was shouting at 3B. 'Calm DOWN! ALL RIGHT!' The words had been an automatic reaction to the clatter of the period six class bursting into the room after the mid-afternoon break. Chris realised that she must have fallen asleep as she tried to read that book on Scottish educational computing. But what a strange dream that was: all that stuff about the future, and the idea of education as the 'No. 1 Priority'. What a fantasy!

Pulling herself together, she rounded on the class: 'Calm DOWN! ALL RIGHT!' What was she supposed to be doing with this lot? Oh yes – Standard Grade Computing Studies, commercial mail-order systems, lesson seven of nine: Printing Sticky Envelope Labels. Where were those Grade Related Criteria assessment sheets? They were somewhere in that pile, surely. Desperately she tried to assert some semblance of order: 'Three to a machine! THREE! Of course they're working. You should know how to start the mail-order program by now. Just get on with it.' She hated herself for talking to them like that but it was the same every day, by period six she was too drained to do any better. Now though the chorus of complaints was rising and Chris began to see that they were justified. None of the machines seemed to be behaving properly – that damned Econet again! She tried hard to fight back the panic which she could feel rising in her stomach: 'Here . . . let me try'. The class were staring at her and they had gone strangely quiet. As Chris leaned over to try one of the errant machines, she caught a reflection of herself in the window. Outside the autumn dark was already creeping in. Then she noticed it: trickling down her cheek, a large tear. Embarrassed, she quickly wiped it away. More fool me, she thought, for having that damn dream. It was only a fantasy. Things could never be like that.

IX

Could they?

INDEX

Acorn 36
Action Plan 49, 68
adventure programs 51, 126
advisers see advisorate
advisorate 15, 16, 34, 73, 100, 106
AI see Artificial Intelligence
AIMS 9, 157, 168
Alvey Report 154
Amstrad 36
Apple 31, 36
Apple Macintosh 93, 128
applications approach 72, 149
applications packages 15
Archimedes 36
Artificial Intelligence 3, 16, 25, 156, 168
Association for Science Education 118
authoring packages 53

Baker, Kenneth 1, 2, 45, 69
Basic 53, 69, 74, 124, 138, 154, 160
BBC Micro 8, 16, 31, 51, 62, 69, 106
Bellis Report 4–5, 7, 39, 136
Benn, Caroline 2
bottom-up development 7
Business Studies 36

CAD 54, 120
CAL 43, 127, 135
Callaghan, James 39
Campbell, Gillian 22
Campus 2000 109
case study approach 61
CCC 6, 13, 14, 28, 32, 34, 35, 114
CD-ROM 47, 108
CDT 113
centraliation policy 84
centralism 28
CNAA 17, 22, 71, 76, 79, 85
Cockcroft Report 154

Colleges of Education 15, 16, 29, 33, 34, 39, 68, 69, 71, 100, 124
Comal 77, 92, 155, 163, 165
Committee of Principals 75
Commodore 31
computer aided instruction 97
computer based learning 39, 56
computer literacy 2, 135, 140
Computer Studies see Computing Studies
computing courses 3
Computing Science 3–5, 7, 16, 144
Computing Studies 10, 16, 21, 24, 30, 39, 41–44, 55, 60, 64, 71, 76, 77, 81, 85, 92, 105, 111, 118, 134, 148, 160
Conlon, Tom 22
consortium 82, 84
control technology 83, 114, 129
core curriculum 3
COSLA 10, 29
creative writing 51, 107
Cromemco 53
CSE 41
curriculum computing 3, 5, 11, 98, 135
curriculum development 20

data handling packages 102
databases 32, 128
Department of Industry see DOI
desktop publishing 43, 51, 120, 129
Diploma courses 15, 71, 76
DOI 1, 6
Doomsday 107
DPSE see Diploma courses
drill and practice 101, 126
DTI 29, 31, 40, 67, 69, 70, 118, 122
Dundee College of Education 117

Education for the Industrial Society Project 48

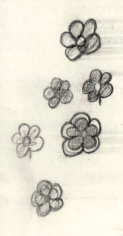